THE SECOND TWENTIETH

A COPY OF THIS BOOK
:: HAS BEEN ACCEPTED BY ::
HIS MAJESTY THE KING

The Second Twentieth
being
The HISTORY of the 2/20th Bn. London Regiment

by
CAPT. W. R. ELLIOT, M.C.
(Adjutant, December, 1916 – March, 1919)

ILLUSTRATIONS BY S. A. COURT
MAPS BY CAPTAIN H. C. LOVELL

The Naval & Military Press Ltd

in association with

The Imperial War Museum
Department of Printed Books

[*Frontispiece*

Photo by T. E. Howe.

LIEUT.-COL. W. ST. A. WARDE-ALDAM, D.S.O.

Published jointly by
The Naval & Military Press Ltd
Unit 10 Ridgewood Industrial Park,
Uckfield, East Sussex,
TN22 5QE England
Tel: +44 (0) 1825 749494
Fax: +44 (0) 1825 765701
www.naval-military-press.com

and

The Imperial War Museum, London
Department of Printed Books
www.iwm.org.uk

In reprinting in facsimile from the original, any imperfections are inevitably reproduced and the quality may fall short of modern type and cartographic standards.

Printed and bound by Antony Rowe Ltd, Eastbourne

To the Memory of

THE OFFICERS, NON-COMMISSIONED OFFICERS
AND MEN OF THE 2/20TH BATTALION THE
LONDON REGIMENT WHO GAVE THEIR LIVES
FOR THEIR COUNTRY IN THE GREAT WAR
THIS BOOK IS DEDICATED BY

THE AUTHOR

FOREWORD

By Lieut.-Col. W. St. A. Warde-Aldam, D.S.O.

It has been truly remarked that to write the history of any one unit in the Great War is a most formidable task. The writer's object is to reproduce the life, the feelings, and the experiences of a community over a continually changing period during which everything was intensive and most things at the time of happening were unintelligible. The difficulty is to thread the story into a larger history in such a way as to make it intelligible, and to keep a proper and proportionate perspective, without depriving it thereby of its freshness and character.

Capt. Elliot is well qualified to undertake the task: he was Adjutant of the 2/20th Battalion London Regiment for over two years; his heart and soul were ever in the Battalion, and he has applied to this labour of love the gifts of a ready pen and unremitting toil and zeal.

The story is that of a lucky Battalion—one imbued with a high spirit of happiness and comradeship, a Battalion that was fortunate enough to avoid the monotony and annihilating experiences of a long, unbroken stay on the Western Front, which managed to keep more than a nucleus of its personnel throughout its service, and thus gained a corresponding wealth of experience and *esprit de corps*. It is a story of high endeavour and of rich rewards : it is not given to many battalions to take part in two victorious campaigns in one year ; yet December, 1917, found the Battalion in the van of the Division which captured Jerusalem, and the following December saw it leading another triumphant Division over the German frontier.

Two things always struck me during our wanderings : one how appropriate it was that troops from London —the greatest seaport of the world—should travel so wide and become acquainted with many lands over which they and theirs were fated to hold so great an influence ; the other was the high standard of conduct invariably upheld by these London men. Theirs was an example of which the Heart of the Empire might well be proud—an example which was patent to all, Australians, Egyptians, Indians, Greeks, French, Italians, Turks, and Germans. The battles in which these troops took their share have had definite and obvious results, but, to my mind, the practical proof that the Londoner is a gentleman, demonstrated alike to our fellow-citizens of the Empire, to our Allies, and lastly to our enemies, will have equally far-reaching effects.

Many men of many counties passed through the ranks of the Battalion, but amongst Battalion Headquarters, the Transport, and more especially the Sergeants' Mess, the majority were invariably old members of the original " Twentieth," and these men never failed to infuse their spirit and character into the new drafts which so frequently joined the Battalion either from home or from other regiments.

I take this opportunity to place on record our extreme good fortune in the commanders and their staffs under whom we served. We are deeply indebted to our Divisional Commanders—Lieut.-Gen. Sir E. S. Bulfin, K.C.B., C.V.O.; Major-Gen. Sir J. S. Shea, K.C.M.G., C.B., D.S.O.; Lieut.-Gen. Sir W. P. Braithwaite, K.C.B.; and Major-Gen. Sir R. D. Whigham, K.C.B., K.C.M.G., D.S.O.—and to our Brigade Commanders—Brig.-Gens. H. W. Studd, C.B., C.M.G., D.S.O. (Coldstream Guards); F. M. Carleton, D.S.O.; C. F. Watson, C.M.G., D.S.O. (Royal West Surrey Regiment); A. J. Hunter, C.M.G., D.S.O., M.C. (K.R.R.C.); and Lord Hampden, C.B., C.M.G. All ranks will join with me in thanking them for their invariable help and consideration. All ranks will also wish me to acknowledge the assistance and comradeship (so fully proved) of the battalions and other units with whom we shared our many adventures. I refer particularly to the 2/17th, 2/18th, and 2/19th Battalions of the London Regiment, the 180th Machine Gun Company, the 1/5th Devonshire Regiment, and the Leeds Rifles; but among all, individually and collectively, we found true friends. Again, we are grateful to our own 1st and 3rd Battalions. The high fighting standard set by the 1/20th (Col. Hubback, C.B., D.S.O.), which preceded us to France by fifteen months, and the practical assistance which Lieut.-Col. A. Pownall, O.B.E., T.D., M.P., and the 3/20th so frequently gave, were deeply appreciated.

This book will serve two purposes—a memorial to our fallen comrades, and a reminder to ourselves. I hope it will tell the kinsfolk of the fallen that they spent their last days amongst happy comrades, and were themselves happy in their set purpose ; and will remind ourselves of that great comradeship produced by the war, and which we shall do so well to emulate in peace.

W. ST. A. WARDE-ALDAM.

PREFACE

THESE pages have been written in the leisure moments of very busy days. They are intended, primarily, as a souvenir—an aid to memory—for all who served in the 2/20th Battalion during the Great War. Perhaps, too, the book will have some interest for those whose dear ones sacrificed their lives while fighting with one or other of the companies of the Battalion.

My thanks are due to Mr. W. T. Massey for permission to quote from his excellent book, "How Jerusalem was Won" (Constable and Co.); to Capt. Churchouse and Capt. Woolfe for permission to quote from letters; to "The Official Record of the Egyptian Expeditionary Force" for a large amount of valuable information; to the Editor of the *Kentish Mercury;* and, finally and most of all, to Col. Warde-Aldam, without whose invaluable suggestions, criticism, and advice it is doubtful whether the book would ever have seen the light of day.

W. R. E.

BLACKHEATH,
May 1st, 1920.

CONTENTS

CHAPTER	PAGE
I.—Training at Home	1
II.—First Days in the B.E.F.	11
III.—Trenches and Craters at Neuville St. Vaast	19
IV.—Raiding the Germans	30
V.—Macedonia: Raiding the Bulgars	56
VI.—Egypt	84
VII.—The Plan of the Palestine Offensive	95
VIII.—The Advance and the Battle of Sheria	103
IX.—Through Huj to the Coast; Across the Plain to Enab; Climbing into the Judean Hills; The Nebi Samwil Fight	119
X.—Surrounding Jerusalem; A Decisive Assault at Lifta; Fall of the Holy City	138
XI.—Jerusalem Before and After its Deliverance	151
XII.—Sight-Seeing; Back in the Line; "D" Company has an Adventure	155
XIII.—Christmas Day in Jerusalem; A Turkish Counter-Attack Defeated; The Advance Continued Northwards; The Battle of Shab Salah; Transfer to the Anata Front; Hebron	164
XIV.—The Battle of Arak Ibrahim; The Fall of Jericho	178
XV.—Raids across the Jordan	188
XVI.—Back to France; Battle of Vaulx-Vraucourt	211
XVII.—Battles of Havrincourt and Flesquieres	234
XVIII.—From Solesmes to Maubeuge	250
XIX.—Germany	273
Roll of Honour	283

APPENDICES

APPENDIX		PAGE
I.—HONOURS AND AWARDS		289
II.—NOMINAL ROLL OF OFFICERS WHO PROCEEDED ABROAD WITH THE BATTALION		291
III.—NOMINAL ROLL OF WARRANT OFFICERS AND SERGEANTS WHO PROCEEDED ABROAD WITH THE BATTALION		292
IV.—NOMINAL ROLL OF OFFICERS WHO JOINED THE BATTALION OVERSEAS		297
V.—NOMINAL ROLL OF WARRANT OFFICERS AND SERGEANTS WHO JOINED THE BATTALION OVERSEAS		300
VI.—AN ACCOUNT OF THE RETURN OF THE CADRE...		302
VII.—AN ACCOUNT OF THE PRESENTATION OF THE COLOUR ON APRIL 10TH, 1920		307

LIST OF ILLUSTRATIONS

LIEUT.-COL. W. ST. A. WARDE-ALDAM, D.S.O.	*Frontispiece*
THE GREAT BLIZZARD, MARCH 1ST-3RD, 1917	*Facing page* 69
"BREAKFAST" (LE PITON BOISÉ), MARCH, 1917	,, 71
BEERSHEBA	,, 105
JERUSALEM	,, 151
JERICHO AND THE JORDAN VALLEY	,, 188
THE ADVANCE TO THE JORDAN, MARCH 22ND, 1918 ("A WINDY CORNER")	,, 195
THE RIVER JORDAN	,, 196
MOVING UP FOR THE ATTACK EAST OF HAVRINCOURT	,, 238
SINZENICH...	,, 273

COLOURED PLATES

ISMAILIA	*Facing page* 85
THE SUNKEN ROAD, SOLESMES—"DIGGING IN"	,, 255
SINZENICH UNDER SNOW, DECEMBER, 1918 ...	,, 277

MAPS

THE "L" SECTOR OF THE VIMY RIDGE ...	*Facing page* 21
PALESTINE	,, 95
FROM DOULLENS TO MAUBEUGE	,, 223

The HISTORY of the
2/20th Bn. LONDON REGIMENT

CHAPTER I

TRAINING AT HOME

THE 20th (County of London) Battalion The London Regiment (Blackheath and Woolwich) displaced the 2nd and 3rd Volunteer Battalions the Queen's Own (Royal West Kent) Regiment when the Territorial Force for Home Defence came into existence in 1907. The new battalion was mainly recruited in the boroughs of Deptford, Greenwich, Lewisham, and Woolwich, and it took over the Headquarters of the 3rd Volunteer Battalion at Holly Hedge House, Blackheath.

For seven years the 20th Battalion did its duty, and prepared diligently for the emergency which cynics said would never come. At the end of that time, when in a flash the veil was drawn aside, and the British nation stood faced with a crisis so momentous that the very future of civilization was clearly in peril, when the Territorial Force was suddenly in all seriousness called upon to be ready to defend the hearths and homes of England, the Battalion was mobilized and took its place with the rest.

Recruiting received a tremendous impetus, and on Wednesday, August 5th, 1914, and the following days Holly Hedge House was besieged by men wishing to enlist. There was no delay in absorbing them. Within only as many days after attestation as were required to arm, clothe and equip them, hundreds of recruits were on their way to Hatfield to join the Battalion at its war station.

It is seldom remembered that, after the dispatch of the Expeditionary Force to France, the pre-war trained Territorial Force was England's only bulwark against invasion. It was more than this. Battalions like the 20th, as soon as the call sounded, set their training machinery in motion, and turned out some of the finest fighting material the country has ever possessed. The fact was proved in the fighting-line very early in the war and the fame of the London Territorial as a fighting soldier soon extended far beyond the limits of our own Empire. The task was no light one. The 20th Battalion was called upon to absorb and train recruits to the number of a hundred per cent. of its peace-time strength, yet seven months after mobilization the Battalion was ready to join the Expeditionary Force. Large numbers of the recruits were of exceptional physique and education, but not five per cent. of them had had any previous military experience.

The Battalion soon attained war strength. The weekly number of enlistments continued to reach a high figure, and the formation of a second battalion naturally followed. On September 3rd, 1914, the 20th (Reserve) (County of London) Battalion The London Regiment came into being, under command of Col. E. J. Moore, C.B., T.D., with Capt. W. F. Marchant as Adjutant and Colour-Sergt. W. J. Dark as Regimental Sergeant-Major.

A long period of organizing and equipping followed, a good deal of delay being caused by the inability of the authorities to supply " service dress " clothing and web equipment. The men lived at home, and paraded daily in mufti for training in route marching and squad and extended order drill, with, occasionally, a lecture and night operations in Greenwich Park. For some time no rifles were available, but one morning the whole Battalion marched to the Tower of London and returned with rifles and bayonets. The 1st Battalion needed all its trained N.C.Os., and there was therefore a dearth of instructors in the Reserve Battalion; but several officers and N.C.Os. were sent off on courses at Hythe and Chelsea, and these, without exception, returned as qualified instructors. Meanwhile the establishment of officers was rapidly filled up, and the Battalion was organized in eight companies.

In September Col. Moore went to Hatfield to take over the 1st Battalion, and Lieut.-Col. H. A. Christmas commenced his period of a year and six months in command of the Reserve 20th.

Though parading daily on Blackheath in the vicinity of the Depot, the men had little opportunity of "feeling" themselves as a Battalion until early in the New Year, when, preceded by an advance party, under Capt. J. O. Cook, the Battalion moved by train to billets round the village of Betchworth (Surrey), under the orders of the 5th (London) Reserve Infantry Brigade, 2nd (London) Reserve Division. The remainder of the Brigade, the Reserve Battalions of the 17th, 18th, and 19th London Regiments, which had been accommodated at the White City, Shepherd's Bush, was now concentrated in the same area.

The move from Blackheath marked a critical point in the history of the Battalion. The eight companies were merged into four. Serious soldiering began; home billets and training in civilian clothes became things of the past. Ration allowance in cash gave way to army rations in kind, and not the least of the many difficulties of settling into first billets was that of preparing and cooking the men's food. In "A" Company, at Wanham Manor, not a N.C.O. or man would own to previous experience as a cook. Starvation stared the company in the face until the oldest man in the Battalion, Pte. F. T. Bottom, though confessing complete ignorance of the duties, offered to try his hand in making the company stew. The result was satisfactory—so satisfactory, indeed, that within a very short time Pte. Bottom received promotion to Sergeant and the appointment of Regimental Sergeant-Master-Cook, a position which he subsequently held for many long months. Though more than sixty years of age, Sergt. Bottom discharged his onerous duties without a break until the spring of 1918, when the hot climate of Palestine forced him to accept less exacting work at the Base. By this time he had gathered round him a staff of cooks second to none in the Division for efficiency and loyalty.

"A" Company probably had the least comfortable quarters. Wanham Manor was a rambling old mansion, unfurnished and devoid of every vestige of comfort. "B" Company was at Brockham, and had the advantage of excellent training ground in Brockham Park. "C" Company was at Buckland, and "D" Company at Brockham Green. Battalion Headquarters, in Betchworth House, though some little distance from the respective companies, was central and close enough for all officers to mess together there. The Battalion was lucky in being pleasantly near London, and week-end leave was regular. The Regimental Band, which had been returned from Hatfield, brought its cheerful influence to bear on route marches and the leisure hours of Sunday afternoon. Training occupied six hours a day, during which companies were often visited in their work by the Brigadier, Col. F. M. Turner, or the Divisional Commander, Brig.-Gen. T. P. Calley, M.V.O., who rode over from Reigate for the purpose. For a time the Battalion was engaged in digging trenches at Merstham, the parties going by train every day from Betchworth.

In February the whole Division marched to Epsom for inspection by Earl Kitchener on the Downs. A heavy snow-storm fell during the march and during the long wait which followed before the distinguished Field-

Marshal appeared and rapidly passed along the front of the Division in his motor-car.

Meanwhile the 1st Battalion had moved from Hatfield to St. Albans, and training and general preparations were receiving final attention for the approaching move overseas. At the last moment reinforcements of officers and men were called for from the Reserve Battalion, and on March 7th a draft of five officers and a party of men left Betchworth for St. Albans. The officers were 2nd-Lieut. C. E. Hamilton, 2nd-Lieut. C. H. Hooper, 2nd-Lieut. T. Gardner, 2nd-Lieut. C. D. Gray, and 2nd-Lieut. H. C. Taylor. (2nd-Lieut. Hamilton and 2nd-Lieut. Hooper, both of whom had been exceedingly popular in the Reserve Battalion, were killed shortly after the 1/20th arrived in France.)

The 1/20th embarked at Southampton on March 9th, 1915, under Lieut.-Col. A. B. Hubback, who had assumed command a few days previously. At the same time Col. Moore received the appointment of Commandant of the 47th Divisional Base Depot, Harfleur, and took as his Adjutant Capt. W. F. Marchant, Adjutant of the 2/20th.

The embarkation of the 1/20th brought a new sense of vocation and responsibility to the 2nd Battalion, which at that time was just settling down to existence as " a battalion with a future." It likewise brought many changes. For long, Col. Christmas had had no Second-in-Command, but on March 9th he had three Majors—Major A. J. Dodd, Major Assheton Pownall, and Major A. H. Franklin. Major Pownall only remained a short time before leaving to take up an important recruiting appointment, and subsequently to command the 3/20th on its formation. Major Dodd was temporarily Second-in-Command of the Battalion, and for a short period at St. Albans commanded it, subsequently leaving to become O.C. Depot at Blackheath. Major Franklin succeeded Major Dodd as Second-in-Command, and continued to hold the appointment until April, 1916. Before proceeding overseas Capt. Marchant handed over the duties of Adjutant to Capt. W. M. Craddock, who had joined the Battalion at Blackheath in September. In April Sergt.-Major Dark received promotion to Lieutenant and Quartermaster, and the new Regimental Sergeant-Major was Colour-Sergt. W. T. Skeer, of the Queen's Own (Royal West Kent) Regiment, who, under Capt. Fitzgerald, had been largely responsible for the musketry training and range-firing of the 1/20th. Lieut. A. Britter continued as Transport Officer, and Lieut. J. H. Chauncey, R.A.M.C., as Medical Officer. The following were the senior officers, warrant officers, and N.C.Os. of the Battalion in May, 1915 :—

"A" COMPANY.

Officer Commanding : Capt. J. O. Cook.
Second-in-Command : Lieut. C. M. Bullock.
Company Sergeant-Major : C.S.M. F. J. Drayton (employed at Officers' School of Instruction, St. Albans). Sergt. J. T. Hills was Acting-C.S.M. for some months.
Company Quartermaster-Sergeant : C.Q.M.S. A. Le Févre.

"B" COMPANY.

Officer Commanding : Capt. D. Watson.
Second-in-Command : Capt. H. I. Barlow.
Company Sergeant-Major : C.S.M. A. E. Dawes.
Company Quartermaster-Sergeant :
C.Q.M.S. E. F. Gunning.

"C" COMPANY.

Officer Commanding : Capt. G. J. Edwards.
Second-in-Command : Lieut. G. Cooper-Willis.
Company Sergeant-Major : C.S.M. J. Drury.
Company Quartermaster-Sergeant :
C.Q.M.S. H. G. Fennell.

"D" COMPANY.

Officer Commanding : Capt. E. C. Russell.
Second-in-Command : Capt. T. G. Moll.
Company Sergeant-Major : C.S.M. E. Mullett.
Company Quartermaster-Sergeant : C.Q.M.S. W. J. Gill.

Regimental Quartermaster-Sergeant : R.Q.M.S. E. H. Clymo.
Orderly-Room Sergeant : Sergt. A. Warren.
Signalling Sergeant : Sergt. F. Powell.
Machine-Gun Sergeant : Sergt. W. G. Bartlett.
Transport Sergeant : Sergt. H. Osbourn.
Sergeant-Master-Cook : Sergt. F. T. Bottom.
Provost Sergeant : Sergt. A. B. Crummey.

Capt. Watson, who had left Betchworth during the first week in March to take charge of the rear party of the 1/20th, remained to make the necessary preparations for the 2nd Battalion to take over the vacated billets, and in April the 2/20th arrived in St. Albans.

The Battalion had many months of home service in front of it. Billets at Braintree, a delightful camp in Hatfield Broad Oak Park, and billets again at Saffron Walden and Haverhill, filled the time until the opening of 1916. But long before this the men had turned their eyes to France, where the 1st Battalion was making history at Loos and Givenchy. Its glorious fighting record created an intense desire (as it was bound to do) among all ranks of the 2/20th to be " doing their bit " as a battalion on active service, and even the many comforts of billets in country towns at home were considered little consolation for being kept in England when the Battalion had volunteered, almost to a man, for active service. It was accordingly with genuine hope that, after two months at Haverhill, we heard of a pending move to Salisbury Plain, the final training-ground of divisions for overseas.

During the summer and autumn, drafts had been sent to the 1/20th to replace heavy casualties, and several officers had left the 2/20th to fill gaps in the First Line. The 2/20th which moved from Haverhill to Sutton Veny in January, 1916, showed many changes from the Battalion which had left Blackheath a year previously. Capt. Cooper-Willis had gone to Brigade Headquarters in September as Brigade Bombing Officer, and Capt. A. Reynolds was now in command of " D " Company. Among the senior N.C.Os., Sergt. J. B. Salkeld, of " B " Company, had been promoted Company Sergeant-Major of " C " Company, and Sergt. H. F. Trevillion (" B " Company) and Sergt. A. G. Robshaw (" C " Company) had been made Company Quartermaster-Sergeants of their respective companies.

The Battalion had been greatly increased in numbers by an energetic recruiting campaign in March and April, 1915, by a selected body of N.C.Os. and men under Lieut. G. Cooper-Willis.

In February, 1916, the Battalion first officially received the title of 2/20th; the Brigade became the 180th Infantry Brigade; and the 2nd (London) (Reserve) Division became the 60th (London) Division, with Major-Gen. E. S. Bulfin, C.B., C.V.O., as its first Commander. Within a very short time Brig.-Gen. H. W. Studd, D.S.O. (Coldstream Guards), arrived and took over command of the 180th Brigade, with Capt. A. O. Oppenheim as his Brigade Major and Capt. H. G. Ash, who had been with the Brigade since its formation, as Staff Captain.

From this time onward the fate of the 2/20th as a fighting battalion (as opposed to a draft-finding one) was never in doubt. Training became physically harder and more advanced, Brigade and Divisional field exercises frequently took the men away from camp all day, and firing on the excellent rifle ranges adjoining the men's quarters filled a considerable portion of the weekly programme. Many changes occurred in the Staff and among the senior officers of the Division. The 2/17th, 2/18th, and 2/19th Battalions each in turn experienced a change in C.Os., Regular officers arriving to take over.

On April 4th, Lieut.-Col. Christmas handed over the 2/20th Battalion to Lieut.-Col. W. St. A. Warde-Aldam (Coldstream Guards), who was to remain in command of it for the rest of the war. This date witnessed the close of a long period of patient waiting and quiet training, in which the majority of officers and men learnt all they had ever learnt of soldiering, and more particularly of life under reasonable discipline under a Commanding Officer whose devotion to the interests of the Battalion, and secondarily to those of every individual in it, laid the foundation-stones of *esprit de corps* and morale in all ranks. It also marked the birth of a new existence for the Battalion, first in the important final stages of active service training, and then in that larger existence of fighting and working on the three battle-fronts where it was to win its name and make its mark under Col. Warde-Aldam. That the foundations had been well and truly laid in the training at Betchworth, St. Albans, Braintree, Hatfield Broad Oak, Saffron Walden, Haverhill, and Sutton Veny, under Col. Christmas, was conclusively proved later on the Vimy Ridge and on countless subsequent occasions—in Macedonia, at Sheria, at Nebi Samwil, at Jerusalem, across the Jordan, at Vaulx Vraucourt, at Havrincourt, and at Flesquieres, to mention only a few of the places where all ranks, rivalling the fighting spirit of the 1/20th, made a prominent place for the 2/20th Battalion in the history of the Great War.

April was a busy month. It witnessed the arrival of a large draft of men of the R.A.M.C. from depots at Ripon, Birmingham, and Sheffield. These men had received no infantry training, and had never fired a musketry course. A programme of rapid training was quickly formulated, and many of the men only completed their firing practices within a week of the Battalion's embarking for France. It says much for the keenness of the men and for the excellence of their short course of infantry training that these men subsequently played a conspicuously large part in the fighting, working, and playing of the Battalion in its two and three-quarter years of active service.

In May the Division was inspected by His Majesty the King. On June 26th long-cherished dreams were realized, and the 2/20th Battalion moved from Sutton Veny to Southampton and embarked for Havre.

CHAPTER II

FIRST DAYS IN THE B.E.F.

THE morning of June 25th, 1916, will be ever memorable to those who disembarked with the Battalion at Havre on that day from the *La Marguerite*. So soon as the ship was made fast at her berth, and gangways were in position, the men trooped off on to the spacious quay, where several unkempt " Tommies," who looked as though they had lived there all their lives, stood against the massive walls of the store sheds, with their hands in their pockets and smoking " cutty " pipes. Beyond a languid interest in us as having so lately left the home of which they thought and dreamed so much, they took little notice of our arrival, and presently ambled off to their day's work in the docks. The Battalion formed up and marched off, intensely interested in its new surroundings. The experience was new to almost everyone. Col. Warde-Aldam, who had passed through Havre in the more fateful days of 1914, and the four officers who had seen active service with the 1/20th, were the only exceptions. Of the latter, Major F. C. Bentley, who was now Second-in-Command, Lieut. H. C. Partridge, and 2nd-Lieut. M. Lane, M.M., had joined at Sutton Veny. 2nd-Lieut. T. Gardner had returned to the 2nd Battalion when invalided from France in May, 1915.

Capt. Bullock was now in command of " A " Company, and Capt. A. Pritchard of " C " Company. Lieut. R. G. Jones had taken over the Transport, and Capt. W. K. Churchouse, R.A.M.C. (T.), had joined at Sutton Veny as Medical Officer. Lieut. L. W. Kempe and Lieut. W. Davies were Bombing Officer and Lewis-Gun Officer respectively.

The complete journey of the Battalion from Sutton Veny to the first billets in France is thus described in the Colonel's diary :—

"*Saturday, June 24th*, 1916.—Left Sutton Veny camp at 5.45 a.m. and Warminster at 7.20 a.m., and arrived Southampton 9.30 a.m. Spent the day in the Docks, and embarked on *La Marguerite* at 3 p.m. Sailed 5 p.m. Passed boom soon after 7 p.m. Rather rough."

"*Sunday, June 25th.*—Arrived Havre about 6 a.m., and began to disembark about 7 a.m. We marched to Halle 3 at Gare Maritime. Entrained at 8.30 p.m., and left about 9 p.m.

"*Monday, June 26th.*—Stopped for thirty minutes at Monterolier Buchy about 3.30 a.m., and at Abbeville at 8 a.m. for one hour. Then went via Frévent to St. Pol, where we detrained, and marched to Blangermont, where we billeted. Very wet night."

Few who have survived them will readily forget those train journeys in horse-boxes which at some time or another formed part of the life of every soldier in France. The wise man chose a comfortable attitude for his body when he first entered the truck, for it was quite impossible to move once the thirty or more others had climbed in. Equipment and rifles were hung on the walls, and every available inch of floor space was occupied. The authorities on occasions expressed surprise that some of the men preferred to travel on the roofs of the trucks, and stringent orders were issued forbidding this dangerous and uncomfortable practice. It occurred to some of us that the preference was in the circumstances a very natural one, and that the best method of overcoming it would have been to add a few extra trucks to each train. When we approached the R.T.O. on the subject, we invariably found that the train had been ordered to consist of so many " K " trucks and so many " L " trucks, and, though willing to help us in any other way possible, he was powerless to increase the number.

On detraining at St. Pol, the Third Army railhead, and the seat of Gen. Byng's Headquarters, the 60th Division was allotted to the 17th Corps (Lieut.-Gen. Sir Charles Fergusson).

The march from St. Pol to Blangermont (our first billets in France) was not a long one, but the Battalion was very glad to get into houses, though the men were " close billeted," and had to march again on the following morning. Rain fell heavily throughout the night, and was still falling at 10 a.m. when the column moved off on trek through Maizières to Penin, a typical French village, fourteen miles west of Arras and two miles south of the Arras—St. Pol main road. 2nd-Lieut. L. E. M. Weatherley and his advance billeting party had made the most of the accommodation available, and on arrival at 3 p.m. companies were able to turn in to their new quarters in tolerable comfort. As the Battalion was to spend some days in Penin, more attention was paid to the selection of billets than would have been worth while for a stay of one night, and straw was obtained for men who had to sleep on the floor. Though at all times appreciative of anything that was done for their comfort, the men on this and many subsequent occasions for the most part preferred to sleep on bare boards rather than run the risk of "picking up something" from the straw. It was one of many ways in which the British "Tommy" showed that he preferred cleanliness to temporary comfort.

Battalion Headquarters was in the village chateau, a fine old building, but "a trifle the worse for wear," as one of the signallers put it. The courtyard was invaluable for "mounting duties" and for parking water-carts and limbers.

It was, perhaps, typical of Gen. Studd—who, of course, had choice of the whole village for his headquarters—that, while Battalion Headquarters was in the chateau, his own was in a small farm at the other end of Penin. It belonged to M. le Maire, and was of a type frequently met with in French villages. Old, and in bad repair, the bedrooms had a habit of leading out of each other in such a way that it was impossible to enter except through the window or through another bedroom. The General had his Mess in the front parlour, and just outside the window lay the familiar steaming muck-pool, where pigs, ducks, chickens, and geese spent the day, and sometimes the night, in grunting, quacking, cackling, and hissing. Under the house was a cesspool, which was the only system of drainage and was emptied into the farm-yard by a pump. At the time of our occupation the pump suddenly ceased to function, and in an unfortunate moment some of us offered to help in putting it right. Our patriotism had got the better of our judgment. We had failed to realize that in helping to cement the *entente* we would be required to stand for some minutes over the open cesspool of a French farm-house, and we learnt a lesson which lasted throughout the war on the subject of interfering with the domestic arrangements of our billetees. Anyway, we mended the pump!

It was often observed during the war how justly a battalion could be judged by its Officers' Mess. Colonel Warde-Aldam always impressed on his officers that the Mess was in a military sense their home, and there was, in consequence, a marked absence of stiffness about the 2/20th Mess which the writer never noticed to the same degree in any other battalion. Guests, whoever they were, were always more than welcome, and especially so the officers of the Brigade Staff and of other battalions of the Brigade. Entertaining was the only way of getting to know one's neighbours. At Penin, Capt. Oppenheim and Capt. Ash had open invitation to the Battalion Headquarter Mess, and one evening after dinner they brought with them M. Mathieu Theodor, the Brigade interpreter. The interpreter was very much worried that evening by domestic happenings, into which there is no space to enter here in detail, but which, it may be said, only went to prove the truth of the old saying that the course of true love never runs smooth. M. Theodor was not, however, too depressed to join in the general merriment, and after several songs had been sung, little persuasion was required to induce him to sing his favourite " La Marseillaise." He sang passionately, and his rendering revealed to some of us for the first time the intense love of country which animates the average Frenchman. The writer has heard the " Marseillaise " many times since, but he will never forget M. Theodor's expression of it in the Chateau at Penin.

Training commenced—or rather recommenced—in earnest on the day after our arrival at Penin, and continued during the few days spent in the village. Platoons and companies visited the Crater Consolidation School at Agnières, about a mile east of Aubigny, and there from the instructing officers and N.C.Os. of the 51st (Highland) Division received first lessons in crater-fighting. The training of specialists—Lewis gunners, signallers, scouts, and stretcher-bearers—and company field training also received attention, and all officers and N.C.Os. went in motor lorries on one occasion to Tinques to hear a lecture by the Corps Commander.

All ranks were gradually becoming acclimatized to the freer, if rougher, conditions of service in a theatre of war after their long period at home. Things were certainly very different. Route marches followed by a hearty meal, perhaps a bath if one had a good billet, and certainly a sound night's sleep, with every prospect of week-end leave in the near future, were now merely a memory—though a very pleasant one—and were consigned to the limbo of the past. What would the conditions of the future really be ? At any rate, we had to be *prepared* now to turn out in the middle of the night, to trek many miles with only the prospect of a fight at the end of it, to dispense with sleep for days and nights on end, to sacrifice comfort, inclinations, pleasure, and maybe even the necessities of life, to the attainment of the one great object to which, with a million others of our fellow-countrymen, we had committed ourselves. Such was the prospect. We have much to be thankful for that the reality was seldom so exacting. The change from home service to active service was everywhere radical. The Pay and Mess Book, that bane of Company Seconds-in-Command and Company Quartermaster-Sergeants, gave place to the Acquittance Roll and Pay Book as the machinery of payment to the troops. Clothing ledgers and elaborate systems of accounting in the Regimental Institutes disappeared. There seemed, wherever one looked, to be a deal more regard for efficiency and a little less for useless show and " eye-wash " than at home. Systems and individuals seemed to be judged more on their merits as war-winning entities, and that was undoubtedly what gave a clearer and freer atmosphere to soldiering on service compared to soldiering at home.

The C.O. from the first had set out to make the 2/20th as near the ideal of the Brigade of Guards as possible. The highest standard of discipline and efficiency alone was good enough, and special attention was paid to parade work. Battalion parades were frequent, and junior officers and N.C.Os. were frequently drilled as a squad by Sergt. S. J. Martin, an ex-Coldstreamer, who not only possessed the Chelsea word of command, but had that inimitable gift of imparting instruction in drill and the handling of the rifle which has come to be regarded as the special prerogative of the British Guardsman. " C.O's. Orders " were held daily wherever the Battalion happened to be. All men who rejoined from hospital, from courses, from detached duty, or from leave, attended, and were marched in front of the Colonel by the R.S.M., who explained the particular reason of their presence. Col. Warde-Aldam would say just a word or two, or perhaps nothing at all, but the name of the N.C.O. or man was not forgotten, nor the particular bit of his history which had brought him to " Orders." Privates for their first stripe and N.C.Os. for promotion would attend to be impressed with their extreme responsibility, and to be told what was expected of them in their new rank or appointment. Company Commanders were always present, and after the N.C.Os. and men had been dismissed they could raise any matter concerning their companies, and have it settled there and then. " C.O's. Orders " was a parade, not only, as in many battalions, of men for trial, but of N.C.Os. and men who, for whatever reason, were figuring prominently in the life of the Battalion at the moment. Whether it were in the line or behind it, the parade was always carried out with the utmost smartness and precision. This daily parade always struck the writer as one of the most prolific sources of the unbounded confidence Col. Warde-Aldam had in his men, and of their great respect for, and confidence in, him.

The very first days in France brought out in the 2/20th that quality of cheeriness which was conspicuous in all ranks as long as the Battalion existed. Probably largely owing to the excellent types of Londoner and north-countrymen of which it was mainly composed, the Battalion never lacked the ability nor the spirit to amuse itself. At Penin there would have been much excuse for a certain amount of homesickness and consequent depression. On the contrary, the men settled down to their new environment at once, and entered thoroughly into the simple pleasures of the country village, and of the novelty of their circumstances. The fine spirit of the Battalion was largely due to its N.C.Os. No battalion was more fortunate in its non-commissioned ranks than the 2/20th. Not only in these early days, but in the many long months which followed, the warrant officers, sergeants, corporals, and lance-corporals never failed to keep alive in themselves, and in the men under them, that spirit which by true discipline brought success.

It was a very interested Battalion which, after a heavy thunderstorm on the night of Tuesday, July 4th, moved up towards the front line on the following day, and went into billets at Acq. "C" and "D" Companies had spent the morning at the Crater School at Agnières, and came straight on in the evening. The Commanding Officer and the Adjutant had reported at the Headquarters of the 152nd Infantry Brigade (51st Highland Division) in the line at 10 a.m., and had spent the day with the 1/6th Seaforth Highlanders, who held the L.2 Sub-Sector of the Vimy Ridge.

CHAPTER III

TRENCHES AND CRATERS AT NEUVILLE ST. VAAST

THE 60th Division was very fortunate in having as its tutor in trench warfare the already famous 51st (Highland) Division. No battalion of the 60th was allowed to take over in the front line without having first undergone a period of instruction, during which companies were attached to the companies of the Highlanders holding the front trenches, and so were able to gain a knowledge of the geography of the sector, and of the routine of trench warfare, before actually assuming responsibility for the defences. On July 6th " A " Company (Capt. Bullock) and " C " Company (Capt. Pritchard) moved forward from Acq into the trenches for the first time, and occupied support dug-outs in the Quarries and in a neighbouring trench, known as Pylones, where they were under instruction by the 1/6th Seaforths. On the following night " A " Company and " B " Company (Capt. Watson) went into the front line to work with the corresponding companies of the Seaforths, and on July 8th these two companies took over stretches of the front trenches. Two days later they were withdrawn to the Quarries, and " C " Company and " D " Company (Capt. Reynolds) had their first turn in charge of the line. On Wednesday night, July 12th, " A " and " B " Companies of the Seaforths were relieved by " A " and " B " Companies of the 2/20th, and the command of the L.2 Sub-Sector passed to Col. Warde-Aldam.

The area taken over by the Division covered three Brigade sectors of the front line lying between Souchez and Arras, and extended westwards as far as Aubigny— a fair-sized market-town with good shops and a busy population—and south to Hermaville, a country village with Divisional Headquarters in its fine old chateau. The 2/20th had Rear Headquarters, consisting of the transport section and the Quartermaster's staff and details, at Ecoivres, under Lieut. Jones and Lieut. and Quartermaster Dark. During the day rations were accumulated at Rear Headquarters, together with all other requirements of the Battalion when in the line, and immediately after dark everything for the men in the trenches went up on regimental transport or on the light railway. Both tasks, of collecting by day and delivering at night, devolved on the same men, the Battalion transport personnel, to whose untiring energy and courage, both at this time and in the many hard months which followed, the writer is glad to be able to pay this tribute. Whatever the dangers or difficulties—there were always plenty of both—the Battalion never went without its rations.

A brief description of the country between Rear Headquarters and the line must suffice. East of Ecoivres lay Mont St. Eloi (where Capt. Ash presided over Brigade Rear Headquarters), La Targette, and Neuville St. Vaast. Between the last-named and Thelus ran the double maze of trenches which formed the opposing front lines. Mont St. Eloi deserves more than passing reference, for here the Battalion spent its "rest" periods in Divisional Reserve, occupying the camp which nestled under the trees of the Bois des Allais and adjoined the ruined village tower. More welcome on relief nights than all the wealth of Crœsus was the sight of the tower of Mont St. Eloi, as it first came into the view of men worn out by the incessant work, the constant strain and monotony and mud of three weeks in the trenches.

The journey to the line forward of Ecoivres could be made by "Roy" and "Territorial" Trenches, passing Brigade Headquarters and the nest of artillery at Aux Rietz cross-roads, and winding through La Targette

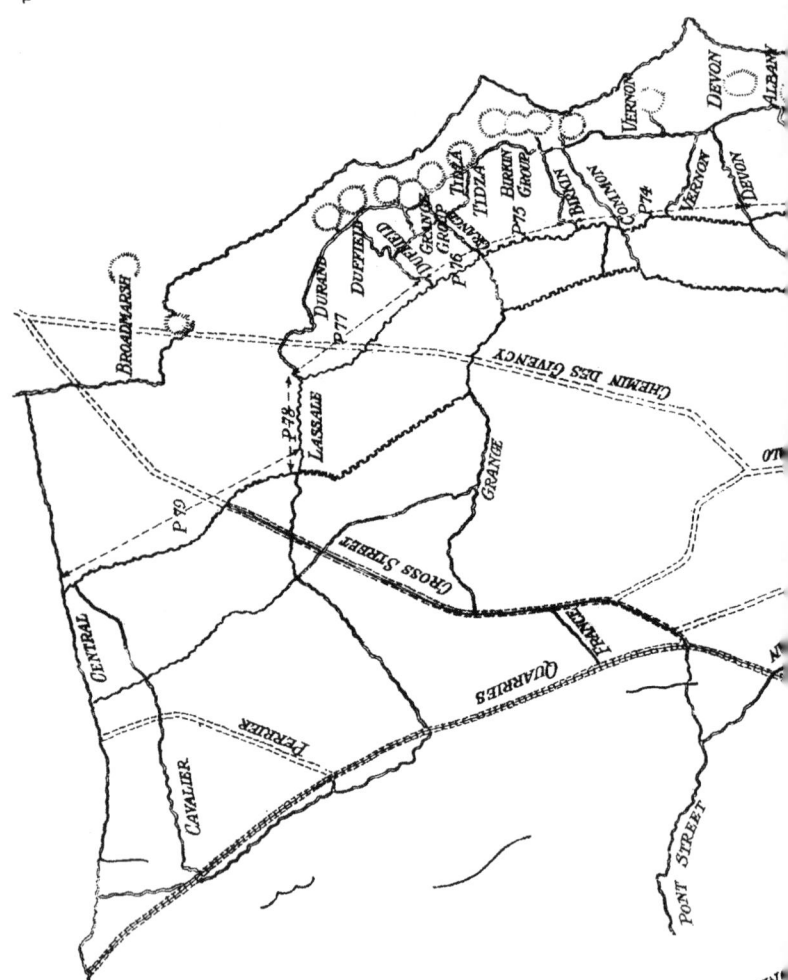

2/10 London Regt

to Neuville St. Vaast, just behind the support line. By night the road could be used, and the journey made more comfortably, especially if there happened to be an empty corner on one of the trucks of the light railway train which plied after dark between Rear Headquarters at Ecoivres and Battalion Headquarters in the line. La Targette and Neuville St. Vaast, as a terrible result of eighteen months of stationary warfare, were little more than occasional piles of crumbling bricks, with a complete wall standing here and there—the only relief in a scene of utter desolation. Just north of St. Vaast lay the Quarries, a wide, sunken road which ran parallel with the front line, and some 300 yards behind it.

The Quarries might aptly have been called Piccadilly Circus. It was the centre of whatever social life was possible in the sub-sector. The Headquarter dug-outs, though roomy enough to provide accommodation for Orderly-Room, Regimental Aid Post, Signal Office, and Headquarters Officers' Mess, certainly bore no faint resemblance to the Piccadilly Hotel. But the Quarries was nevertheless the hub of the "L.2" universe. It was the terminus of the light railway; it was the distribution point for rations and that ever-welcome Godsend, the mail from home; and it was the point at which many visitors to the sector suddenly discovered that they had seen all there was to see, and it was high time they were getting back! True enough, it was not a place to stand and loiter in, especially on nights when the Boche had a fit of "machine-gun fever," for he usually selected the Quarries as one of his objectives. But it was more comfortable than those battered trenches in front, where dug-outs hardly existed at all, and things became decidedly unpleasant when "Fritz" started throwing some of his "rough stuff" over on to the men who held the fire steps.

Nothing could be brought from Rear Headquarters in daylight, so that material, when it arrived at night, was formed into dumps in convenient parts of the sub-sector. Close to Battalion Headquarters in the Quarries was the R.E. store of pickets, wire, tools, and timber, known as " Birmingham Dump," where working parties would assemble after dark to collect their " doing irons " before climbing the parapet to mend the wire or dig fresh trenches. Here, too, alas! the small shed used as a mortuary, where the bodies of the dead might rest by day until in the darkness they could make their last journey down to the cemetery at Ecoivres on the returning railway trucks.

Companies had their headquarters in dug-outs scattered along the front line. Communication trenches connected the Quarries with the main line of resistance —the " P " line—in front of which lay an unfinished series of trenches, known as the Retrenchment Line. Out of the Retrenchment Line ran a series of saps with sap-heads, held as observation posts. The majority of these were situated on the near lips of the craters, which latter had been formed by the mining activities of both sides, and with which No Man's Land was well studded.

Mining had, indeed, come to play a very important part in the tactical situation in this part of the Vimy Ridge. New craters were constantly being formed as each side saw the opportunity to improve his local position or outlook. The names of the craters in July, 1916, though not likely to be forgotten by those who came to know almost every inch of them, are given here for reference :—

> Vernon.
> Common.
> Birkin.
> Grange.
> Durand.
> Duffield.
> Broadmarsh.

The last-named was completely in No Man's Land, and was too far from *our* front line for us to hold. We had at least one post on the near lip of each of the others—on Grange we had three—and the N.C.Os. and men who occupied them had no enviable task. In many cases the post was only 40 yards from the enemy's front trench or crater post, and in some it was much less. On one occasion the Huns threw over a copy of the *Berliner Illustrite Zeitung* tied to a stone. The garrison of one of our posts quickly replied with a packet of British cigarettes. Having thus succeeded in his attempt to locate our post exactly, the Boche had the third and last say in the matter by throwing over a bomb, which caused casualties, 2nd-Lieut. G. S. Morris being among the wounded.

By a remarkable coincidence the sector next on the left of the 60th Division was held at the time we took over by the 47th Division, the 1/20th being its right battalion. This was the only time that the 1st and 2nd Battalions came near to each other on active service. Two days later the 1/20th commenced to trek for the Somme, and no fraternization was therefore possible.

The first casualty in the Battalion occurred on July 8th while companies were in the line under instruction, Lce.-Cpl. R. J. Hill being wounded. Pte. S. Eunson, who was killed on July 12th, was the first fatal casualty. On the same day R.S.M. Skeer and Sergt. Martin were wounded.

The first night spent by the Battalion in the trenches is thus described in the War Diary :—

" ' A ' and ' B ' Companies relieved ' A ' and ' B ' Companies Seaforths at 6 p.m. and 6.30 p.m. respectively. Casualties nil. The night passed quietly and without incident, a few sling bombs being thrown, and enemy machine guns being active."

The inevitable stagnation of mind and morale which must accompany long periods in the trenches, with no opportunity of attacking or advancing, was amply appreciated by Gen. Studd, who, as soon as the Brigade took over, laid down very clearly the object which all ranks must definitely set before them as long as they were in the line. That object *must* be attained at whatever cost. The Boche must be made to feel his moral inferiority. No opportunity must be lost of impressing upon him that he was only there on sufferance, and until such time as we chose to advance and drive him out. No Man's Land must be denied to his patrols. His miners must be outwitted and out-manœuvred; weak spots in his trenches must be covered by our snipers; his machine guns must be located as soon as they fired, and must be knocked out by our artillery; his gunners must be put in mortal terror of our bombardments. His very life must be made a burden to him. And all the time, by active patrolling and work with Lewis gun, rifle, and bomb, we must be cultivating in ourselves the aggressive spirit which, when the opportunity came, would assure success in attack. That opportunity never came, but the account which appears in the next chapter of the raids in September and October proves that the 2/20th Battalion, at least, was ready for it. Only second in importance to aggressive morale—and in a sense largely contributory to it—was unceasing work on our own trenches, dug-outs, crater posts, and barbed-wire entanglements. There was no illusion, either in the mind of the Brigadier or in the minds of the men, as to what the translation of these two objects into practical soldiering would mean. So long as the Battalion was in the line there could be little sleep or rest for anybody, and the men would need, like those citizens in the Old Testament to whom was entrusted the rebuilding of Jerusalem after its fall, to have a weapon in the left hand while they dug with a shovel with the right. But in both cases the object to be achieved was worth any sacrifice, and in the modern case the fact that it was achieved has long since obliterated memories of the irksomeness of the means employed.

From the first in the 2/20th Battalion particular emphasis was laid on the importance of patrolling, not only in order to keep the Boche behind his own wire, but to give confidence to our own men and enable them to gain a thorough knowledge of the geography of No Man's Land and of the habits of the enemy. To be on patrol was, certainly at first, not exactly a pleasant occupation, though on occasions it could be quite an exciting one. Patrolling was, of course, only possible at night, and perhaps the worst feature of it in the L.2 Sub-Sector was that a large part of it had to be done on the stomach. It meant crawling out in the long grass and waiting, watching an enemy working party, perhaps, or listening to the tramp of the German officer in his front-line trench as he visited his sentries, and thus disclosed to you their position. And the whole time Véry lights, our own and the enemy's, were lighting up the ground for yards, and German machine guns, which seemed to be about ten yards ahead of you, spat out their bullets, which whistled overhead. Then perhaps you began to feel sleepy, so much so that you were confused as to which were our trenches and which the Huns'. The Véry lights gave no clue. But you pinched yourself and looked round for the remainder of the patrol, and were glad to find them at varying distances around you. No; patrolling, even when one got used to it, was no bed of roses. All the time one had to be prepared with rifle and Mills bomb for hostile patrols. But it had beneficial effects, especially on the Boche: it taught him that the safest place for him was behind his own wire, and when he had learnt that, the first fruits of the Brigadier's plan became evident.

Both sides were fairly equally matched in artillery, but the enemy had a decided ascendancy in heavy trench mortars and *Minnenwerfer*. The conditions of trench warfare gave little scope for machine guns, but at night the Quarries were always well searched by the enemy, and the guns of the 180th Machine Gun Company (under Major E. H. Oxenham) would play on the enemy's dumps in and around the village of Thelus. Reference has already been made to mining in the sector. Probably in this branch of the fighting, to which more detailed reference will be made later, the British superiority was more marked than in any other. The work on our side was carried out by the officers and men of a R.E. Tunnelling Company, whose bravery, efficiency, and capacity for hard work soon became the admiration of all ranks of the 2/20th. The 180th Trench Mortar Battery, to which 2nd-Lieut. E. J. C. Vint, Cpl. J. De Bolla, and a number of 2/20th men were attached, had two Stokes mortars in emplacements in the sub-sector. These did excellent work on many occasions by themselves, and also in combination with the artillery and with Lieut. Hicks and his 2-inch mortars.

The 2/19th Battalion (Lieut.-Col. D. C. Sword) went into the right half of the Brigade sector at the same time as the 2/20th took over the left, and a constant *liaison* had to be maintained between the two battalions. In order the more easily to pick out officers and men of the different units, each Brigade in the Division had a " flash " as a Brigade sign, the emblem being worn on each side of the steel helmet, and by officers also on the back of the jacket just below the centre of the collar. The colours of the triangle worn by the 2/17th, 2/18th, 2/19th, and 2/20th Battalions were respectively black, green, blue, and vermilion. The four battalions were grouped in pairs for purposes of relief. The 2/17th Battalion (Lieut.-Col. H. M. Birkett) and the 2/19th Battalion alternately occupied " L.1 " Sector, and the 2/18th Battalion (Lieut.-Col. W. H. Murphy) and 2/20th Battalion relieved each other in L.2 Sector. Periods in the line were approximately of eight days. Each tour in the front trenches was followed by one " in support," then by a return to the line, and finally by a period in Divisional Reserve.

The first period of " rest " for the 2/20th came on

August 3rd. The Battalion, having handed over the line to the London Irish Rifles on the previous night, moved back before dawn to Divisional Reserve in the hut camp at Mont St. Eloi.

The War Diary, characteristically brief, thus sums up the activities of the eight days which followed:—

"*August 3rd.*—Rest. Concert in evening.

"*August 4th.*—Kit inspection and general clean up. Work on cook-house begun.

"*August 5th.*—Company training 10—1 and 2—4.30. Commencement of soap-pit and drain for ablution trenches.

"*August 6th.*—Church of England service in the wood. Inspection of companies by C.O.

"*August 7th.*—Company training and route march. 2nd-Lieuts. Hearn and Cresswell reported for duty. Officers' dinner with Brigade band playing.

"*August 8th.*—Company training. Sergeants' dinner in Brigade Canteen.

"*August 9th.*—Visit of His Majesty the King to Mont St. Eloi. Company training continued.

"*August 10th.*—Battalion relieved 2/18th Battalion in the trenches. Relief complete at 11.45 p.m."

On the 9th the Battalion informally lined the road when the King arrived, and afterwards there was an excellent cricket match in a field adjoining the camp.

The sergeants' dinner on August 8th was the first of those many happy functions which were always a healthy symptom of the life and spirit of the warrant officers and sergeants of the 2/20th, and which were subsequently held with unvaried success in Salonica, in Egypt, in Jerusalem, in France (in 1918), in Germany —in fact, wherever the Battalion has been. It needed no large dining-room or elaborate arrangements to make the affair a success (though it was a great help at Sinzenich in February, 1919, to have almost ideal conditions); at least one of the dinners was held in the open air under the star-lit sky of the East. The personalities of the sergeants themselves insured merriment, and if something more than rations and rum could be found to eat and drink, that were so much the better. The R.S.M. was *ex-officio* chairman, and if Sergt.-Major Skeer was away, as when he left the Battalion wounded, the duty fell on either C.S.M. Drayton, C.S.M. Salkeld, C.S.M. Hills, C.S.M. Martin, or C.S.M. E. H. Chappell, whoever happened to be the senior with the Battalion at the time. No matter who the chairman, there was sure to be a cheery evening, and when the Commanding Officer and the officers came in as guests before the " smoker " which followed the dinner, fun was sure to follow. The items of the concert were usually punctuated by speeches from the members of the Sergeants' Mess and from their guests, the officers. The speeches, being frequently of an original and informal type (memory recalls particularly vividly one in France by 2nd-Lieut. Slaughter, and another at Shellal by Sergt. Fielder), as a rule contributed in no small degree to the good humour of the evening. It was usual to invite the Brigadier or the Commanding Officer of another Battalion, and the writer well remembers the delight of Brigadier-General Viscount Hampden on one occasion, long after this first sergeants' dinner, in attending one of these functions.

The Battalion possessed no band of its own, but it had supplied a number of men to the Brigade Band, which during rest periods frequently played to the men in the afternoon and to the officers during Mess.

The time spent in support, though affording rather more time for sleep than tours in the front line, was one of almost unceasing manual labour, and most of the men preferred to be holding the line. Digging parties at night and carrying parties by day took all available N.C.Os. and men, and there was the additional strain of knowing that, in the event of trouble, companies would have to muster at short notice, and give a hand in repelling the enemy from the front line.

Schools for officers and N.C.Os. were becoming an established feature in the back areas in July, 1916, and following months. The opportunity of learning the very latest lessons in practical soldiering from instructors who had themselves had considerable experience in the firing line was of great value, and, in addition, the time spent in the seclusion of some village many miles behind the line came as a breath of fresh air to those who had been bearing the burden and heat of the day in the fire zone. Capt. Watson, Capt. Reynolds, and Capt. T. S. Travers in turn attended the course at the 3rd Army School, Auxi-le-Chateau, and all obtained first-class reports. In August Capt. Travers took over " A " Company from Capt. Bullock. Capt. H. C. Partridge had already succeeded Capt. Pritchard in command of " C " Company.

The N.C.Os. and men to whose lot it fell are not likely to forget the experience of watching in the crater posts on the Vimy Ridge, nor, indeed, will the officers whose duty it was to pay frequent visits to each post to receive the report " All correct, sir." The writer, who had no part in these experiences, beyond surveying them from the quieter atmosphere of Brigade Headquarters, would dearly like to write at much greater length of the general routine and atmosphere of those days. He could tell much of the fortitude and cheerfulness of the men amid conditions almost indescribably horrible : of their devotion to duty as they kept their weary watch, and carried out their manual labours in mud and slush and danger, with the ever-present possibility of the bomb or " Minnie " or shell which might come at any moment and blot out a dozen men. But he must resist the temptation, and ask the reader to follow him into a new chapter, where account shall be given in greater detail of the doings on certain days.

CHAPTER IV

RAIDING THE GERMANS

No history of the 2/20th (or any other) Battalion would be complete without many personal references to individuals. Ignorant people have argued that the best soldier is he who has lost his own personality in the crowd, but the experience of the war completely disposed of this theory. On the contrary, the successful battalion was that which set out to use each man in that capacity where he could be of greatest service, and undoubtedly this was one of the guiding principles of Col. Warde-Aldam's command. No one, except he, was allowed to promote N.C.Os., or to select those for specialist work. In many battalions these duties devolved on the Adjutant ; in the 2/20th the Commanding Officer made them his special prerogative. The Adjutant reported the vacancies as they occurred, and the Company Commanders forwarded their recommendations, but the decision always lay with the Commanding Officer himself. No trouble was too great for him to take to ensure that promotion came as soon as vacancies occurred to the well-deserving, and his personal interest in, and knowledge of, every individual concerned made it certain that his decision would be just. In the same way, in submitting names for awards for gallantry, every case reported to him was most carefully considered, and it is safe to say that every medal won in the 2/20th on the field was thoroughly deserved. The Colonel did not believe in lowering the standard of qualification for awards in order " to make a show for the Battalion," and only those deeds which reached the highest level were chronicled and forwarded to the Brigade. In no Battalion, whatever the number of honours gained, was the standard of individual gallantry higher than in the 2/20th.

Personal references are sometimes invidious on account of the people they omit, and it is hoped that the writer may be forgiven if in the lines which follow he fails to refer to some who deserve recognition.

A nominal roll of officers appears as an Appendix to this volume, but the present appears a suitable opportunity, and, moreover, one which may not recur, to digress for a few moments on some of those parts of the Battalion which contributed to its life in a measure out of all proportion to their size or numbers. The first of these were the four Company Sergeant-Majors and the four Company Quartermaster-Sergeants. By coincidence, all the Company Sergeant-Majors were schoolmasters by profession. To the influence of these warrant officers and senior N.C.Os. the Battalion owed a very large part of its efficiency and high morale. The second—and the largest numerically—was the Transport Section. For long the N.C.Os. (Sergt. H. Osbourn, Lce.-Sergt. O. W. Mahoney, Cpl. G. W. Henney, and Lce.-Cpl. F. Lelean), the drivers, grooms, farriers, saddlers, and wheelwrights who formed that cheery, hard-working family under Lieut. Jones, lived a separate life to the rest of the Battalion. At Ecoivres they spent their time each with his own team or rider. Ride-and-drive limber work in all weathers was no child's play on those roads close behind the line during the day, but it was simple and safe in comparison with the long journeys with precious loads to the line at night, over a road well known to the enemy's artillery. And then, when the double journey was completed, and long after midnight, teams and drivers had finally rumbled over the cobbles of Ecoivres, there were the horses to be seen to first, ere the men could turn in for an hour or two's sleep before early morning stables marked the start of another day. It was a point of honour, and one which was frequently put to the test, with the Transport men of the 2/20th, that whatever left Ecoivres on Regimental Transport for the men in the trenches reached the Quarries somehow. The work of the Section changed much in later days, as subsequent chapters will show, but the Transport never did better work than in those days when the Battalion was just "feeling its feet" on the Vimy Ridge. Much of the *esprit de corps* of his men was undoubtedly due to the splendid example of Lieut. Jones, and much also to the sterling qualities of the individuals themselves.

Ecoivres, too, was the home of that strange medley of employed men that will be easily recognized by all who served abroad in the war when we pen the name Rear Headquarters. It included all those N.C.Os. and men, from the Regimental Quartermaster-Sergeant to the post-corporal and the butcher, who were so invaluable on the administrative side of the Battalion, and for whom each day was full of hard work very much like the last, except that when the Battalion was out of the line the work increased by 100 per cent. Quartermaster Dark was in charge of this part of "the firm," as he was wont to call it. His N.C.Os. and men were always liable to be called on for an urgent journey to the trenches if the need arose, and many of them visited the line on duty pretty frequently after their day's work was done.

Certainly R.Q.M.S. Clymo and Sergt. J. Bose, the Quartermaster's assistants in the commissariat department, came to know the Quarries very well. The shoemakers and tailors, under Sergt. A. E. Watkins and Sergt. A. D. Barnard respectively, at this early stage at Ecoivres, and at all times, did invaluable work for the Battalion. Part of the Orderly Room work was done at Rear Headquarters. The complicated returns required for higher authority and much of the routine correspondence were handled in the comparative peace and quiet of Ecoivres by an N.C.O. well known throughout the Battalion, Cpl. M. W. Gathercole. The immediately important clerical work which had to be done in the rough condition of the trenches fell to Sergt. S. G. Giles, who worked under Capt. Craddock in the Quarries. Sergt. A. Warren, who had seen the Orderly Room through its infancy in England, had gone to the Records Section to take charge of Battalion records at Rouen when the unit first arrived in France. The Signalling Section, still, as at Betchworth, in possession of that inimitable instructor, Sergt. F. Powell, was at this time almost identically the same section as in those early days. The Signalling Officer had changed more than once, but the men—Lce.-Cpl. A. C. Crate, Ptes. Owen, Maxted, Crawley, Richardson, Stamford, Mann, Bagwell, Joyce, Targett, Meyer, the two brothers Nash, and several others—remained. 2nd-Lieut. H. L. Goldby was now in charge, with Cpl. J. W. Johnson as his second N.C.O. The communications of the Battalion were in eminently efficient hands, and if the work in France was light compared to that demanded later by the open warfare of Salonica and Palestine, yet never a day passed without some call upon the courage and endurance of the Battalion telephone operators and linesmen. The 2/20th owed much—very much—to its signallers. Closely allied to them were the Headquarter runners, under Cpl. L. F. Jones, who likewise had under him one of the most efficient sections in the Battalion. The runners' task was no easy one. If the Hun artillery " strafed " and, as usually happened, the telephone cable was cut, it was the signallers' job to repair the wire, but it was the duty of the runners to maintain communication until the line was again restored. At normal times, by day and night, the runners had to be prepared to take a message, verbal or written, to any part of the Battalion area, of the geography of which they had to possess a greater knowledge than the Colonel himself, if that had been possible. Their devotion to duty was never at fault. Of the bombers and Lewis gunners it is more difficult to write, as the latter were always with their companies ; and though the bombers were organized as a Headquarter Section for a time under 2nd-Lieut. Kempe and Sergt. A. J. L. Smith, they also worked mostly with their companies. The Battalion was always exceptionally proud of its Lewis gunners. The foundations of their training had been laid by Capt. (then Lieut.) Travers at home, and now, under 2nd-Lieut. W. Davies and highly efficient instructors, Sergt. W. G. Bartlett, Sergt. A. Backhus, Sergt. F. L. Pringle, Sergt. R. T. Jones, and Cpl. J. Linklater, each company had its own complement of gunners, and thought so well of them that a proposal to make " duty " N.C.Os. of some of the " Nos. 1 " not only met with the obvious disinclination of the privates concerned, but was strongly opposed by all the Company Commanders. The Sniping Section was under the charge of 2nd-Lieut. Weatherley, the Assistant Adjutant and Billeting Officer, who had the assistance of Cpl. G. D. Myers. The personnel were responsible for manning the " O.Ps." in the line, for obtaining as much detailed information as possible about the enemy, and for sniping any of his men who dared to show themselves over the parapet or in parts of his trenches which failed to provide adequate cover. The Section undoubtedly contributed much to the destruction of Hun morale.

Of the individual officers, N.C.Os., and men who bore the brunt of all the work in the actual duties of the front-line trenches, it would take more space than is here available to write. Something of their dangers and hardships may be gathered from the concluding stages of this chapter, though no words can adequately describe the monotony, the physical and mental strain of their task, and its utter hopelessness, had they not been supported by the comradeship and mutual support of each other and of their people at home. The future at that time bore no faint signs of that glorious victory which lay more than two years distant, and though it seemed impossible to realize that one day these narrow, muddy trenches would be left far behind an advancing Allied Army, yet there was never any absence of cheerfulness or humour, and almost every day brought out fresh incidents which kept all ranks interested and amused.

Before we turn to the War Diary for an account of some of the more conspicuous days which the Battalion spent in the L.2 Sub-Sector, yet two more personal references must be made. The first is to the cooks, and the second to the officers' servants. Sergt. Bottom and Cpl. J. Goreham needed no reminder of the old adage that an army marches on its stomach. The 2/20th had good reason to congratulate itself on the fact, for never was Battalion better looked after in the cookhouse. The cooks, among whom may be mentioned Pte. Lawes, Pte. Bailey, Pte. Crane, Pte. Alvin, and Pte. Mather, made expert use of whatever rations were issued, and were ready at all times to provide a hot meal at any hour of the day or night. The officers' servants, under Sergt. F. W. Watkins, and headed by Pte. J. Deuters (servant to the Commanding Officer) and Pte. A. Bertram (to the Adjutant), had perhaps slightly more in the way of comfort than the majority of men in the line, but they made ample amends later, when the Battalion was on the march, and they had two people—their master and themselves—to look after. In the trenches they were at the side of their officer whenever he moved about in the line, orders being very strict that no officer was to walk about in the fire zone unaccompanied. The Commanding Officer had a special runner, Pte. J. Collinson, who went with him at all times when he made his tours round the sub-sector twice or three times daily. The servants of the company officers, very often entirely without any previous " domestic " experience whatever, were responsible for the company officers' messes and discharged their responsible duties with that amazing adaptability which is so characteristic of the Britisher in emergency.

The utter unselfishness and devotion of the majority of officers' servants in the infantry battalions of the war have seemed to the writer to have received far less than their due measure of recognition.

As has already been stated, Col. Warde-Aldam took over the line for the first time on Wednesday, July 12th. The events of the 13th and three following days are thus chronicled in the War Diary :—

"*In the Trenches, July 13th*, 1916.—Considerable enemy activity throughout the day with *Minnenwerfer* and rifle grenades. In each case artillery retaliation had desired effect and silenced enemy. At midnight enemy working party was observed in front of P.79 (trench) and dispersed by our Lewis guns."

"*July 14th*, 1916.—The night passed quietly, enemy artillery being active on left sector in front of P.79, and his snipers being busy on Broadmarsh Crater and in direction of Lassale. Our snipers claim a hit. A new sniping post was established overlooking Duffield and Grange, Lassale and Cavalier."

"*July 15th*, 1916.—There was considerable activity in the afternoon along the whole front, the enemy sending a large number of rifle grenades and *Minnenwerfer* into Lassale Trench, causing casualties from blown-in parapet. We retaliated with Stokes gun and 18-pounders. A little machine-gun activity during night. Coloured streamers were seen in enemy trench left of Durand. Sombard and Cavalier trenches improved."

"*July 16th*, 1916.—Continued activity during the day from trench mortars and rifle grenades. Stokes gun dispersed opposition. A working party of six of the enemy dispersed by our rifles. Our snipers claim three hits."

The initiative at the moment undoubtedly lay with the enemy, but these were only the opening days, and later, as we shall see, the tables were turned.

The first recorded instances of gallantry under fire in the Battalion formed the subject of the following notice, which appeared in Battalion Routine Orders dated July 19th, 1916 :—

"The Commanding Officer wishes to bring to the notice of all ranks the gallant conduct and devotion to duty of the undermentioned N.C.O. and men of this Battalion :—

No. 2342 Lce.-Cpl. Keating, F. L. 'A' Company
No. 5563 Pte. Waterhouse, J. ... 'C' Company
No. 5630 Pte. Smith, A. ... 'C' Company
No. 1590 Pte. Hubble, W. G. ... 'A' Company

"These men, in face of heavy fire from the enemy snipers, rifle grenades, and machine guns, coolly proceeded to dig out four of their comrades who had been buried by the bursting of a shell in the trench, and did not stop until the buried men had been released.

"The Commanding Officer deeply regrets to announce that No. 2342 Lce.-Cpl. F. L. Keating and No. 5563 Pte. J. Waterhouse have since succumbed to the wounds which they received whilst carrying out this work."

It was announced on August 7th that the Military Medal had been awarded to Pte. A. Smith and to Pte. W. G. Hubble for their gallant conduct. These two medals were the first to be awarded in the 60th (London) Division.

The Battalion went into support on the 17th, and was disposed as follows :—

Battalion Headquarters : La Portique.
Two Companies : Pont St. and Quarries.
One Company : Ross St. Dug-outs.
One Company : Cenot Cave.

Throughout the time, the men were employed in assisting R.E. working parties to improve the front trenches.

A draft of 80 other ranks from the 1/15th London Regiment joined the Battalion on July 22nd. Three days later all four companies were again in the line, the order from right to left, as before, being "A," "B," "C," and "D."

The aggressiveness of the enemy was seen in a fresh form on July 26th. At 2 a.m. he exploded a mine between Durand and Duffield, and, though little damage was done, the event is of importance as introducing a new feature into the life of the 2/20th. Our reply, in the shape of another mine, was made at 9.12 p.m. on the same day. The resulting crater, which was situated between Birkin and Grange, and was described officially as approximately 50 yards north and south and 120 yards east and west, came to be known as "Tidza."

Tactics, whether on a large or small scale, are very much a matter of the configuration of the ground, and when the whole contour of No Man's Land opposite a length of 50 yards' frontage is changed, there must of necessity be, at least locally, an altered tactical situation. The R.E. tunnellers had advised the Brigadier as to the best psychological moment for the mine to be sprung. That was their job—to pit their knowledge and labour against those of the enemy's tunnellers, whose burrowing and tamping they could hear as they worked in their own shafts. Each side was seeking to improve his position by blowing his mines in such a direction as should afford better observation or better chances of concealment, and at such a time as would thwart the intention of the enemy's miners by blowing in his galleries as they approached completion. When a German mine went up, all available men were hastily collected into parties for "making good" at least the near lip of the crater, and if in anywise possible the far lip too. Similar arrangements were necessary when our own tunnellers "blew," but in their case, of course, the exact moment of the explosion (though not the shape of the crater) was known beforehand, and consolidating parties were prepared accordingly.

Immediately the explosion which was to result in

Tidza occurred, our artillery put a barrage on the enemy's lines, but no sooner had the earth resettled than the Boche rushed a strong bombing-party on to the ground between Grange and the new crater, and waited there to catch our consolidating parties in enfilade. Every attempt to fight our way on to the near lip was met with a murderous shower of bombs, rifle grenades, and trench mortars from the enemy, who had obviously determined that we should have no footing on the crater at all.

After dark on July 27th-28th a party of seven men reached the near lip, and gallantly held on to it throughout the night. Despite continued harassing by the enemy, a working party made good the ground, and under heavy fire dug in on the near lip. In the fighting which preceded the consolidation 2nd-Lieut. C. T. Hellicar and Lieut. T. Gardner lost their lives, and 2nd-Lieut. K. G. Malcolm was wounded.

Much credit for the ultimate success of the consolidation was due to those N.C.Os. and men who, having once reached the crater lip, refused in spite of all opposition to be driven off. Posts with loophole plates were constructed on the near lip, and as time went on these were gradually improved by working parties.

The details of mining and counter-mining which went on almost as a matter of routine in the weeks which followed were known only to very few. Gen. Studd gave unceasing attention to the subject, and his conferences with the tunnelling authorities were long and frequent. To such good purpose was the vigilance of the Brigadier and his experts applied that on no occasion was the enemy ever able to effect a surprise by " blowing " a mine without the previous knowledge of our authorities, nor did he blow up any section of trenches by mining without our having first removed the garrison.

At 9.40 a.m. on Sunday, July 30th, the enemy, preceded by a hurricane bombardment, made a strong bombing attack from his posts at the back of Duffield Crater. His advance was completely repulsed by rifle fire, rifle grenades, and bombs, and within an hour the situation was again restored to normal. The Boche continued to " show his tail " in a disagreeable way for some days, the while the 2/20th awaited the opportunity of humbling him. On August 2nd the Battalion left the line for its first period in reserve, and on the 7th drafts of 20, 60, and 10 other ranks respectively joined from the 7th, 9th, and 12th Battalions London Regiment.

The return of the Battalion to the line on the 11th synchronized with a heavy bombardment by us of Broadmarsh Crater, as a result of which considerable damage could be observed through glasses. At 2 a.m. on the 13th our artillery barraged the enemy's lines in conjunction with a raid by the 2/19th Battalion in the " L.1 " Sub-Sector, and the Hun trenches were seen to be badly knocked about. The enemy made a feeble reply, which caused us no casualties.

On the morning of the 15th Lce.-Cpl. A. Smith and Pte. W. G. Hubble received their Military Medals from Lieut.-Gen. Sir Charles Fergusson, the Corps Commander. In the evening we bombarded an enemy strong point on the north-east lip of Birkin with howitzers and Stokes mortars, obviously with excellent effect.

On Wednesday, August 16th, we put up a mine on our lip of Grange, as the Germans were working hard towards us. The War Diary account states :—

" At about 7 p.m. a small mine was blown under Grange Crater, destroying, and at the same time raising, a portion of our lip. Covered by the fire of our Stokes guns and by rifle fire both from the flanks and the edge of the crater, the consolidation party got on to the lip of the crater, and in about ten minutes new plates had been established. By the morning the consolidation was complete. During the early part of the work the enemy threw ' whizz-bangs ' into the support lines, causing a few casualties, and blocking a portion of Grange Trench. A *Minnenwerfer* fell in the Retrenchment Line, between Birkin and Tidza, lowering the parapet considerably. The damage in both cases was soon repaired. During the night the enemy made some attempts to attack between Tidza and Grange, but they were driven off."

Gen. Bulfin and Gen. Studd visited Grange on the 18th to see the new feature. The Battalion was in support throughout August 19th—23rd, and took over the line from the 2/18th Battalion again on the night of the 24th. Capt. G. J. Edwards and 2nd-Lieut. E. K. James reported for duty on the 23rd.

Col. Warde-Aldam had one of his many lucky escapes about this time. Having attended a conference of Battery Commanders of Col. Bayley's Brigade of Artillery at Berthonval Farm, he went on to spend the night with " A 303 " Battery. The enemy threw some shells over into the neighbourhood of Battery Headquarters, and finally obtained a direct hit on the Officers' Mess, which it demolished. The shell came at a lucky moment, or there must have been many casualties. The C.O. walked across to Col. Bayley's Headquarters, and dined and slept there.

On the 25th and 26th our artillery and trench mortars did some good work on the enemy trenches and crater posts, considerable damage being observed in each case. On the second day our trench P.79 was knocked about by the enemy's retaliation, 2nd-Lieut. J. A. C. Hasslacher and three men being buried. All were extricated, and none were seriously hurt. 2nd-Lieut. Lane was slightly wounded in a bombing attack launched by the enemy against the right sap of Tidza on the morning of August 29th. In the afternoon our artillery bombarded the back of Common Crater, but, owing to very heavy rain and mist, no satisfactory observation of the results could be obtained. As a result of the rain, the trenches were soon in flood, and in many places the parapets collapsed. Wednesday, August 30th, was spent in making good the damage as far as possible, and in draining off the water. In the evening the Battalion went into reserve. Lieut. J. Crafter had joined for duty on the 28th, and on the last day of the month a draft of 35 other ranks reported.

The period out of the line on this occasion was confined to six days, the first of which was observed as a complete rest for everybody.

On the night of the 5th, after a "compulsory rest" from 3 to 6 p.m., the Battalion once more took over in the trenches. Our artillery gave the Germans snuff in the form of 18-pounders, 60-pounders, and howitzers on the following days and nights, and the enemy replied at frequent intervals. On the 7th we commenced wire-cutting in front of Durand Crater, and, as if to lower our morale before we attempted to use the gaps as openings to his trenches, the Boche put up a big notice-board in his front line containing the bare announcement: "20,000 Rumanian prisoners." After being exposed for some hours, the board was removed.

On Monday, September 11th, the Battalion carried out its first offensive operation in the form of a raid on the enemy's front line north of Durand Crater on a frontage of 100 yards. The raid had as its object "the capturing of prisoners, identifications, and stores, and the infliction of as much damage as possible on the enemy trenches." The raiders, of whom Lieut. J. Crafter was in command, had been training behind the line for some time previously. The composition of parties, their duties, and their entire training were placed by the Commanding Officer in the hands of Capt. W. M. Craddock, for whom 2nd-Lieut. Jones acted as Adjutant temporarily. The officers taking part numbered three (Lieut. Crafter, 2nd-Lieut. B. T. Woolfe, and 2nd-Lieut. W. G. Thompson), the N.C.Os. ten, and the men fifty-eight. Every detail had been thought out and practised, so that every man who went " over the top" knew exactly what part he had to play. In addition, every man of the party had been across No Man's Land at least once by night by the route which he would take on the night of the raid. The men were organized in two main groups, "marauders" and bombing parties. The former, designed to carry out the main object of the raid, consisted of five sub-groups —*i.e.*, three parties of one N.C.O. and five men, each under an officer, one party of one N.C.O. and five men, three booty parties of three men each, and three connecting files of three men each. The duty of the bombing parties (right and left), which comprised three N.C.Os. and ten men each, was to take up positions at the extremities of the frontage of the raid in the enemy lines, and to form bombing blocks to prevent the "marauders" being enfiladed by the Boche. At 3.28 a.m. the whole raiding party climbed the parapet and crept stealthily forward. At 3.30, under an intense barrage from our artillery, assisted by machine guns and trench mortars, the raiders, with blackened hands and faces and armed with rifles (with bayonets fixed), bombs, and in some cases "knobkerries," doubled forward into the enemy trenches. Certain men, who had been specially detailed, ran out a tape from our lines to the enemy parapet to act as a guide for the return journey. On the party entering the trenches, a white board was stuck on the German parapet to mark the end of the tape, and here the " booty men " had orders to remain. The connecting files remained near the tape half-way across No Man's Land, so that no risk was taken of the "marauders" and bombing groups losing the way home. The raiders found repairing material on the enemy's parapet close to the gaps which had been cut in the wire, so that the raid had not come an hour too soon. The "marauders" quickly set to work searching the dug-outs. Cpl. E. J. Painter knocked down and captured a German; Lieut. Crafter captured two Red Cross men in a dug-out; and one

German gave himself up to 2nd-Lieut. Woolfe. Altogether four prisoners were taken, all of the 122nd Regiment, and a quantity of booty providing identifications. In addition, several of the enemy had been killed in their trenches, which had been badly knocked about by our artillery. By 3.49 all the raiders had returned except three, who remained unaccounted for. Our casualties amounted to three other ranks wounded. The three men missing were, unfortunately, later found to have been killed.

That the objects of the raid had been achieved to the satisfaction of the authorities was soon made evident by the following letter, which was received by the Corps Commander later in the day :—

"*From the G.O.C. First Army.*

" I should be glad if you will direct the G.O.C. 60th Division to convey to Brig.-General Studd, Commanding 180th Brigade, my thanks and appreciation of the action of the 2/20th Battalion the London Regiment, under the command of Lieut.-Col. Warde-Aldam, last night in carrying out their successful raid into the German trenches. The identification they obtained by the capture of prisoners is of exceptional value at the present time, and this information will be of the greatest service, not only to the British Army, but to the Armies of our Allies who are fighting in all theatres of the war.

(Sgd.) " R. C. HAKING, *General,*
11/9/16. *Commanding First Army.*"

The Divisional Commander wired to the Brigadier :—

" Congratulate you and OX [code name for the 2/20th] on success of raid. Hope all have returned, and wounded sent back."

In forwarding the Army Commander's message, Gen. Studd wrote to the Commanding Officer :—

"The success of the raid was, in my opinion, due to the very careful way in which the enterprise was planned and organized by you, and to the determination and fine spirit in which it was carried out by the officers, non-commissioned officers, and men of the raiding party. I congratulate you on the very great value of the information obtained. This first offensive enterprise of the Battalion under your command will, I feel sure, be but one of many fine exploits which will establish the reputation of the 2/20th as a Battalion remarkable for its hard fighting and hard work."

Congratulations were also received from the other Battalions of the 180th Brigade.

In addition to Col. Warde-Aldam and Capt. Craddock, both of whom had taken infinite pains with the organization and preliminary arrangements, and the officers who actually went "over the top" in the raid, useful work in connection with the operation was done by 2nd-Lieut. Weatherley, who carried out very valuable reconnaissances beforehand, and Capt. Partridge, who checked the men as they returned to our lines.

Lieut. J. Crafter received the Military Cross, and Sergt. J. C. McCafferty, Cpl. Painter, and Pte. Castel the Military Medal for gallantry in the raid.

The Colonel's diary relates that on September 11th Major-General J. S. Shea, who months afterwards took over the 60th Division from Gen. Bulfin, visited the sub-sector accompanied by Brig.-Gen. Charles, the B.G.G.S. of the 17th Corps.

From the night of the 11th to the 17th the Battalion was in Brigade Reserve. "A," "B," and "D" Companies were employed on a special scheme of work, widening and deepening the observation line from Watling Street to Birkin and the saps leading from the "P" line to it. The work was practically complete when companies relieved the 2/18th in the front trenches on the night of the 17th. "C" Company was employed on Brigade fatigues and guards. During this period

2nd-Lieuts. R. G. Grant, G. Tweedie, A. Stone, E. A. Clarke, and D. R. Blundell reported for duty.

Heavy rain set in on September 19th, and continued for two days, transforming the trenches into running water-courses, and necessitating much work on parts of the parapet which had collapsed. The enemy was quiet, but our 18-pounders and trench mortars are reported as doing considerable damage on September 20th. At 6.30 on the 21st we exploded a mine between Grange and Duffield. The enemy offered no opposition, and we consolidated the near lip without casualties. On the 22nd and 23rd our trench mortars asserted themselves, and did considerable damage to enemy posts on Broadmarsh. On the evening of the latter date the London Irish came into the line, and the 2/20th took their third turn at St. Eloi in Divisional Reserve.

Sergt. McCafferty, Cpl. Painter, and Pte. Castel received their medals from the Corps Commander on a special parade on Tuesday, September 26th, and afterwards the General remained to witness a demonstration of *Flammenwerfer* and various smoke bombs. Intensive digging, attack practice, and anti-gas training received special attention during this period out of the line. Lieut. W. G. Elder, who had been seconded from the Battalion to take charge of the Divisional Gas School at Frévent Capelle, lectured to the whole Battalion on gas warfare on the morning of the 29th.

In the evening the men were once more in the trenches. The night and the following day are described as "extremely quiet." There was practically no enemy artillery or trench-mortar activity; our own fired intermittently throughout the day. A striking contrast to the enemy of earlier days! The enemy blew two *camouflets* early on the morning of October 1st, one between Grange and Tidza, and the other under the southern lip of Common. Slight damage was done to the left post of Tidza, but the ground was not broken, and no casualties were sustained.

At 2 a.m. on October 2nd a party of two officers, eight N.C.Os., and thirty-two men, under 2nd-Lieut. M. Lane, raided the enemy line near Vernon. The party was subdivided into right and left parties, the former being under 2nd-Lieut. B. T. Woolfe, with Sergt. G. W. Osborne as Second-in-Command, and the latter under 2nd-Lieut. Lane, with Sergt. F. N. Harding as second-in-command. Other N.C.Os. taking part were Cpl. W. C. Davies, Cpl. E. J. Fuller, Cpl. A. E. White, Lce.-Cpl. A. Otterburn, Lce.-Cpl. O. S. Midwood, and Lce.-Cpl. C. H. Nixon. Lieut. Crafter was in command of the immediate operations from a point in our front trenches. A heavy barrage was put down at " zero," and the raiders followed hard on its track into the enemy trenches. The trenches they found badly knocked about, and practically deserted. Two of the enemy were seen. They fired at our men and ran away, but were pursued by Pte. J. Garland, who knocked one down. Being badly wounded, he found it impossible to pursue them farther, and they made good their escape. No other signs of the enemy could be found. We had seven slight casualties, all of which occurred just as the party entered the trench.

On the night of Wednesday, October 4th, 2nd-Lieut. A. W. Pilbeam, Sergt. McCafferty, M.M., and four men raided an enemy post between Durand and Duffield. They crawled out and lay for a short time under the parapet until they heard voices. The officer and N.C.O. then mounted the parapet, and, while within a few yards of a party of Germans, emptied their revolvers into them and dropped some bombs among them, killing four. The enemy retaliated with rifles and bombs, and our party withdrew, one of the men being killed and two wounded. An attempt was also made to bomb the enemy's post on Common, but it was found impossible to get through the German wire.

The recent activities of the 2/20th were beginning to have their effect on the morale of the Boche. On the night of the 4th the enemy betrayed every sign of nervousness, and sent up many Véry lights and intermittently threw bombs at his own wire. Our Stokes guns and machine guns were abnormally active, but there was very little reply except for a few rifle grenades. The Battalion handed over to the 2/18th on the 6th, and was in Brigade Reserve, supplying fatigue and carrying parties, until the night of the 11th, when companies went into the front line for the last time for many long months.

This final period was noteworthy for great activity on our part in wiring and patrolling. Twice in the seven days the enemy put up his S.O.S. signal—the first time as a result of two N.C.Os. of the Battalion crawling out and bombing a small crater which had been formed between Tidza and Birkin ; and the second when, on October 15th, we bombed the enemy's front line from several points for ten minutes, and put over a trench-mortar barrage. At 7 p.m. on the 16th 2nd-Lieut. Weatherley and three men crawled out on the right of Tidza, each carrying a Stokes shell. They reached the enemy right post on Tidza, into which they threw two shells, and threw the other into the small crater. The party returned safely, and the enemy post was badly damaged.

The last day in the line, October 17th, appears as follows in the War Diary :—

"At 2.25 a.m. the enemy were active with trench mortars, doing further damage to the ' P ' line. Patrols were sent out on either flank, and in both cases valuable information was obtained. Further wiring was completed. A further reconnaissance was made of the small crater between Birkin and Tidza. Save for enemy trench mortar activity, which again caused damage to our ' P ' line, the day was quiet. The Battalion was relieved by the 2/18th London Regiment in the afternoon."

On October 24th the relief of the whole Division, preparations for which had been going on for some days previously, brought to a close three months of very satisfactory work. The change, in the "L.2" Sub-Sector at least, since the 60th Division first took over was more than remarkable. The subdued attitude of the enemy in the last few weeks was in creditable contrast to his assertiveness in the first days of July. The fighting ideal laid down by the Brigadier and the Commanding Officer had been attained in many particulars. In addition, our own defences had been developed and improved throughout. Trenches had been connected up, crater posts enlarged and new ones added, and the barbed wire strengthened everywhere. The sub-sector as taken over by a battalion of Princess Patricia's Canadian Light Infantry, 3rd Canadian Division, was in every way safer and more comfortable than when it was taken over by the 2/20th in July, and the enemy had been humbled and deprived of initiative. On relief the 60th Division moved back to a training area.

Before leaving the line we must add one brief word on the work of the Commanding Officer and his officers in the three months which had just passed. The strain thrown upon all ranks by the conditions in which they were fighting and living was bound to fall more heavily on those who had the responsibility, not only of men's lives, but also of the safety of the whole of the Allied Armies on the Western Front. A break-through at any one point might, and probably would, involve the whole line. Such a break-through could be carried out by the enemy at any moment of the day or night, and without his giving the slightest possible warning, so short was the distance from his front line to ours. The responsibility of a Battalion Commander, his Adjutant, and his Company Commanders, was truly immeasurable. Col. Warde-Aldam made a complete tour of the front trenches at least twice every day. He organized the greater part of the work on the trenches himself. His courage, if there was trouble on, was unlimited. Needless to say, he knew every inch of the sub-sector. Capt. Craddock, as Adjutant, had an enormous amount of administrative work to get through, and in addition assisted Col. Warde-Aldam in a hundred and one ways in the trenches. Like the C.O. in that he was never happy in a dug-out, Capt. Craddock usually threw as much of the clerical work as possible on to 2nd-Lieut. Weatherley, the Assistant Adjutant, who in turn never lost an opportunity of spending time in the trenches with his snipers. The result was a minimum of clerical work for everybody, especially the Company Commanders. Major F. C. Bentley had a great deal to do with the construction of crater posts and the general improvement of the trenches, besides being P.R.I., and when Col. Warde-Aldam went home on special leave on October 11th, Major Bentley assumed temporary command. The Company Commanders—Capt. Travers, Capt. Watson, Capt. Partridge, and Capt. Reynolds—probably had the most difficult task of all. The high morale of their men and the low morale of the Boche were undoubtedly largely due to their gallant and untiring efforts.

The casualties up to the date of leaving the line were as under :—

	Officers.	Other Ranks.
Killed in action	2	35
Died of wounds	1	13
Wounded	5	187

Individual mention has already been made of the officer casualties, except that of 2nd-Lieut. E. A. Clarke, who was wounded by a rifle grenade on September 30th, and died of wounds on the following day, only seventeen days after joining the Battalion, and Lieut. W. R. Elliot who was slightly wounded on August 14th. A complete Roll of Honour of all ranks who were killed and who died of wounds will be found in the Appendix.

The following N.C.Os. were wounded :—

Lce.-Cpl. R. J. Hill.	R.S.M. W. T. Skeer.
Sergt. S. J. Martin.	Sergt. L. G. Fry.
Cpl. B. H. Lymbery.	Lce.-Cpl. H. D. Deacon.
Cpl. C. Dickens.	Lce.-Cpl. H. Wood.
Cpl. E. J. Clifford.	Lce.-Cpl. E. Hallam.
Lce.-Cpl. J. Powell (twice).	Sergt. A. J. Spittle.
Lce.-Cpl. J. Skeen.	Lce.-Cpl. C. H. Slatter.
Cpl. E. H. Chappell.	Lce.-Cpl. A. E. Taylor.
Cpl. J. K. Overall.	Lce.-Cpl. R. J. Lowe.
Sergt. H. J. Mitchell.	Lce.-Cpl. P. A. Hodges.
Sergt. H. A. Walker.	Sergt. F. Speer.
Sergt. G. W. Phipps.	Lce.-Cpl. R. Bell.
Lce.-Cpl. E. Barrett (twice).	Lce.-Cpl. A. Howe.
Sergt. J. G. Rennie.	Sergt. J. H. Mould.
Sergt. E. A. Funnell.	Lce.-Cpl. J. O. Garbutt.
Sergt. S. N. Seager.	Lce.-Cpl. W. E. Cowell.
Cpl. J. Greer.	Sergt. G. W. Osborne.
Cpl. W. C. Davies.	Sergt. J. McCafferty.
Lce.-Cpl. J. C. Howell.	Lce.-Sergt. W. R. Herbert.
Lce.-Cpl. C. W. Purvis.	Lce.-Sergt. S. J. Collins.
Cpl. S. G. Bird.	Cpl. A. S. Churchill.
Lce.-Cpl. A. V. Minter.	Lce.-Cpl. H. Ingham.

On Monday, October 23rd, the Battalion left Mont St. Eloi and all its many experiences behind, and billeted in Penin for the second and last time. Houvain (on the 24th), Bonnières (on the 28th), and Heuzecourt (on the 29th) were occupied and left behind in succession ; then a prolonged stay was made at Yaucourt. From here a few officers and N.C.Os. were granted short leave home, though in some cases it meant less than twelve hours there. There was no general leave.

Rumour had been hard at work in the meanwhile, and the prospect of the Battalion being on its way to the Somme battlefield found general acceptance. The Division had received frequent praise for its fighting spirit and hard work, and it was generally felt that these qualities would find their expression most usefully in what was up to that time one of the greatest British offensive battles of the war. These rumours, though true as representing the original intention of the Higher Command, were not destined to be fulfilled. On November 4th, while the Battalion was at Yaucourt, a warning order was received that the whole Division would very shortly proceed to join the British Salonica Force in Macedonia.

To say that the news came as a surprise can give no idea of the effect it had. It was a veritable bombshell, though the complete ignorance of everybody on the subject of Salonica, its climate and conditions of warfare, soon produced a general attitude of "better to wait and see," and the Battalion, beyond a certain amount of ill-concealed speculation, resigned itself to the inevitable. A pink pamphlet, "Salonica Establishments," followed the warning order, and organization and equipping on the new scale soon occupied attention to the exclusion of all else.

It was now announced that Gen. Studd would not accompany the Brigade, and that he had been appointed B.G.G.S. 11th Corps. This was the saddest news of all. No man had done more for the 180th Brigade than he. The writer had had the privilege of being attached to his staff from the time that Gen. Studd took over the Brigade at home until the middle of August, and had had special opportunities of knowing all that its four battalions owed to him. He had put the finishing touches to the training of officers and men at Sutton Veny; he had watched their preparation and organization before battalions first took over the line; he had undoubtedly saved many lives by insisting on the provision of steel helmets for the men before they went into the trenches (though the authorities protested that steel helmets could not be provided), and in countless ways he had looked after the welfare and comfort of his troops, appreciating their every discomfort and sympathizing in their every difficulty. Above all, in spite of chronic lameness caused by his old wound, he had been indefatigable in touring the trenches at all hours of the day and night, so that he might have a thorough knowledge of the conditions in which the men were placed, and of the physical difficulties in which their work was carried out. In his daily tours the General would always spend a long time in the actual front trenches examining the enemy line through his periscope. As a proof, if any were needed, of his intimate knowledge of the minutest details in the German defences, Gen. Studd would frequently amend the Brigade daily intelligence report on such an apparently small matter as the exact position of an enemy machine gun emplacement or the thickness of the German barbed wire at a particular point. On returning from the line, he would spend long hours poring over aeroplane photographs of the enemy positions, in consultation with his mining and artillery experts, and would frequently produce these photographs at conferences of Commanding Officers to illustrate his orders and intentions. In his tours of the trenches the General was invariably accompanied by Pte. T. Helyer, who, as his orderly, always carried a rather massive periscope. (Pte. Helyer, who returned to duty with the 2/20th when the Battalion left France, was unfortunately captured by the Bulgars in Salonica, and met a sad end from typhus whilst a prisoner of war.) The Brigadier's departure was in a very real sense a personal loss to the officers of the Brigade ; it was certainly no less regretted by the men. On a special parade at Ailly on November 8th Gen. Studd said farewell to the Brigade, and after congratulating all battalions on the work they had already accomplished, wished them good luck in that which lay before them.

Lieut.-Gen. Sir Chas. Fergusson, the Corps Commander, personally visited the Battalion to say goodbye.

Gen. Studd was succeeded by Brig.-Gen. F. M. Carleton, D.S.O., Reserve of Officers. Capt. Oppenheim's place as Brigade Major had been taken some months before by Capt. H. E. Macfarlane, M.C.

The disappointment felt in leaving France, with its close proximity to home, was somewhat mitigated by the fact that the whole 60th Division was embarking. The 2/20th had made many friends among the artillery officers, and with the officers and men of the 180th Brigade Machine Gun Company and Trench Mortar Battery, and it was some consolation to know that these friends were proceeding to Salonica at the same time.

The Battalion left Yaucourt in pouring rain on November 19th, and marched to Longpré, where entrainment for Marseilles took place. The journey took rather more than twenty-four hours. After a somewhat uncomfortable beginning (on the pitch-black night of our arrival the guides led us many miles out of our way, and to Valentin Camp instead of Mussot), a very delightful period of eight days was spent in Mussot Camp, Marseilles, and the Battalion embarked for Salonica by the s.s. *Ivernia* on November 30th.

The following letter, received by the Divisional Commander, was published in Battalion Routine Orders on October 26th, 1916 :—

" MAJOR-GEN. E. S. BULFIN, C.B., C.V.O.,
" *Commanding 60th Division.*

" I should be very sorry to let the Division leave the 17th Corps without expressing to them, through you, my thanks for all the hard work they have done, and my appreciation of the soldierly spirit they have shown throughout. It is a great pride and pleasure to have had such a Division under one's command, and a real regret to part from them.

" I am very grateful indeed to you and your staff for all the loyal co-operation shown to myself and the Corps.

" I am absolutely confident that the Division will make a name for itself whenever the chance comes, and I wish you and them the best of luck and success.

  (Sgd.) " CHARLES FERGUSSON, *Lieut.-Gen.,*
25/10/16.   *Commanding 17th Corps.*'

CHAPTER V

MACEDONIA : RAIDING THE BULGARS

OUR account of the period spent in Macedonia must be compressed into a single chapter. Not that the front in the Near East was in any sense unimportant—Ludendorff's " Memoirs " have exposed that fallacy of the arm-chair critics—but for the 60th Division the time lacked much of the excitement and adventure common to France and Palestine, though its discomforts and difficulties were incomparably greater than those on the Western Front. In allotting space, it is vital to the true perspective of our " History " to give no more than their due number of pages to events which, however novel and interesting, yet paid no contribution to the unit's fighting record. For this, after all, is the only sure test of greatness in any battalion. In the case of the 2/20th the one addition which Macedonia made to that record may well be regarded as one of the finest achievements of the Battalion—but of that more anon.

The Battalion had left Marseilles without Major Bentley, who had been evacuated sick, and a large number of N.C.Os. and men who had not recovered from wounds or sickness. Some of them, including R.S.M. Skeer, followed to Salonica when they left hospital, but the majority, unfortunately, never rejoined. Capt. Craddock received promotion to Acting-Major, and became Second-in-Command. Lieut. W. R. Elliot became Adjutant. 2nd-Lieut. F. D. Parker had joined the Battalion a few days before it left France.

The discomforts of the Macedonian theatre of war were unparalleled on any other front, with the possible exception of Mesopotamia. The main reasons appear to the writer to resolve themselves into three, viz.—the extremes of climate ; the lack of roads, rivers, and other means of communication ; and the submarine peril in the Mediterranean. Of these the last was undoubtedly the most potent. Had the sea journey home been without risk, and had ships been available to take leave parties at least on the same scale as the cross-Channel leave boats from the Western Front, the British Salonica Army could have put up cheerfully with any extremes of climate, and endured all the discomforts of a roadless country. Then, too, if the Mediterranean had been free, mails would not have gone to the bottom of the sea with that obstinate persistency which was more demoralizing than all the " strafes " of the Bulgars, and the British Salonica Force would have received at least its share of good things from home. As it was, the army in Macedonia was by compulsion of circumstance almost entirely self-supporting in everything but the bare necessities of life. Every tin of bully beef and milk, every box of biscuits and tea, every gun and shell and round of ammunition, had to pass through an avenue of German and Austrian submarines before it reached its destination ; and, of course, reinforcements were exposed to equal risk. There was a price on the head of everybody and everything sent from home. How frequently that price was paid is now a matter of history. The comparative safety of the English Channel brought many comforts to the troops in France which were denied to the men in Macedonia, Egypt, and Mesopotamia ; but these were an insignificant loss compared to the loss of leave. The way home was barred to all. Even the sick and wounded were detained at Malta and other Mediterranean stations equally far from " Blighty," and casualties might consider themselves lucky if they even got as far as Malta before they were pronounced fit and were ordered to rejoin their units.

The Battalion got no farther than Marseilles before

its attention was directed to the submarine menace. The *Ivernia* left harbour at 5 p.m. on November 30th, and she seemed to be making good headway when everyone, except the crew and the officers and men on submarine guard, turned in at 10 p.m.; yet on waking in the morning we found ourselves back in Marseilles Harbour as surely as though the ship had never moved. Nor did she leave her berth again until forty-eight hours later, by which time two practice alarms had been held, and the men were already heartily sick of the confinement and stuffiness of the troop-deck.

In addition to the 2/20th (36 officers and 855 other ranks strong), there were on board the 2/21st London Regiment (whose Commanding Officer, Col. F. D. Watney, T.D., was O.C. Ship), the 2/5th Field Ambulance (Lieut.-Col. R. Corfe), and the Divisional Commander and his Staff. Major Craddock was Ship's Adjutant. The *Ivernia* was making her last completed voyage, for on her next journey she was torpedoed and sunk in the Mediterranean. She carried her cargo of the 60th Division safely into Salonica Harbour soon after sunrise on Friday, December 8th, and we had our first view of the picturesque Balkan city as it lay glittering white on the slope facing the sea. Whether it were that distance lent enchantment to the view, or that first appearances, as commonly taught, are always best, certainly Salonica never seemed so attractive again !

The day was oppressively hot, and the Battalion was ordered to remain on board until the evening. At 5 p.m. the *Wave*, a commodious lighter, capable of holding all four companies and Headquarters, carried the men to the quayside, where there was no delay in setting out on the march of seven miles to Uchantar Camp, on the northern outskirts of the city. On their way through the narrow, sordid, cobbled streets, companies had their first glimpse of the tawdry estaminets, the dingy cafés, and the squalid dwellings of the Balkan people, and as we passed, the shopkeepers—mostly Greeks, Spanish Jews, and Turks—strolled leisurely to their doors to look on with unconcerned indifference. Their lack of enthusiasm (to put it mildly) was in noticeable contrast to the crowded windows, the cheers, and the patriotic songs which had greeted the Battalion so recently as it marched down the main thoroughfares of Marseilles.

Rain fell heavily before Uchantar came in sight. A gale sprang up and played havoc with the tents which had been pitched by the men of the 2/19th London Regiment. Hot tea was all ready, and after consuming it officers and men crowded uncomfortably into those tents which were still standing. The night was black as pitch and wretchedly cold, and as the blankets had not come up, mackintosh ground-sheets had to serve the double purpose of protection from wet and cold. Rain fell in torrents all night, and the gale increased. By morning the camp was under water, and the number of tents standing could be counted on two hands. Officers and men were thoroughly drenched. One Company Commander, who had turned in in the dark, woke up in the morning to find that he had spent the night sharing the covering of a Greek private, who had joined the Battalion as interpreter on the previous day, and into whose tent he had inadvertently strayed.

As if ashamed of her chilly reception, Nature produced a glorious day to follow. Taking advantage of the hot sunshine, all spare clothing and all equipment were hung out to dry, tents were newly pitched, the camp was drained, and ornamental stone paths—the delight of the Brigadier—were made.

Uchantar was sited on a sandy plain, dotted with numerous prehistoric tumuli, and situated on the extreme outskirts of Salonica.

Neither officers nor men were slow to take advantage of leave to the city in the afternoons which followed. They found Salonica at once the most crowded and the most cosmopolitan place imaginable. Jews and

Jewesses, Greeks, Turks, Albanians, and Balkan peasants, soldiers of all ranks and colours, and British and Australian nursing sisters, rubbed shoulders together in its streets. Venizelos Street was almost one solid mass of human beings at all hours of the day, and for long after dark, and one could certainly have walked from one end of it to the other on the heads of the people. The babel of shouting and conversation—a mixture of every known language on the earth—which rose from the crowd was occasionally drowned from a neighbouring street by the ugly clang of a passing tram, which was never by any chance anything but absolutely full, and usually had a jostling knot of Greek men, women, and children hanging on anxiously to the small rear footplate. Rattling springless carts, army lorries, and motor ambulances formed the greater part of the traffic in those streets where any traffic was allowed. (There were no vehicles in Venizelos Street.) In the middle of it all, and controlling and directing it, was the British Military Policeman.

The shops were for the most part small and dingy, and contained little that was useful. The prices charged put even those of home profiteers well into the shade. A five-drachmæ note (worth rather more than four shillings) purchased practically nothing, and it was quite obvious that the Greek shopkeepers were out to exploit to the full their monopoly of goods, poor as these latter undoubtedly were. The city abounded in cafés of the open Continental type, Floca's being undoubtedly the most attractive. The impression left on the mind by this half-restaurant, half-public-house is a curious medley. The perspiring waiters, the multi-coloured clothes of the customers seated at the tables, the coffee and the rich chocolate cakes, the ices and the thin Salonica beer, the flies buzzing here, there, and everywhere, and the Greek newsvendor wending his way among the tables selling the *Bawkanoose* (*Balkan News*) —these were the most memorable features of a house which was the rendezvous and talking-place of all nations in this city of Jewish prosperity.

A different house of call was the Hotel Splendide, facing the sea. This was the favourite resort of officers on three days' leave from the line, needing a bath, a bed, and breakfast. Such luxuries were worth more than money at that time, and it was as well for the proprietors that they were, for otherwise they could never have charged such extortionate rates. The officer on leave had a busy time. Little of it was available for his own pleasure ; most of it was spent in purchasing some of the innumerable wants of the Mess and his brother officers. But the evenings at least were free, and when, after visiting the principal attractions, he would turn in between the welcome sheets at the Hotel Splendide, he would wonder how phantoms so empty as these cafés, drinking-shops, cinemas, and skating rinks could hold sway over this strangest of eastern cities, and masquerade as pleasure. And as he wondered, he thought of those at home, and what he would give to be with them—and so fell asleep. Next evening he would have dinner under the stars in the big pleasure garden of the White Tower to the strains of a Greek orchestra, and perhaps would afterwards adjourn to the French Club.

The docks and camps and offices of Salonica are an integral part of its memory, and many a man in the 2/20th spent weeks in one of its marquee hospitals tossing in bed with P.U.O. or sand-fly fever. But for the majority of men the city of Salonica was to play but a small part in their life in the Balkans. It was soon to be left behind and almost forgotten as the 60th Division marched northwards into Macedonia, that depressing land of barren scrub and rocky hills, of quagmire-tracks in winter and of dusty, parching plains in summer, a land of lizards and of tortoises, a land which seemed as bare and rough and inhospitable as any land could be.

The days spent at Uchantar were busy days—days

of organization principally. The equipment table (A.F.B. 1098, wasn't it?) was rather different from the scale used in France. Every man of the Salonica Army carried his own little shelter. For there were no billets in Macedonia; we bivouacked instead. Each man was supplied with a bivouac sheet (in common parlance a " bivvy sheet "), a pole, and some rope and pegs. To make his dwelling he combined with another man, and between them they erected a little roof-shaped shelter which served as housing for both. When complete, it was just big enough for two men to lie in on their backs; they could neither stand nor kneel. These " bivvies " were the homes of officers and men for more than a year.

The Transport Section, which with fifteen horses and nine mules had made the journey from Marseilles in the *Manitou*, put in an appearance only a few days after the Battalion, and almost immediately was subjected to a thorough reorganization. Wheeled transport was not included in the establishment of battalions in the B.S.F., and all baggage, it was explained, would in future have to be carried by pack-mules. The personnel of the section had to be considerably augmented as a result of 136 of these hardy animals joining the Battalion on December 12th. They had been described by the Remount authorities as " trained mules," but it was hard to see in what possible sense they could be called trained. No form of coaxing or coercion seemed to influence them, and when the Battalion came to leave Uchantar it was not surprising to hear that the " signal mules " had made a rush for the Y.M.C.A. tent half an hour previously, and had not been seen since, and that the Officers' Mess baskets had been found outside the camp derelict, with no mule in sight. By practice, common sense, patience, and good-humour, however, all difficulties were eventually overcome, and by the time that the Battalion left the country six months later it was not unusual for the transport to arrive in camp after a long march all complete! This very desirable result was largely due to the Transport Officer, Lieut. Jones, who spared neither patience nor good-humour in obtaining it. Each company and headquarters from Uchantar onwards was to have its own transport section of men and mules, carrying its Lewis guns and S.A.A., its blankets and other belongings.

Reorganization was not the only employment of the Battalion at Uchantar. Training occupied all the morning, and within a week all four battalions of the Brigade were hard at it. A memorable Brigade field day under Gen. Carleton near the tumuli at Dautbali, a Battalion route march and field day, and a lecture by the Brigadier to all officers and senior N.C.Os. in the Y.M.C.A. tent come to mind even now.

The various units comprising the 180th Infantry Brigade were separated into two columns for the move towards the line. Col. Warde-Aldam, who had as his staff officer Capt. C. G. Ross, of the 2/17th, was in command of the second column which set out on the afternoon of Tuesday, December 19th, and included the 2/18th Battalion (now under Lieut.-Col. A. E. Norton), the 2/20th Battalion, one section R.Es., one section 2/5th Field Ambulance, and one section of the Divisional Train.

There were only three roads leading northwards out of Salonica. The column took the centre one, to Naresh. Those on right and left were the Seres Road to the Struma Valley, and the Monastir Road, the latter being principally used by the French and Serbians. The only arteries of supply to the British sector of the line were the right and centre roads, and a railway which was seldom in working order for long at a time. Five divisions were fed, equipped, and supplied with munitions and reinforcements through these three unreliable traffic routes. Truly a remarkable achievement!

The Naresh Road led to the Doiran Front. It probably would not have been called a road in any other country but Macedonia. North of Naresh it became one continuous stretch of mud, more than a foot deep after a few hours' rain, and from Sarigol the route was completely lost in a broad quagmire which stretched to Janes.

The column pitched bivouacs at Naresh the first night, and moved on in the morning to Salamanli, and on the 21st, through mud more than ankle-deep, to Sarigol, where two nights were spent. Simultaneously with our arrival at Gerbazel, where we found a tent camp waiting, the various units, together with the remainder of the 60th Division, came into the 12th Corps (Lieut.-Gen. Sir Harry Wilson).

It was soon obvious that battalions were not going to be hurried into the line. Brigades were widely separated, and battalions of the 180th found themselves scattered over an area of many miles. The 2/20th at Gerbazel was set the special task of constructing the Corps Defence line of trenches, and was to work directly under the orders of the Chief Engineer of the Corps, Brig.-Gen. G. Walker. The authorities were, fortunately, in no great hurry, and the start of the work was delayed until after Christmas.

The Battalion had much reason to be thankful that its first Christmas Day on service was to be spent out of the line. But facilities for making the day other than ordinary were nil, and though not ungrateful for the small mercy of release from the trenches, we pined for the luxuries of Haverhill of a year previously.

The camp at Gerbazel lay on the slope of a hill only separated from Brigade Headquarters by a small valley and the railway. The men, in accordance with Brigade orders, were soon hard at work laying out the new camp with paths and ornamental designs in stones. The result certainly did them great credit, though it seemed unfortunate that their energies could not be more usefully employed, or at least conserved for the important work of the future.

The Brigade Padre, the Rev. C. Jenkins, took the services on Christmas Day in the old ruined Greek church at Vergetor, close to the camp. After church there was an impromptu sports meeting, organized by Major Craddock and Capt. Travers. The affair was a huge success. Two bare-back mule races figured in the list of events, part of the course being on the Brigade Headquarters side of the Deccauville Track. The results were exciting from every point of view. The writer has often wondered whether Gen. Carleton ever realized how nearly his mess marquee was to being swept away by the leading jockeys in the second race. Complaints were received from " Higher Authority " that an organized (!) race had taken place over the railway line, but on examination it was found that the metals had received no damage, and on a promise being given by the Colonel that no more Christmas Day sports would be held (not a very difficult undertaking), the matter was allowed to drop.

The officers' Christmas dinner in the evening, though no different from an ordinary night as regards comestibles, was a very merry affair, and was much enlivened by a party of carol-singers under C.S.M. J. B. Salkeld and Sergt. J. H. Mould, who gathered near the ammunition boxes which served as our dinner-table under the star-roof. The visit of the officers to Brigade Headquarters after the meal will not readily be forgotten by those who took part. Fortunately the Brigadier had gone out to dinner!

It was a habit of Col. Warde-Aldam to inform new drafts of men, when he welcomed them to the Battalion, that they would find active service soldiering to be, more than half of it, hard manual work. The truth of this theory was amply borne out in the ensuing weeks. The Vergetor-Janes defence line had first to be completed before the bigger work on the Janes-Kurkut switch was commenced. The ground had been thoroughly reconnoitred by the Commanding Officer, Major

F

Craddock, the Adjutant, and the Company Commanders on the 24th, and on the 26th, under the direction of Major Phillimore, R.E., work was commenced on four strong points east of Vergetor, and on trenches east and west of that place. On the following day " B " Company moved bivouac to Hadzi-Junas in order to be nearer their task; and on the last day of the year, for the same reason, " A " Company moved to Armutci, west of Janes.

In spite of the scattered dispositions of the Battalion, a sergeants' dinner was held at Gerbazel on the last night of the year, and the sergeants of the two outlying companies came and spent the night at Headquarters.

The strong points round Vergetor were completed on January 6th, and labelled with the names of the respective Company Commanders. " A " Company's special task at Armutci was not complete, but the remainder of the Battalion was able to commence work on the Kurkut switch, a line extending from Janes eastwards to Kukus, and across the River Spanc to Kurkut. The siting of machine gun positions, of tactical barbed wire, and of infantry trenches was left by Corps Headquarters to Col. Warde-Aldam, who, after deciding the various positions, handed over the task of their construction to the three companies available. The high ground on which the Corps Commander had decided to make his reserve line was a ridge overlooking a pleasant stream, and the front was covered by a strong belt of wire entanglements.

The fresh task involved a move from Gerbazel and the neighbourhood of the Pic de Kretchovo. The new bivouac was located in one of the most charming spots in Macedonia, a ravine about one mile east of Janes. Headquarters and the Transport were quartered on beautiful turf beside a rippling stream. The position would have been even more attractive but for mosquitoes, which made the ravine almost intolerable at night. " B," " C," and " D " Companies were dotted in that order up the length of the stream, " D " Company being on a slope adjoining the inhabited village of Sermenli.

In their new areas companies had a happy life of hard work and simple comforts. Major Craddock had spared no effort to make the regimental canteen the " William Whiteley's " of the Salonica Force, and by dint of purchasing from Greeks and other cosmopolitans in Salonica, and from the E.F.C. at Janes, Sergt. F. W. Watkins was able to sell a large variety of eatable and useful articles otherwise quite unobtainable in the houseless wilderness of Macedonia. It was in these days when prices were cheap that the solid foundation was laid of the 2/20th Canteen Fund, at once the envy of other battalions and the subsequent source of innumerable small comforts for the men of the 2/20th.

The opportunity provided by the Battalion being absorbed in digging was used to send small parties of the senior officers for periods of a day in the line, the 2/18th Battalion at Gugunci supplying a night's hospitality.

The tactical situation deserves some notice. The first impression was overwhelming. The Bulgar held all the important geographical features. Wherever one looked, he was on the mantelpiece and we were on the carpet. Every movement across the plain, almost as far back as Salonica itself, could be seen from his O.P. on the Grand Couronné. One almost laughed to think how easy it would be for him to drive the whole British Salonica Army into the sea—the thing seemed so simple.

The Allies had come to the Balkans originally to rescue the gallant little Serbian Army. Their attempt had failed by being too late, and in their withdrawal they had had no opportunity of choosing their own positions or of dictating the enemy's. He had dug in on the formidable line of the Pip Ridge and of the

mountain, Grand Couronné, with outposts on the Petite
Couronné spur. We had no alternative but to sit down
opposite to him, and hope for the best. He held the
healthy heights ; we had to be content with the malarial
plain and the still more malarial Struma Valley. A
visitor to the line was bound to be surprised, disappointed, and indignant. But there was no way out
of the position save by an offensive, and the mere thought
of that made one shudder. Those frequent evening
telegrams which came to us at Janes warning all units
behind the line that the men must be prepared to turn
out at short notice in the night, had a special meaning
for those of us who had visited the right of the line and
seen by how slender a thread hung the security of the
British Salonica Force.

The work on the defences made good progress, and
by the third week in February had been completed as
far east as the Spanc. A start was then made east of
the river, and Headquarters, " A," " C," and " D "
Companies moved to bivouacs near Gramatna.

Sunday, February 25th, was a day of hospitality.
The weather left nothing to be desired (unless it were
that the sun was too powerful for football), and after
lunch a " Rugger " match against the Lothian and
Border Horse was followed by an Association game
against the 22nd Battalion the Rifle Brigade. Both
encounters were won by the 2/20th amid much excitement. Col. Curties, who commanded the 22nd Rifle
Brigade, was among the guests, as also were the Divisional
Commander's A.D.Cs., Capt. Oliphant and 2nd-Lieut.
Bulfin, several officers of the Lothian and Border Horse,
and some of our own Brigade Staff. The band of the
22nd Rifle Brigade was a welcome addition to a very
cheery gathering.

The same evening, after the Battalion had turned
in, orders arrived for a move by stages to Mihalova in
Corps Reserve to the line, in view of an expected attack
by the Bulgars. Leaving a rear party, under Lieut.

H. C. Lovell, at Gramatna, the Battalion concentrated in the old bivouac in the ravine near Janes on the following morning, and remained concealed while eleven German planes bombed Janes in the afternoon. The march to Mihalova took place on the following evening, eighteen enemy planes having bombed Salonica at 4 p.m. Fortunately our column was not discovered.

The whole Brigade was concentrated at Mihalova, and the 2/20th came once more under the orders of the B.G.C. 180th Brigade. The Battalion bivouac adjoined " Dead Man's Ravine," an unhealthy title of an unhealthy spot. The Colonel's diary records the fact that on February 28th he saw two wolves.

In the afternoon a railway accident occurred to some Scottish troops who were on their way up the line by the Deccauville Railway, running close to the 2/20th bivouac. Sergt. W. J. Lee, Sergt. W. Narroway, and Pte. H. A. Bean, the Medical Officer's orderlies, and Capt. Churchouse himself, did much good work for the injured, and everybody on the train was taken to the Battalion cook-house and given hot tea. Two men, unfortunately, were killed in the accident.

About 6 p.m. a driving storm of wind and sleet commenced, and gave the men their second bitter experience of the Balkan climate. During the night the velocity of the wind increased, and by midnight the full fury of the " Vardar Blizzard " was raging. The storm lasted without intermission until 6 p.m. on March 1st. The men's " bivvies " had been drenched and rendered useless by the storm of the previous evening. The camp, which was flooded within two hours of the rain commencing, was in the open, and possessed neither shelter, cave, nor dug-out. The men, surrounded by water and comforted by a rum ration, huddled together in their bivouacs and waited for twenty-four hours for the storm to abate. It is safe to say that never in its whole experience did the Battalion spend a more miserable and helpless night and day. Fortunately the expected Bulgar attack did not materialize.

The issue of an elaborate training programme by the Division synchronized with the visit of Company Commanders to " J " Sector of the British line between Lake Doiran and the River Vardar on Monday, March 5th, and three days later the 2/20th Battalion took over the sector from the 13th Manchester Regiment, of the 66th Infantry Brigade.

The western bank of the Vardar was held by the French. The British line, with its left flank resting on the left of the river, consisted of a series of disconnected strong points, sited on the first ridge after crossing the plain from Salonica. On the right, near Doiran, where the country became mountainous, the peaks and crests were held ; on the left the defence works lay some little distance down the forward slope of the ridge. The Bulgars had selected their position with great care, and had utilized to the full the opportunity of siting their defences on commanding ground. They completely overlooked the British position from the Bellashitsa Mountains, where they had spent many months entrenching and wiring in.

The war in " J " Sector was open warfare with a vengeance ! The strong points were backed by a wide ravine, the Cidemli Dere, among the trees of which companies were bivouacked, and where the men not on duty lived during the day. Small garrisons were left in the works during daylight, and at night companies moved out of the ravine, occupying the works and improving the defences, returning to the Cidemli Dere at dawn. On the left of the sector was the deserted village of Reselli, and in the ravine close by was Battalion Headquarters, consisting of a series of dug-outs and shelters carved out of the sheltered bank of the Cidemli Dere. Down the centre of the ravine ran a water-course, which rose to great heights after heavy rain. It was here one night while the river was in flood

that the Quartermaster's horse, "The Camel," fell into the stream while being led by its master over a narrow bridge. It was small wonder that the poor animal bolted some weeks later, and was never seen again!

"J" Sector boasted at least one important tactical feature, Piton Boisé. This was a small spur which had been put in a state of all-round defence, and was held by one company. It provided the best observation post in the sector, and was capable of holding out for some days against an attack. To this end a supply of small-arm ammunition, bombs, and reserve rations was permanently kept there.

No Man's Land was approximately a mile deep. The country consisted of an undulating valley, intersected by ravines and stretches of low-lying grassland. A deeply bedded water-course, the Selimli Dere, ran parallel with our front, and could not be forded in wet weather on account of floods. This was an important factor, as it was impossible for either side to reach the other's line without crossing the Selimli Dere. The most commanding position on this part of the enemy's front was "The Nose," a prominent tactical feature (so named from its shape), which had been converted by the enemy into a valuable stronghold. "The Nose" had twice been raided by British troops, but as a position it was almost impregnable. It completely dominated the British line far below it, and here, behind wire many yards thick, and in trenches which had taken many months to construct, the Bulgars watched every movement of the British troops a mile away on Piton Boisé and its environs. West of "The Nose" was a work less strongly fortified, "Les Mitrailleuses," and east of it lay Boyau Hill and the Crête des Tentes.

The conditions, tactical, geographical, and climatic, were as different from those on the Vimy Ridge as could be imagined. The rifle came into its own, and the bomb, which was so much in evidence in France on account of the slender depth of No Man's Land, faded into its true position as a secondary weapon. The climatic conditions varied uncomfortably. Spells of rough weather with drenching rain were interspersed with periods of oppressing heat. Later, when the sun became even more powerful, an issue of sun-helmets, combined with a uniform of shorts and shirt-sleeves, brought a maximum of coolness.

Following its successful precedent in France, the Battalion set out to explore No Man's Land as soon as it took over.

The Bulgar, though active in patrolling, was found to be unenterprising unless attacked. He was never seen near our wire, but his parties were known to visit a hill called Bergerie, which lay some 400 yards from our line, and where on one occasion he left a written notice in English, telling us to go home to our wives and families, and not to disturb a peaceful nation who wished us no harm. Enemy patrols were always strong in numbers, presumably because the men had not sufficient confidence to risk moving in small parties.

Our daylight patrols sometimes occupied sheltered parts of No Man's Land. The normal activities of the day were confined to short harassing bombardments by both sides, but on occasions more prolonged "strafes" took place. One of these occurred on March 17th, on which day the enemy in the early morning commenced a heavy bombardment of the British line from the Vardar to Piton Boisé. During the day about 1,200 shells fell on Piton Boisé and in " J " Sector, including a large number of gas shells. No infantry action followed. Our casualties, which included 2nd-Lieut. D. F. Spurgeon wounded, were not heavy. During daylight a patrol searched the Selimli Dere and the ground round Bergerie to make sure that no attack was being launched. The men returned to our lines by the Bogorodica Track, having seen no signs of the enemy.

The Bulgars were very strong in aircraft, and the " Travelling Circus," a fleet of sixteen to twenty battle-planes, caused much annoyance, and did a considerable amount of bombing on our dumps and lines of communication. On Sunday, March 18th, they visited the transport lines and Rear Headquarters of the 2/20th in Caussica Ravine, adjoining the Cugunci Road, and, besides causing casualties to personnel, did considerable damage to the animals on the horse-lines. Lce.-Sergt. F. W. Watkins, the canteen sergeant, and Lce.-Sergt. E. B. Gibbins, post sergeant, and Pte. Mayhew, his assistant, were severely wounded; two horses and twenty-one mules received injuries, two of the latter having to be destroyed. During the air raid Pte. R. Jones, of the Battalion Transport Section, showed great gallantry in going in the open to the assistance of a man of the 10th Loyal North Lancs. Regiment who had been severely wounded, and round whom bombs were falling thickly. Pte. Jones was subsequently mentioned in Gen. Milne's Dispatch for his bravery. On another occasion hostile aircraft carried out a destructive raid on the Karasouli Dump, causing much damage.

The Battalion was relieved by the 2/17th Battalion (now under command of Lieut.-Col. H. J. Dear) on the night of March 21st-22nd. The few days immediately prior to relief had been characterized by greatly increased artillery activity on the part of the enemy, but our day and night patrols which searched the Selimli and Sejdelli Ravines, and visited Bergerie and the Bogorodica Track, failed to discover any increase in hostile patrolling. "A" Company remained in support to "J" Sector in a small ravine 400 yards west of Reselli. "B" Company proceeded to Lothian Ravine in support to "K" Sector, and the Battalion (less two companies) moved to "The Crag," and came into Brigade Reserve. Hot baths at Karasouli and work on bombardment slits in the bivouac occupied the following two days, and on March 26th the Battalion concentrated, and moved by platoons to Gully Ridge for special training. Meanwhile several drafts of reinforcements had joined from the base since the Battalion left Uchantar, including Lieut. M. F. C. Willson, of the 1/20th, R.S.M. Skeer, who had now taken over his old duties from C.S.M. Drayton, and Sergt. E. H. Chappell. A draft of N.C.Os. and men from the K.R.R.C., which included Sergt. H. K. Holmes and Cpl. R. Pallister, reported at Gully Ridge on April 5th.

In the same month all preparations were in hand for a British offensive against the formidable Bulgar positions immediately west of Lake Doiran. The advance was to be made in conjunction with an attack by the French opposite Monastir. The 60th Division was allotted no part in the major operation, but was ordered to carry out two demonstration raids on its own front. These raids were entrusted to the 2/19th and 2/20th Battalions respectively. The former was to have as its objective the hill already referred to as " Les Mitrailleuses." The objective of the 2/20th was " The Nose." Both operations were to be carried out at night, and the tactics employed were to be much the same as those used for trench raids in Flanders. The last week in April was decided as the approximate date. Owing to the heavy concentration of artillery on the right of the British front and the consequent lack of guns elsewhere, the raid by the 2/19th Battalion had to be cancelled at the last moment.

The objects of the 2/20th operation were stated to be the capture of prisoners and identifications, the destruction of the enemy's trenches, and the infliction of casualties ; but the main object was to make the enemy believe that the principal British attack was coming at that point, so as to distract his attention from the real centre of operations, which, as has already been stated, was some miles farther east. There is good reason to believe that this object was in a measure achieved. So thoroughly was deception practised that the 2/20th erected a dummy camp, consisting of empty tents and some horse-standings at Oreovica, near Gully

Ridge, to lead the Bulgar airmen to exaggerate the strength of the British force opposite " The Nose."

Capt. Watson was in command of the raid, which was fixed for the night April 24th-25th. The operation had been repeatedly practised on life-size trenches at Gully Ridge until every man knew his part. Patrols had been sent out into No Man's Land nightly for a fortnight before " D " day, and all the officers and most of the men had been over the ground as far as the enemy's outside wire at least once beforehand. The difficulty of the operation lay in the concentration of the raiders in No Man's Land. For raids in France it had been possible to " jump off " from some position in our own trenches. On this occasion the raiding parties had to be allotted " jumping off " positions just outside the enemy wire, and the move across a mile of No Man's Land to these positions on a night which had been particularly chosen for its blackness was not without great difficulty. The plan was for three parties to enter the enemy trenches at selected points. These assaulting parties were respectively under command of 2nd-Lieut. A. H. Hunt (left), Capt. Watson (centre), and Lieut. Kempe (right). Each party had at least two belts of wire to pass, and the artillery had been ordered to cut six gaps accordingly. These means of entry had to be made some twenty-four hours before the raid, and it was hoped to prevent the enemy repairing them by directing machine-gun fire on to each at frequent intervals until zero. A party under Capt. Reynolds was to protect the right flank of the raiders, and was to meet any enemy counter-attack from Boyau, or any attempt on his part to send a party round the right flank.

Capt. Reynolds's party was established on the Bogorodica Track one and a half hours before our barrage opened, and was only about 60 yards from an enemy advanced post which had on the previous night caused casualties to a party under Capt. Partridge, who had himself been wounded. The suspicions of the enemy garrison were soon aroused, and the Bulgars opened fire. A special patrol from Capt. Reynolds's party, under Sergt. F. N. Harding, made a rush for the enemy's post, but was not in time to capture the occupants, who made good their escape, and doubtless gave the alarm to the enemy. A left flank guard was placed under command of Lieut. R. C. Hearn (now O.C. " C " Company). This party, with a machine gun, was ordered to deal with any trouble from the left. No such trouble occurred, but when the enemy artillery opened fire, Lieut. Hearn's party found itself on the line of the enemy's heavy artillery barrage, and was, in addition, subjected to intense trench-mortar, machine-gun, and rifle fire. They found it impossible to open up communication owing to breaks in the wire and to the necessity of the telephonists having to wear box respirators as protection against enemy gas shells.

The three assaulting parties already referred to were in position in front of the enemy wire at 10.40 p.m. The signal that all was ready for our artillery barrage to open was to be given by Capt. Watson over the telephone, the code word " Vimy " being used, as soon as the raiding parties were opposite their respective gaps in the wire. Owing to the extreme darkness of the night and to the extraordinarily complicated nature of the enemy's wire entanglements, difficulty was experienced by the scouts in finding the gaps which had been cut by the artillery. It was subsequently discovered that, in spite of the machine-gun fire directed on to them before the raid, these gaps had been repaired by the Bulgars. The enemy had already suspected trouble, and a varied display of coloured Véry lights betokened that his S.O.S. barrage might be expected at any moment. At 10.55 p.m. he put down a murderous barrage of heavy trench mortars. Simultaneously three powerful searchlights came into operation from Boyau and behind " The Nose," and No Man's Land became as light as day.

On Capt. Watson giving the signal "Vimy," the British barrage opened within five seconds. Capt. Watson, with C.S.M. Dawes and about fifty men, doubled through the heavy trench-mortar barrage. They found that the gaps in the wire had been recently mended, but by means of wire-cutters, mats, and a ladder, the majority of the party got through the five thick belts of wire which stood between them and the enemy. At one point the wire was found to be too thick for wire-cutters. Here it was blown by a Bangalore torpedo, which made a very good gap, and enabled Capt. Watson and his men to enter the enemy's trenches. By this time casualties had considerably reduced the strength of the party. No Bulgars were to be seen, as the whole of the enemy garrison had withdrawn to the high ground in rear, and was holding it strongly. In anticipation of an attack, he had blocked portions of his front trenches by filling them with wire, and from his position in rear he directed trench-mortar, machine-gun, rifle-grenade, and rifle fire on to the raiders in his trenches during the whole time that they occupied them. The fact that they were throwing downhill enabled the Bulgars to attain a large measure of accuracy in bomb throwing. Conversely, our men had great difficulty in throwing uphill. A Lewis gun was brought into action, and by this means, together with bombs and rifle grenades, the enemy was prevented from forcing his way back into his front trenches. Meantime demolition parties were getting to work, wrecking the trenches and their machine-gun emplacements and dug-outs with gun-cotton. Thirty minutes after entering the trenches Capt. Watson gave the signal to withdraw, and the party commenced to move back by the same route as they had used on entering. This route had been marked by a white tape, which was now found to be invaluable.

The parties under 2nd-Lieut. Hunt and Lieut. Kempe had both caught the full fury of the enemy's barrage, and had suffered considerable casualties. Lieut. Kempe was himself wounded early in the operation. Neither party had been able to penetrate the enemy's wire.

By 2.25 a.m. the raiders were reported back, with the exception of twenty, who were missing. A search party was sent out, but failed to reduce the number. Of the twenty, three (including Pte. Helyer, who died as a prisoner) were subsequently proved to be prisoners-of-war, and the remaining seventeen, though reported as missing, were later officially reported as killed. Sergt. W. O. Smyth, who, though severely wounded and exhausted by exposure, managed to crawl back into our lines during daylight on November 25th, after having lain for many hours in No Man's Land unattended, died of his wounds the same day. His loss was a great blow to " A " Company, and indeed to the whole Battalion. Lce.-Cpl. L. G. Nash, the Signalling Corporal, a most gallant and reliable N.C.O., who was last seen in the middle of the enemy's barrage attending to the signal wire from Capt. Watson to Battalion Headquarters, was among the killed. The wounded included Lieut. Kempe (seriously), 2nd-Lieut. D. C. Bacon, C.S.M. Dawes, Sergt. S. Collins, Sergt. W. G. Bartlett, Sergt. J. G. Rennie, Sergt. G. W. Phipps, Lce.-Sergt. E. G. Oliver, Lce.-Sergt. A. Backhus, and Lce.-Sergt. A. E. White.

Total casualties were as follows :—

Killed (originally reported missing) : 17 other ranks.

Died of wounds : 2 other ranks.

Prisoners-of-war : 3 other ranks.

Wounded : 2 officers and 68 other ranks.

During the raid an advanced Battalion Headquarters was established in the Selimli Dere, under Major Craddock. Capt. Churchouse had his regimental aid post here, and, in spite of the darkness and the enemy's artillery, he attended to over thirty casualties.

A party of twelve sappers from the 519th Field Company, R.E., under command of Major R. Steers, was attached to the Battalion for the operation for demolition work and for exploding Bangalore torpedoes under the wire. Only one torpedo was used, and that, as has been stated, was a complete success.

Considerable assistance was furnished by the 180th Brigade Machine Gun Company, under Major Oxenham.

Viewed in the light of the considerable difficulties attending it and of the fact that the enemy had made elaborate preparations to meet the raiders (as, indeed, he was meant to do), the operation was generally believed to have proved the fighting qualities of the Battalion. Talking of the raid on the following day, the Divisional Commander remarked that he had watched events from " The Crag," and, seeing the Bulgar searchlights playing on the men as they went over, he never expected to hear that any of the men had reached the enemy trenches.

A great deal of valuable preliminary reconnaissance work was carried out by 2nd-Lieut. Lane, Sergt. E. H. Chappell, and Sergt. F. N. Harding, and a number of officers, N.C.Os., and men, who, in addition to taking part in the raid, patrolled No Man's Land night after night for some weeks before the operation in order to obtain all possible information about the ground and the habits of the enemy.

The C.O. received the following letter from the Brigadier on April 28th :—

" With reference to the recent operation carried out by the Battalion under your command on the night of April 24th-25th, the G.O.C. Brigade wishes you to convey to all ranks who took part therein his appreciation of the manner in which this enterprise was carried through. The action of Capt. Watson and his party in effecting an entry into the enemy's lines under such difficult conditions is particularly worthy of praise, and the Brigadier has had much pleasure in drawing the special attention of the Higher Commands to the gallantry displayed by this party, whereby the instructions controlling the enterprise were carried out, and the enemy was led to believe he was being seriously attacked."

Capt. Watson received the Military Cross, and C.S.M. A. E. Dawes (who was wounded three times in the raid) the Distinguished Conduct Medal, for their gallantry.

After the raid the Battalion (less " D " Company, who remained at Reselli in support of " J " Sector) concentrated at La Pyramide; and two days later Battalion Headquarters, " B " and " C " Companies were once again in Brigade Reserve at " The Craig," where, memory recalls, an excellent concert was given one evening by Lieut. Willson, Pte. Beeby, and others. " A " Company had moved to Lothian Ravine in support to " K " Sector. On April 29th the Battalion again took over " J " Sector from the 2/17th Battalion.

The offensive on the right flank of the British line had failed to attain its objects, and the mountain " 535," La Grande Couronné and Petite Couronné, the enemy's strongholds, still remained in the hands of the Bulgars.

The 10th Black Watch came into the line on Saturday, May 19th, and took over in " J " Sector. Leaving Reselli and the Battalion garden there (which had been carefully tended by Pte. J. Bromage, under the close personal supervision of the Colonel) for the last time, the 2/20th returned to the old bivouac site at Mihilova.

Brigade Headquarters was in Galovanci Church, and the writer well recollects a memorable ride with Col. Warde-Aldam about this time through Galovanci, by Lake Ardzan, to Dragomir, where we saw fields of white poppies, storks' nests on the roofs of the ruined houses, and a church containing old Greek vestments, books, and pictures. As commonly in Macedonia, we hardly saw a human being throughout our ride. The shepherds on the hills and the priests in the churches were the only inhabitants likely to be met outside Salonica itself, though in Sermenli "D" Company became very friendly with the peasants of the village, and the officers and some of the men were kept well supplied with eggs. Such villages as Janes, Hadzi Junas, and Gerbazel, even where they possessed any houses at all, were mere spots on the map, without inhabitants. Its travelling khaki population alone seemed to save the country from an appearance of utter desolation and desertion. Some parts, like Dragomir and Lake Ardzan, were certainly picturesque, but the general impression of Macedonia was then—and remains to this day—one of severity of climate, barrenness of soil, and scarcity of population.

Training at Mihilova included a Brigade field day on ground near the Pic de Kretchovo on Saturday, May 26th. On the following Monday a short march was made to a new bivouac at Bare Hill (one mile north-east of Cugunci), and on Tuesday, in considerable heat, the Battalion (less "A" and "B" Companies) made a further move to bivouacs in the Vladajah Nullah, in order to be ready to take part in a renewed attack against "535." The two detached companies went into support to the 2/17th Battalion in "C" Sector, and bivouacked behind the hill "La Tortue," on the right of the British front, close to Lake Doiran.

"A" and "B" Companies carried out reconnaissances of the line and of No Man's Land, but the same evening sudden orders were received for the withdrawal of the 180th Brigade from the line, and within twenty-four hours all companies were concentrated once more in bivouac at Bare Hill.

The Battalion marched to Hadzi Junas on June 1st, and by marches on successive nights through Sarigol, Ambarkeuy, and Naresh, reached Uchantar Camp at 11 p.m. on Tuesday, June 5th, when first official intimation was received that the Division was leaving the country. Not, however, until the ship was actually quitting harbour did we know our new destination to be Alexandria.

During the ten days at Uchantar pending embarkation every effort was made to induce the hospital authorities to release men of the 2/20th who were anything like fit, so that as few as possible might be left behind, and a number of N.C.Os. and men who had been wounded in the raid on " The Nose " came from hospital to ask the Commanding Officer to do his utmost to influence the authorities. The happy results were a draft of 105 men to the Battalion on June 8th, and small drafts each day until the date of sailing. The instructors at Summerhill Reinforcement Camp also rejoined before the Battalion left, as did Lieut. W. G. Elder, who had held the appointment of Chemical Adviser to the Salonica Force at G.H.Q. for some months, and who was very anxious to get back to regimental duty. Among the N.C.Os. left behind was Sergt. F. J. Barber, who had done invaluable work as Pioneer Sergeant since the very early days of the Battalion, and who was now succeeded by Cpl. A. W. Hollands. Sergt. H. Osbourn, the Transport Sergeant, had been at Brigade Headquarters as Camp Sergeant-Major, and his regimental duties had recently fallen to Lce.-Sergt. Mahoney.

The effective strength of the Battalion on leaving Salonica was 32 officers, 815 other ranks.

Casualties in Macedonia were as follows :—

Killed	20 other ranks.
Died of wounds ...	2 other ranks.
Accidentally killed ...	1 other rank.
Died of disease ...	2 other ranks.
Wounded	{ 4 officers. 101 other ranks.

N.C.Os. wounded, in addition to those already referred to as casualties in the raid on " The Nose," included Lce.-Cpl. F. H. Dutton, Cpl. O. S. Midwood, Lce.-Cpl. H. J. Weir, Lce.-Sergt. E. B. Gibbins, Lce.-

Sergt. F. W. Watkins, Sergt. J. Fowler, Lce.-Cpl. W. Lloyd, Cpl. A. Lewis, Lce.-Cpl. P. E. May, Lce.-Cpl. O. Curran, Lce.-Cpl. E. P. Garstone, Lce.-Cpl. B. Parmley, Lce.-Cpl. A. J. Pridgeon, Cpl. H. G. Kennedy, and Sergt. A. B. S. Crummey.

There were few regrets at leaving Macedonia when the *Kashmir*, escorted by two destroyers, carried us out to sea on the morning of Saturday, June 16th. Our six months' stay in the Balkans had not been without its pleasures, but these had been more than balanced on the other side by the lack of leave, of billets, and of civilization generally. Campaigning in such a climate was bound to involve a maximum of discomfort. The sterile country, the pack transport, the chlorinated water, the quinine parades, the septic sores and " P.U.O.," alone were sufficient to induce depression and lethargy. Above all, the tactical situation seemed to give no hope of a successful offensive against enemy positions, which, so far as the British front was concerned, seemed wellnigh impregnable. (Even the final offensive, months after, which drove the enemy out of Serbia and forced an armistice, was only successful by encircling his right flank from Monastir.) In the circumstances it was no wonder that the move to—wherever it was—was welcome.

There had been a few changes in the Battalion in April—2nd-Lieut. D. R. Blundell had replaced 2nd-Lieut. J. B. West as Assistant Transport Officer, and 2nd-Lieut. Woolfe had become Signalling Officer for a short time in the absence of 2nd-Lieut. Goldby, on a course at Janes.

The men had enjoyed a certain amount of football, both Association and Rugby, and this, with the daily arrival of the *Balkan News* and occasional concerts arranged by Lieut. Willson, had done much to counterbalance depressing tendencies. Finally, the absence of malaria among the men had been noteworthy.

CHAPTER VI

EGYPT

IT was always a sore point with the troops in the Eastern theatres of the war that the public at home had no eye for any campaign but that on the Western Front. However brilliant the achievements in the smaller theatres, public opinion at home, led by the Press, seemed to be in an organized conspiracy of reticence on the subject. This lack of publicity, which was falsely interpreted by the troops as due to lack of appreciation, did much to damp the enthusiasm of men who were in most cases fighting against heavy odds, and in all cases were campaigning in difficult and adverse conditions. *The Times* has put the matter in a nutshell :—" These men in our Eastern Armies have had the dust and toil, without the laurel of the race to victory." The ignorance of the outsider on the subject of the conduct and progress of the war in the minor parts of the one great Allied frontage was only fully brought home to some of us when we found ourselves landing in a country to fight, knowing nothing of its campaign. We had done it in Macedonia, and here we were again about to do it in Egypt. Our knowledge of the local conditions of warfare was as small and unreliable as our knowledge of the fighting in the Balkans had been seven months previously ; but our ignorance was no evidence of inaction on the part of the troops in Egypt. The Egyptian Expeditionary Force, under Gen. Sir Archibald Murray, though not heralded at home, had driven the Turks from the Suez Canal in February, 1915, and had now established a front line in Southern Palestine which pinned the

ISMAILIA.

enemy down to positions extending from the sea at Gaza, the famous city of the Philistines, along the main Gaza—Beersheba road to Beersheba, the ancient home of Abraham. Gen. Murray's line formed an impenetrable barrier between the enemy and his cherished ambitions of Egypt. But the front line does not concern us so much for the moment as does Egypt itself.

There is probably no portion of its history which holds happier recollections for the 2/20th Battalion than these first days in Egypt. A land of plenty, of vast stretches of well-watered cultivation and of busy agriculture, Egypt seemed as far removed from the land of Vardar blizzards and arid plains as the sun is from the earth. To an ideal climate was added the fascination of Ismailia, with its quaint native dresses and ox-drawn wagons, its fresh-water lake, and its picturesque palm-grooves and cool glades on the banks of the Suez Canal. Small wonder that, after the barren wastes of Macedonia, it seemed like some glimpse of fairyland.

The glare of perpetual sunshine on white buildings and light yellow sand was a little distressing to the eyes at first, but we soon got used to it, and came to love the glorious deep blue sky and all the varied Eastern colours. The heat was intense but dry, and not uncomfortable to men clad only in drill shorts, shirts, and sun-helmets. The shops had abundant supplies of melons and other cooling fruits. The lake gave many of the men their first swim since leaving Sutton Veny, and the Officers' Club brought visible reminder of home and London to many who had almost forgotten what a table-cloth and dining-table looked like.

There were yet greater joys ahead. A strong rumour that the battalions of the 179th Brigade, which had arrived some days before the 2/20th, were already sending leave parties to Cairo was not long in being confirmed, and within a few hours of detraining at Ismailia from Alexandria on June 19th the first of many parties of the 2/20th was on its way to Cairo for three days' furlough. What that meant to those who had been away from any sort of civilized city for so long (the civilization of Salonica was negligible) can perhaps better be imagined than described.

The three hours' train journey from Ismailia across the fertile plain of Egypt was an experience in itself. The scenery from the train was full of interest. Here were oxen treading out the corn, women grinding at the mill, camels in yoke drawing the plough, and donkeys trotting along the roads with heavy burdens, the man usually " up " and the woman or child running behind. At Cairo the train came to a standstill in a large well-roofed station with many concrete platforms, and the first impression was as of a typical provincial railway-junction at home. If we soon had to revise that impression, yet we found much in the city that was European. There was one characteristic, however, which was peculiar to Cairo, and which struck troops from the Western Front and the Balkans immediately. This was the absence of almost every sign of the great world-war. It seemed impossible that any city on the earth could be so little disturbed by the gigantic conflict. The surface of its daily life was scarcely ruffled. The shops had no lack of goods to sell, and betrayed no trace of unusual circumstance beyond the many khaki figures which thronged them all day long. Here was a place where one could forget the war, and it was a wise decision of the Commander-in-Chief that every man possible from the front line should have a spell in Cairo before the autumn offensive began. Hotel accommodation in the city was comfortable and ample. The men mostly stayed at the " Anzac Hostel," an excellent " home from home " provided by the Y.M.C.A. The officers turned in at Shepherd's or the Continental Hotel, where the joys of a bath and the prospect of two nights between sheets soon banished care. The three days were all too short when sight-seeing began. The

Pyramids, the Sphinx, and the Tombs of the Caliphs were probably the most popular objects of interest, but few men returned to the Battalion without visiting the native bazaars or taking a trip up the Nile. Many spent their first two days (and nearly all their money) in purchasing souvenirs to send home. Some found their way round the old mosques and tombs, escorted by guides whose beautiful flowing white gowns were soon found to be no criterion of their moral character. Sportsmen mostly spent much time at the Gezira Sporting Club, where they were sure of seeing polo or cricket at its best. The race meetings, too, were invariably well patronized. Golfers found a delightful course, and chose their caddies from the long line of Arab boys who squatted along the hedge in front of the club-house by the first "tee," waiting their turn to be employed. Many officers had their first experience of " putting " on sand " greens." After the game there was the delightful cool of the club-house, and the shower baths if one felt so inclined. Then, Cairo in the evening was never dull. Bands and concert parties invariably drew large audiences, and the moonlight Nile trips were perhaps the most delicious of all the attractions of that memorable time. No seaside holiday at home can compete with those first three days in a city which none of us will ever forget.

The anniversary commemorated by June 24th could not be allowed to pass unobserved, and the conclusion of the first year of active service was marked by a concert and special dinner with beer for the men, and by sergeants' and officers' dinners. Lieut.-Col. Sword, commanding the 2/19th, Lieut.-Col. Norton, commanding the 2/18th, and Capt. Macfarlane, the Brigade Major, were the guests of the evening at the officers' dinner, and also at the smoking concert which followed the sergeants' dinner.

It was perhaps a little unfortunate that the award of the D.S.O. to the Commanding Officer was not published in time to give the Battalion a double reason of rejoicing on June 24th. The announcement was made on parade three days later by Major Craddock, and was received with loud cheers. The honour was felt to be a fitting recognition of all that Col. Warde-Aldam had done in leading and directing the Battalion through the fighting and hard work of its first year of active service.

The joys of Ismailia lasted for but a fortnight. In the comparative cool of the evening, on July 5th, the Battalion marched to El Ferdan, and on the following evening, by a road running along the bank of the Suez Canal, to Kantara. The latter was rapidly being transformed into the advanced base of the Egyptian Expeditionary Force. In pre-war days it had been but a collection of shacks, and of no importance other than that attaching to all places on the Canal, and especially to those possessing traffic bridges across it. Now it was literally a town of tents, pitched on the sand, and occupied by thousands of troops. This transformation had made it a suitable landing port for supplies and an important railway centre. In their pursuit of the retreating Turks many months before the time of which we write, when the enemy had made his futile attack on the Suez Canal, British troops had laid a single-line railway track from Kantara up the coast to Deir-el-Belah, and by this means the front troops had been maintained in reinforcements and supplies. A pipe line had also been laid, carrying water far up into the desert. The journey from Cairo to Belah could now be made by train, the traveller having to change stations at Kantara. Not many months afterwards passengers leaving Cairo in a sleeping-car in the evening could wake up the next morning and find themselves in Jerusalem. The capture of the Holy City, the construction of a railway bridge over the Suez Canal, and the connection of the military line with the main Jaffa-Jerusalem track, had combined to produce what in pre-war days would have been regarded as a miracle. It will readily be appreciated that Kantara was an eminently suitable advanced base for the rapidly increasing British force which was occupying the desert east of Suez.

The 2/20th spent two days in Kantara, and after dumping kit-bags at the Divisional Base Depot, was on the move again, this time by train eastwards to Deir-el-Belah. But for the signboard on the railway station, Belah would probably never have been found by an uninitiated traveller. Shade was, of course, the first thing we looked for on arrival. We saw no house or building, not even a tent camp, but only a clump of trees by the sea, and this was already " inhabited " by the Royal Flying Corps. In the bivouac area allotted to the Battalion there was one patch of shade, a group of fig-trees 20 yards square. This was required for the Battalion Orderly Room. The men pitched their " bivvies " on the sand, and were glad to have even a thin waterproof sheet between them and the scorching sun. In the days which followed all training was carried out in the early morning, and the day was spent perspiring in bivouacs. After tea, sea-bathing parties made full use of the evening coolness to march the mile which separated the camp from the Mediterranean.

The Eastern Desert presented transport difficulties greater even than those of Greece. The single-line railway to which reference has already been made, and stretches of rough wire tracks which lay beside it, were the only traffic routes. Wheel transport was again out of the question, and camels took the place of pack-mules. Accustomed to long periods without water, and capable of crossing the vast, untracked sandy desert, these beasts did wonders in carrying water, ammunition, and supplies over country which no other means of transport could have negotiated. No less than half of the fifty-two camels which joined the Battalion at Belah and remained with it throughout the Palestine campaign were water-carriers, and as such were one of the most vital parts of its organization. Led by natives, these animals covered miles of country on their journeys. The water was carried in fantasses—12 and 15-gallon zinc tanks—and each camel carried two when filled. The camel convoy comprised the animals and their leaders, and a small section of men from the Battalion, the latter's duty being to load and unload. This section, first under Cpl. J. W. Wilgress and later under Sergt. E. F. Fuller, never failed to bring water to the Battalion if it was possible to obtain it. Frequently their quest took them many miles across the desert in the heat of the day (when the remainder of the Battalion was resting), or in the darkness of the night (when the remainder of the Battalion was sleeping), perhaps to find that the well was dried up or did not exist, meaning a fresh search and another long tramp. Always they walked, and many times, having found their way back with filled fantasses, they would have to return at once for a fresh supply in order that the Battalion might carry a reserve ration of water when it marched the next day. (Fantasses were never allowed to lie empty if water could be obtained from any source reasonably near.) The native Egyptian camel-leaders caused endless amusement, especially when singing their unmelodious camel choruses on the march—" *Kam layla ? Kam yôm ?*" How many nights ? How many days ? (to next leave). In their blue galabias they looked very attractive (from a distance !). Later in the campaign, when, without boots or shoes and only wearing thin linen clothing, they followed the infantry through the floods of the plain and the bitter cold of the Judean hills, their wailing was pitiable to hear. It was little comfort to us or to them to know that they had been issued with Army boots, but in almost every case had sold them. The camels and their native leaders were under the watchful eye of Lieut. Dark, the Quartermaster, whose handling of the situation in any case of difficulty with either was masterly, and invariably effective.

The first glimpse of the front line came early in August. The Battalion had left Belah, and spent one night at Sheikh Nuran, and had moved forward to Es Shauth in support, taking over bivouacs from the 1/1st Hereford Regiment on July 30th.

Much as the line in Macedonia had amazed us after the trenches of Flanders, the contrast was as nothing to that afforded by this front line in the desert, surely the most amazing front line on any of the many fronts ! Never to hear a shot fired or a mine going up, to be able to do battalion drill and skirmishing in No Man's Land, to mend the wire in daylight, and to receive rations and mail some time in the early afternoon—these are things we had often dreamt of ; here they were in reality. The tactical situation calls for some few words by way of explanation here. It shall receive fuller treatment later.

The second battle of Gaza, on April 19th, 1917, had failed. The ancient city on the coast still remained in the hands of the Turks, whose position, as has been explained, extended as far east as Beersheba. The British line, with its left flank opposite Gaza and its right at Gamli, covered a sandy length of 22 miles, approximately along the line of the Wadi Ghuzzee. The breadth of No Man's Land increased as one travelled eastward, and only opposite Gaza were the two front lines within striking distance. The British right flank, held by the Desert Column (Maj.-Gen. H. G. Chauvel, C.B., C.M.G.), lay far out in the desert, where the Turks held Beersheba across a No Man's Land more than 10 miles broad. It was in the Gamli Sector that the 60th Division was placed early in August, the 2/20th being in the line, with Battalion Headquarters in the Wadi Ghuzzee, adjoining the gigantic natural mound Tel el Farah. The line here consisted of a series of disconnected strong-works (similar to those in Macedonia), in front of the wadi, with a thin belt of wire along its whole length. It was separated from the Turkish line by a waterless desert many miles deep.

The enemy was never seen, except when, as a tiny speck many thousand feet high, his planes carried out their spasmodic air reconnaissances. The British line was thinly manned, and while holding it the Battalion carried out training daily.

There were ample water-supplies near us in the Wadi Ghuzzee, as a result of the magnificent achievement of the R.Es. in carrying the waters of the Nile from Kantara through 130 miles of pipe line to Shellal.

On August 27th Lieut.-Col. Warde-Aldam left the Battalion and proceeded home on leave, and Major Craddock assumed temporary command. A few days later Capt. Watson, who had " gone sick " at Ismailia, rejoined from hospital and became Second-in-Command ; and Capt. Partridge returned from the Senior Officers' Course, Heliopolis, and took over " C " Company from Lieut. J. A. C. Hasslacher, who had been in charge of it for a month.

Leave to Cairo and Alexandria, and to an excellent rest-camp on the coast at El Arish, continued on a liberal scale throughout the autumn. Training, which had been somewhat light at the beginning of August, gradually became more strenuous, and, in spite of great heat, a full programme of range-firing, company training, and field-days was carried out. Several " Allez-Allez Schemes," plans of attack and defence without troops for officers and N.C.Os., took place under the Brigadier. On one occasion the Commander-in-Chief was present at a practice attack carried out under a smoke barrage in the Wadi Ghuzzee, and took the salute during the march past at the conclusion of the exercise. On a subsequent date the Battalion was drawn up for inspection on parade by the Divisional Commander, who, however, rallied the men in an informal way around him, and addressed them quietly on the forthcoming operations against the Turks.

The evenings were spent in sports, the men mostly favouring football and the officers hockey. At a

Brigade Boxing Tournament the Battalion figured prominently in supplying the referee (Lieut. Dark), the winner of the light-weight competition (Pte. Harris), and the runners-up of the " heavies " and " middles " (Lce.-Cpl. Whight, of the Transport, and Pte. Stacey respectively). On another occasion, in a competition open to the whole Division for the best-turned-out company, the Battalion was represented by " D " Company. The prize, however, went to a company of the 2/18th Battalion.

The time at Shellal was undoubtedly one of the most trying the Battalion ever had. Though the heat was intense, training could not be relaxed. Bivouacs were pitched on the bare sand. There was no diversion close at hand, not even the sea to bathe in. The daily sick-list mounted up, and septic sores and " P.U.O." took a heavy toll of all ranks. Such conditions are the breeding-place of low morale, and the Battalion which triumphs over them has good reason to congratulate itself.

Entertainments and recreation were not neglected. " The Roosters," a divisional concert party, gave a performance at Shellal, and this was followed later by a series of excellent impromptu concerts arranged by Lieut. Jones and Lieut. Willson, to which, if memory serves aright, the principal contributors were Pte. G. Cook, Pte. G. Edwards, Pte. J. Kent, Pte. Nash, Lce.-Cpl. W. J. Mashman, and Lce.-Cpl. A. C. Crate.

The Egyptian Expeditionary Force had undergone great changes since June. On the 28th of that month Gen. Sir E. H. H. Allenby, G.C.M.G., K.C.B., had succeeded Gen. Sir Archibald Murray as Commander-in-Chief. Six weeks later the formations of the Eastern Force (Lieut.-Gen. Sir Philip W. Chetwode, Bart., K.C.M.G., C.B., D.S.O.) and the Desert Column, which had shared the honours and responsibilities of the campaign on this front up to that time, were merged into the newly-formed Desert Mounted Corps, 20th

Corps, and 21st Corps, placed respectively under command of Lieut.-Gen. Chauvel, Lieut.-Gen. Chetwode, and Lieut.-Gen. Bulfin. The 60th Division joined the 20th Corps.

Universal regret felt throughout the Division at the departure of Gen. Bulfin was tempered by the knowledge that he was receiving promotion long deserved. During the eighteen months of his command Gen. Bulfin had frequently had to make calls on the men which had taxed the capacities of physique and morale to the utmost. Those calls had invariably been answered with loyalty and enthusiasm. No Divisional Commander had earned the confidence and respect of his officers and men in a larger degree, as the writer had peculiar opportunities of observing. Probably no Division had a greater measure of divisional *esprit de corps* than the 60th. Certainly none was more infused through and through with the spirit of mutual help between units. How far this feeling was due to Gen. Bulfin's personality and leadership only those who actually served under him in the Division will ever realize. To the 21st Corps as B.G.G.S. Gen. Bulfin took Lieut.-Col. E. T. Humphreys, D.S.O., who had been his G.S.O.1. in the 60th Division since the old days at Greenhill, Sutton Veny.

The new Divisional Commander was Maj.-Gen. J. S. Shea, C.B., C.M.G., D.S.O., Indian Army. Brig.-Gen. J. Hill, C.B., D.S.O., A.D.C., relieved Gen. Carleton in command of the 180th Brigade at the end of August, and a month later left to command the 52nd (Lowland) Division, being succeeded by Brig.-Gen. C. F. Watson, C.M.G., D.S.O., Queen's (Royal West Surrey) Regiment.

At the end of October a change in the tactical situation occurred. The important events which followed deserve a new chapter.

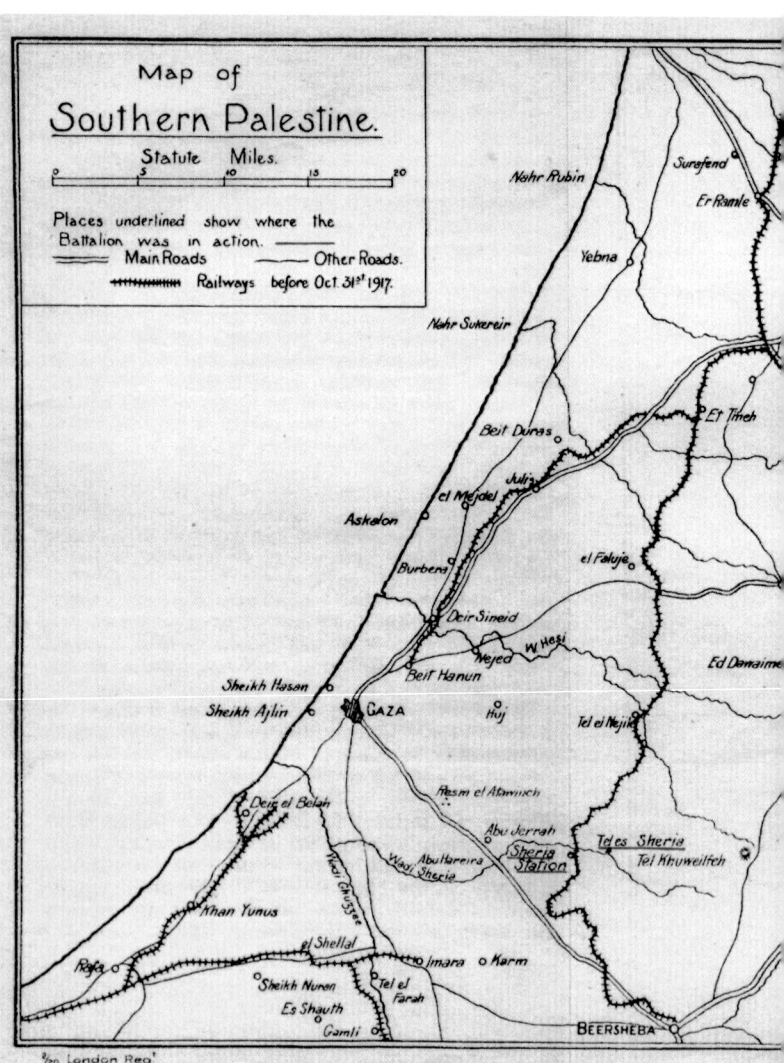

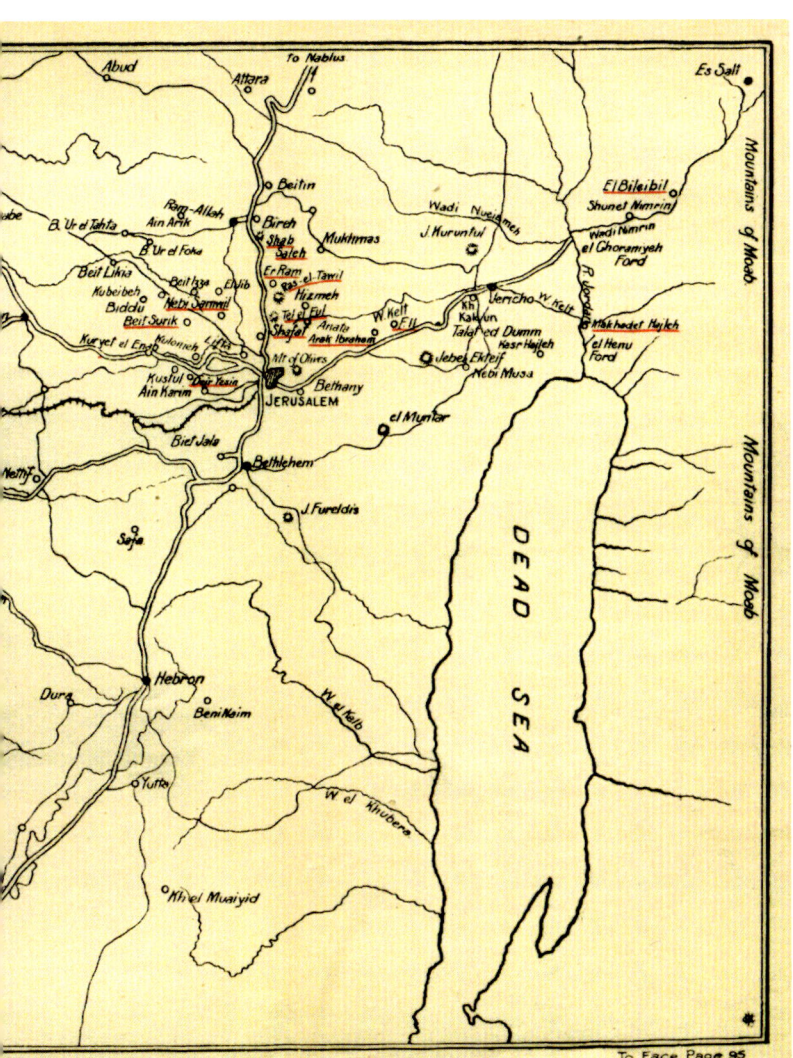

To Face Page 95

CHAPTER VII

THE PLAN OF THE PALESTINE OFFENSIVE

THERE had been no offensive movement of any importance on the Palestine Front since the second battle of Gaza in April. Much that had happened since the arrival of Gen. Allenby betokened that the lull would not last. The speeding up of training, the largely increased leave allotments to Cairo and Alexandria, the arrival of heavy reinforcements of personnel, artillery and aeroplanes, the various changes in formations and staffs, and the mass of paper which, in the form of Intelligence Summaries, reports by the Air Force, orders, instructions, and memoranda, was issued from the Brigade Office, were all sure portents of a coming offensive. If any further proof were needed, it was to be found in the numerous dumps of supplies and ammunition which were being formed at many points immediately behind our front line. The railway had been carried out to Shellal, and branched from there to Gamli. A 2ft. 6in. gauge line from Belah to the Wadi Ghuzzee now completed the journey from Kantara. Still further tokens of the Commander-in-Chief's intentions were to be found in a great increase of activity in patrolling on the part of the cavalry, and in the arrangement of long mounted reconnaissances of various important points in No Man's Land, such as Goz Mabruk, El Buggar, Rashid Bek, and Bir el Esani, by the cavalry, accompanied by senior infantry officers. For long the details of the offensive were wrapped in mystery. About the middle of October they began to assume a definite outline, but even then the extent of the operations was not disclosed. Many conferences at Brigade Headquarters divulged to a privileged few that the coming movements would be of considerably more than local importance. But to the majority of those who were about to take part in events, which can now be seen to have been among the most brilliant and the most important achievements of the war, the affair was simply an attack on Beersheba. All the suppressed excitement of September and October—the early morning training in the desert; the physical training and bayonet fighting; the field work; the night schemes; the conferences; the detailed instructions regarding first reinforcements, equipment, rations and water-supply, camels and transport generally; and, finally, the moonlight march from Es Shauth and the desert bivouac at the position of readiness in No Man's Land—all have been crystallized into one lasting impression, " preparing for the attack on Beersheba." Secrecy about the whole matter was remarkably well preserved, and few except those on the Staff whose duties necessitated the knowledge had any definite idea of how far it was expected that the advance would be pushed. Certainly Jerusalem was as little dreamed of by the majority of us as Aleppo or Damascus. Even when Beersheba and Sheria had fallen, the prospect was no clearer. Then, as the advance continued day after day without a halt, Jerusalem suddenly came into view, and the whole campaign bore a new meaning. Now we know that the events which so unexpectedly brought us from the edge of the desert to far beyond the gates of Jerusalem paved the way for those dramatic days in the autumn of 1918, when, by one incisive stroke, Beyrout, Damascus, and Aleppo were overthrown, and the Turkish Army was finally reduced to a fleeing mob.

The whole story of the offensive in the autumn of 1917 and the early months of 1918 forms a complete picture of its own, and can be studied by itself. No more fascinating picture is contained in the vast collection left to us by the war, and as time goes on this brilliant campaign, which restored to Christian civilization its holy birthplace, and freed Syria and Palestine (we hope for ever) from the infidel and barbarous Turk, will take its place among the greatest military achievements of all time.

Because of the compactness, if we may so term it, of the Palestine Campaign, the limelight which stationary warfare in France and Salonica has enabled us to keep centred on the 2/20th Battalion almost exclusively hitherto must from now onwards, if we are to give an accurate account of the important part played by the Battalion, light up the whole stage, and bring into view much that is only indirectly connected with our subject. The narrative is so closely bound up with the general plan of the campaign and with the doings of other units that it is doubtful whether the doings of the 2/20th would be intelligible unless fitted into their place in the larger plan. No apology is therefore made for entering somewhat deeply into the whole Palestine offensive, and for explaining at some length its object, its difficulties, the course which was planned for it, and the course which it actually took.

The main reason which prompted the original conception of it is to be found far from the Holy Land. To drive the Turk off the Sinai Peninsula and deprive him of his last hold on Egyptian territory was a worthy enough object in itself, but there was a deeper one behind Gen. Allenby's plan. The collapse of Russia had freed a large Turkish force in the Caucasus, which was now available for use in Mesopotamia, where our victory at Bagdad had had an enormous moral effect on the peoples of the East. The German General Staff were loud in urging that an attempt should be made to retake Bagdad, and so rehabilitate the name of the Triple Alliance in the Mohammedan world. Gen. von Falkenhayn was dispatched to Constantinople to press the Turkish Government to embark on the Yilderim undertaking (as the scheme for the recapture of Bagdad was called), and to use the Turkish divisions freed from the Caucasus for the purpose.

Meanwhile the Allies had decided that an offensive in Palestine on a large scale was necessary in order to pin down this new enemy reserve and prevent any move towards Bagdad. The arrival of Gen. Allenby and the sudden growth of the Egyptian Expeditionary Force had the desired effect. The Turks saw that their army on the Sinai Peninsula must be strengthened, and no large reinforcements were sent to Mesopotamia. As one writer has well said, " Gen. Allenby's attack on the Gaza line wiped the retaking of Bagdad out of the list of Germany's ambitions." The object of our offensive, then, was to attack the enemy on the Sinai Peninsula and drive him back through Palestine, in order to divert his reserves from attacking us in a much more vulnerable spot—Mesopotamia. What, then, was Gen. Allenby's strategical plan?

We have already described the respective front lines held by ourselves and the enemy in August. The Turks greatly strengthened their positions in September and October by joining up their several groups of defence works—the Sihan group, the Atawineh group, the Baha group, and the Abu Hareira-Arab el Teeaha trench system—until the whole formed a continuous and formidable line of entrenchments from the seashore at Gaza to Beersheba.

In his first Dispatch Gen. Allenby tells us that it was against the enemy's left flank—the Hareira and Sheria positions—that he decided to direct his blow. (Both of Gen. Murray's attacks had formed up opposite Gaza.) His reasons were mainly three. The enemy's works were less formidable on the left of his line than elsewhere, and were easier of approach. Once Beersheba was captured, the enemy's left flank would be exposed, and full use could be made of our superiority in mounted troops. Finally, the chances of exploiting a preliminary success were much greater on the left than elsewhere, the Turks having no prepared line on which to fall back, as they had behind Gaza, where the Wadi Hesi would give them an excellent chance of protracted defence.

The Dispatch adds that early in October our aircraft reported an increase of activity behind the Turkish lines, and deserters who came over confirmed the inference that the enemy were expecting to be attacked and had decided to offer strenuous opposition on their present line.

It was vital to the success of the operations that the point at which the attack was to be made should be concealed from the enemy, and that he should be led to expect it in some quarter other than the right one. To this end, Gen. Bulfin's Corps of three divisions, assisted by a naval bombardment from the sea, was ordered to prepare a demonstration on as large a scale as possible against Gaza, commencing with a heavy bombardment on October 27th, four days before the assault on Beersheba was due. This feint attack was designed to draw the enemy's attention away from Beersheba, and pin as many of his reserves as possible to the Gaza area. The actual assault on Gaza was not to be launched until the result of the Beersheba operation was known. The success of the main attack, it was realized, would be largely dependent on the water-supplies of Beersheba being captured on the first day of the offensive, so that infantry, cavalry, and camels could go forward to the assault on the enemy's main position, the Hareira-Sheria line, with ample supplies of water behind them.

To say that the attack followed, almost to the minutest detail, the course which had been planned for it is the greatest tribute that can be paid to the genius of Gen. Allenby and his staff. Their calculations had omitted nothing, and had gauged the position to a nicety.

But even now that the plan of the operations had been decided upon, the difficulties of carrying it out might well have daunted the new Commander-in-Chief. These difficulties lay more in the matter of water and supplies than in tactical questions. The initial concentration of a force of several divisions of all arms in the desert of No Man's Land, and the provision of sufficient water for men and animals, was in itself a task of great magnitude. Some idea of the obstacles which the nature of the country presented to such an advance as was contemplated may be gleaned from the words of the Commander-in-Chief himself in his Dispatch :—

" The chief difficulties were those of water and transport, and arrangements had to be made to insure that the troops could be kept supplied with water while operating at considerable distances from their original water base for a period which might amount to a week or more ; for, though it was known that an ample supply of water existed at Beersheba, it was uncertain how quickly it could be developed, or to what extent the enemy would have damaged the wells before we succeeded in occupying the town. Except at Beersheba, no large supply of water would be found till Sheria and Hareira had been captured.

" The transport problem was no less difficult : there were no good roads south of the line Gaza—Beersheba, and no reliance could therefore be placed on the use of motor transport. Owing to the steep banks of many of the wadis which intersected the area of operations, the routes passable by wheeled transport were limited, and the going was heavy and difficult in many places. Practically the whole of the transport available in the force, including 30,000 pack camels, had to be allotted to one portion of the eastern force to enable it to be kept supplied with food, water, and ammunition, at a distance of fifteen to twenty miles in advance of railhead. Arrangements were also made for railhead to be pushed forward as rapidly as possible towards Karm, and for a line to be laid from Gamli towards Beersheba for the transport of ammunition."

The troops at General Allenby's command were seven

infantry divisions, three mounted divisions, and the Imperial Camel Brigade. The Turkish line was held by ten infantry divisions and one mounted division. We held the advantage in artillery, and by the time that the operations commenced our airmen had obtained control of the air. The enemy was better supplied with roads than we were, having the excellent Hebron Road to feed the left of his line, and a somewhat poor metalled track from Junction Station to carry supplies as far as Julis for the Gaza and centre areas. The Jaffa-Jerusalem Railway at Junction Station, about 6 miles southeast of Ramleh, sent out a single narrow-gauge line to Beersheba, with a spur running from Deir Sineid to Beit Hanun, behind Gaza. The Turk was known, however, to be very short of rolling-stock and of fuel. In the circumstances it was highly creditable to his Staff that he was able, by means of these hopelessly inadequate communications, to provision more than sixty battalions and a large force of artillery. Certainly we were no better off, but rather worse. On the coastal belt, where the country was a vast stretch of drifting sand, camels alone could do the work of transport. A similar position existed on the right—a state of affairs which could only be improved, as it actually was, by continuing the railway forward from Shellal.

While the whole energies of the " Q " branch of the Staff were concentrated on overcoming the supply and transport difficulty, those of the " G " Staff were applied with equal vigour to the training of the men, and assuring that all ranks were as fit as it was possible to make them when they lined up for the advance. It was recognized that the severest test would be that of the physical endurance and fighting morale of the troops, and the training in the extreme heat of September and October was mainly directed to developing these two essentials. There had been a good deal of minor sickness in the form of septic sores and " P.U.O.," the result, no doubt, of the continuous diet of dry Army rations. But rations improved, and leave to Cairo, Alexandria, and El Arish had wonderfully increased the morale of the Army. Almost equally important with the health of the men was the health of the horses, thousands of which had lost condition on account of short rations, the extreme heat, and no grazing. These poor animals were to be sorely tested later, when the water question became acute, though they always had the first call on whatever water was available. Very nobly did they carry out their part of the Palestine offensive.

The conditions in which the men would be required to fight necessitated slight variations from the equipment normally carried by troops in the East. The webbing valise was to be carried on the back, and all personal and other property for which no room could be found in the pack was to be left behind. Officers and men were to carry two water-bottles, one being a reserve which was not to be touched without a special order from Headquarters. Throughout the offensive all ranks were in possession of a mobile ration in addition to their " iron " ration.

By the last week of October all preparations were nearing completion. Vast dumps of munitions, supplies, and stores had been accumulated by the efforts of the Egyptian Labour Corps at the various railheads. The men had been equipped for their coming task. Finishing touches were put to training, detailed instructions for the preliminary concentration in No Man's Land were issued, and the four divisions of the 20th Corps—the 10th, 53rd, 60th, and 74th—to whom the attack had been allotted, prepared to leave the Wadi Ghuzzee and commence the offensive.

To the 60th Division was to fall the preliminary assault on the enemy's works covering Beersheba. This honour was on a par with later events, when, as we shall see, Jerusalem surrendered to General Shea, and the 60th Division was the first of Gen. Allenby's force to cross the Jordan.

CHAPTER VIII

THE ADVANCE AND THE BATTLE OF SHERIA

MAJOR CRADDOCK wished every man in the Battalion to know the plan of operations so far as it had been divulged, and many were the conferences of Company and Platoon Commanders held at Headquarters in the Wadi Ghuzzee. The operation orders provided that a certain proportion of officers, N.C.Os., and specialist privates should be left out of action as " first reinforcements," and should be used for work on communication behind the fire zone. They would thus be available to reinforce the Battalion when casualties had depleted the ranks. In the event of the Battalion being " wiped out," they would form a nucleus on which it could be reformed. The provision of " first reinforcements," though of course very necessary, meant that some of the most valuable officers, N.C.Os., and men were away from the Battalion while it was in battle, and, incidentally, it meant that several platoons went into action commanded by a sergeant. Capt. Partridge was in charge of the party of 5 officers and 108 other ranks of the 2/20th who, as " first reinforcements," left Es Shauth for Gamli on Saturday afternoon, October 28th. These officers and men had a strenuous time during the first part of the operations, the officers acting for the most part as guides, and the men as loaders to camel convoys bringing supplies to the troops in action.

Captain Watson was in charge of the brigaded regimental water convoys, Echelon " A," and had the heavy responsibility of seeing that all units had water whenever it was possible to get it to them. 2nd-Lieut. Blundell was in charge of the Battalion camels. 2nd-

Lieut. Woolfe went into action with the Battalion as Signalling Officer, 2nd-Lieut. Goldby, who had been Signalling Officer for nearly two years, being now Assistant Adjutant, and left with " first reinforcements."

October 31st was the date chosen for the opening of the offensive. The 180th Brigade was to play no part in the first stages of the fighting, and was to be in Divisional Reserve. Though there was little doubt that the Turkish position would be carried, yet the importance of capturing the water-supply of Beersheba without delay made it necessary that the 180th should be prepared to be called into battle before nightfall.

After a particularly hot day, which was spent in resting, the Battalion struck bivouacs at Es Shauth on the evening of Sunday, October 29th, and at 6.30 p.m. moved off into No Man's Land. The whole Brigade was on the march, and in order to lessen the dust evil considerable distances were observed between battalions. Maps were almost useless as guides, even if there had been light to see them, and direction was maintained by compass. The Brigade starting-point was a red lamp placed just outside our wire opposite Tel el Farah. Gen. Watson and his Brigade Major, Capt. N. R. Crockatt, M.C., waited to see units pass and vanish into the dark, and then galloped ahead to Bir el Esani, where bivouac sites had already been allotted to battalions at the positions of readiness. The large number of troops—artillery, cavalry, and infantry—who were moving forward did not interfere with each other, as there was no track worthy of the name, and each Brigade more or less chose its own course across the open country. Arrived at Bir el Esani, the men turned in to sleep in a sheltered bivouac in the Wadi Mirtaba, and a limited supply of water was found in the wadi for the animals, from sources which had already been developed by the Divisional Engineers. In some of our reconnaissances enemy cavalry patrols had been met in the Wadi Mirtaba, but now we had a strong

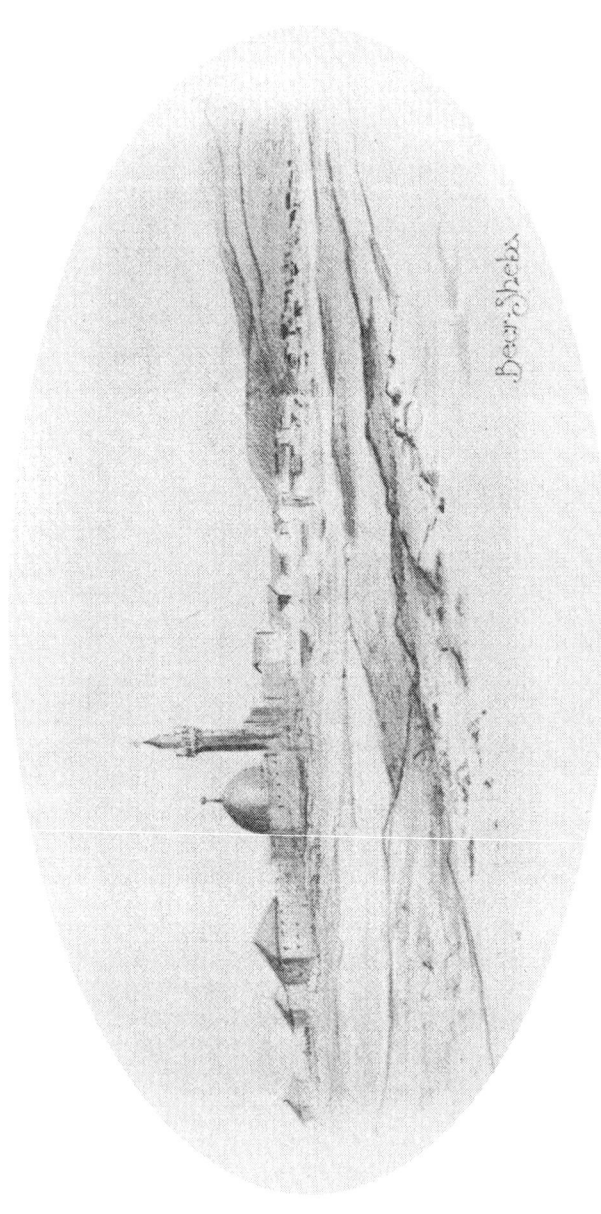

cavalry screen out, and there was little fear of interruptions during the night. The period of daylight on October 30th was spent in bivouac, all except necessary movement being forbidden. Immediately after dark the whole Brigade moved by moonlight down the Wadi Shanag to their assembly positions, the 2/20th being located at Hill 970. A party of " B " and " C " Companies, under Lieut. H. F. Baker, did invaluable work moving in advance of the Brigade and making a track for the guns. Bivouacs were pitched behind Hill 970, and the Battalion flag set up to mark the position of Headquarters. There was little rest for anyone until dawn.

The attack by the 60th Division was timed to synchronize with a wide encircling movement by the cavalry, who had orders to turn the enemy's left flank and enter Beersheba from the north-east. The assault was led by the 2/14th and 2/15th Battalions and by the 2/22nd and 2/24th Battalions. From a small knoll near the assembly position of the 2/20th it was possible to watch the progress of the attack. The operation of wire-cutting by the artillery in front of the enemy's advanced works commenced soon after dawn, and was continued, with short checks owing to dust clouds, until 8.30 a.m., when the leading waves of the 181st Brigade, who had been lying in extended order some distance in front of the wire, were seen to advance in line after line up the ridge towards the enemy's trenches, under cover of an intense artillery and machine-gun bombardment. The last that could be seen of them as we watched through glasses was as they made their final charge and disappeared in the maze of trenches on the enemy's stronghold " 1070." In less than an hour news arrived that the enemy's front line had been captured, and that the assault on the second line would commence as soon as the artillery had made the necessary gaps in the wire. By 3 p.m. further progress had been made by the infantry, and a line had been secured and was being consolidated on the high ground overlooking Beersheba. In the afternoon the Divisional Reserve was ordered to move forward, and the 2/20th advanced to a bivouac in Westminster Wadi. Guns, camel convoys, and infantry were all pushing forward down the various wadis and nullahs towards the Turkish lines. The capture of the first ridge meant that whole bodies of troops could move without being seen by the enemy. Fortunately, the sky was clear of his 'planes.

As we wended our way forward, now halting to allow a long chain of water-bearing camels to pass, now pressing on to maintain connection with the 2/17th in front, a large batch of Turkish prisoners—the first to be captured in the offensive—was being escorted to the rear. They seemed well clothed, though dirty, and did not appear to have been underfed. The men marched in front and the officers behind, and the escort was on both flanks and in front and rear. The usual salutations passed between the men of the escort and our men as they went by, and one of the prisoners, a somewhat learned-looking Turkish doctor, with thick, dark-rimmed spectacles and an astrakhan hat, was subjected to much friendly chaff in the form of questions as to whether his mother knew he was out, and who he had been with " last night." The Londoner is nothing if not a humorist, and the N.C.O. who started " We haven't seen the Kaiser for a h—— of a time " was soon joined by the whole of the rest of his company. Incidentally, these prisoners were the best clothed Turkish prisoners we saw on the Palestine Front. Those captured later were of much lower morale, and showed the fact plainly.

Soon after dark the sky over Beersheba was lit up with a glow which left no doubt but that the mounted troops had effected their entry. This was confirmed later by a signal message, which added that a large number of prisoners had been captured, and that the water-supply of Beersheba was little damaged and abundant. The Brigadier came round to advise everybody to have as much sleep as possible, and companies turned in, and realized that they were lucky to be able to do so.

Everybody was astir early on the following morning, and by 7.30 the Battalion was on its way to a captured enemy work (" Z 8 ") to bury the dead and assist in clearing the battlefield.

The insanitary condition of the enemy trenches did not make the unsavoury task any less unpleasant. The bivouac sites, where apparently the Turks had slept when not actually on duty in the trenches, were now masses of filthy rags, paper, and refuse, haunted by millions of flies. Here and there small shelters had been dug into the banks of the wadis, and these, too, were unimaginably filthy. It was some encouragement to see the many evident traces of our artillery bombardment. The wire, though many yards thick, had been well cut in several places. The trenches for great stretches were filled in and blocked by débris and fallen chalk. The surroundings presented a picture of the utmost desolation. Here and there one found the bodies of the dead, and in one place where the enemy's defence had been particularly resolute the bodies of one British officer and five of his men were found beside those of ten Turks. In many parts of the battlefield Chaplains were saying the words of the Burial Service over the graves of the British dead, after the bodies had been lowered to their last resting-places. The Rev. C. Jenkins having fulfilled this office in respect of the dead whose graves we had prepared, the Battalion returned to Westminster Wadi for the night.

A move was made on the following afternoon, November 2nd, to a site about 1½ miles south-west of Beersheba. Enemy airmen dropped a number of bombs round the new bivouac in the evening, but inflicted no casualties. They were similarly unsuccessful on the following day when hostile 'planes attacked the Brigade column on the march.

The capture of Beersheba and of the enemy works on the hills around that town ended the preliminary moves necessary for the launching of Gen. Allenby's main assault. This assault was now imminent, and orders were issued for the 60th and 74th Divisions to attack the powerful works on the left of the enemy's main line of resistance—the Kauwukah System—on November 6th. The retirement of the enemy from Beersheba had been in the direction of north and north-east, and the massing of a quite considerable number of his troops a few miles up the Hebron Road made it obvious that he anticipated our next advance along that excellent route. He was wrong. Detaching the 53rd (Welsh) Division and some mounted troops to Khuweilfeh to deal with this portion of the enemy, Gen. Chetwode decided to throw all the weight of his Corps against the enemy's strong works in the Kauwukah line, to exploit to the fullest extent any preliminary success, and to press on the Turks as hard as possible, and secure the water-supplies of Sheria. On the night November 5th-6th the 60th Division concentrated for the attack.

The plan was for the 74th Division on the right to roll up the enemy's works from the flank, and to hold these while the 60th Division on the left made a frontal assault. This sequence would prevent the Londoners' attack being enfiladed. The 179th and 180th Brigades were detailed to carry out the task of the 60th Division, the assaulting battalions of the 180th being the 2/18th and 2/19th, with the 2/20th in close support. The Battalion had moved on the afternoon of the 4th through the outskirts of Beersheba to a bivouac just south of the Wadi Muweilah, and at 5 a.m. on the 6th was assembled at the position of readiness allotted to it for the attack.

As the 74th Division made progress, the troops of the

60th Division were able to move gradually forward in artillery formation. The 2/20th advanced down the Wadi Pitt behind the 2/19th. The wadi was being harassed, somewhat heavily at times, by enemy artillery, and every few minutes the platoons in artillery formation used the cover afforded by the steep banks to avoid unnecessary casualties. A long column of howitzers and 18-pounders was winding down the wadi at the same time, and by raising clouds of dust was attracting the unwelcome attentions of the Turkish gunners. About noon, the writer well recollects, the Battalion " in blobs " had halted, preparatory to making the next step forward across open ground, the Wadi Pitt having ended in a cul-de-sac. The Brigadier was on a small knoll about 400 yards ahead, and, seeing the Battalion approaching, he sent Capt. Crockatt over at the gallop for Major Craddock and the Adjutant. From the knoll Gen. Watson pointed out the Kauwukah System, and added that, the attack on the right having succeeded, the 60th Division was now to go forward to the assault on its objective.

Orders had been given for the 2/18th and 2/19th Battalions to press on with all speed over the undulating ground to the chalk ridge in the distance, where the enemy's trenches could be plainly seen. These battalions were now advancing to their jumping-off positions, and two companies of the 2/20th were ordered to keep close up to them and be at the disposal of their respective Commanding Officers. The remainder of the 2/20th was to move in rear at 500 yards' distance.

Major Craddock gave immediate orders to " A " Company (Capt. Travers) and " D " Company (Capt. Reynolds) to hurry forward to support the 2/19th and 2/18th Battalions respectively, while " B " Company (Lieut. H. F. Baker), " C " Company (Capt. R. C. Hearn), and Battalion Headquarters followed in rear. From this moment the Commanding Officer completely disappeared, and was not heard of again for some hours.

The enemy's shelling, at first intermittent, increased into a heavy barrage, and an unlucky " 5.9," which fell on Battalion Headquarters, killed Pte. Deuchars, of the Intelligence Section, and wounded several other men. The camel carrying signalling equipment was killed by the same shell.

The assault, the first ever made by the 180th Brigade, was completely successful. The 2/18th and 2/19th Battalions drove the enemy out of his works. " D " Company of the 2/20th, finding a gap on the right of the 2/18th Battalion, filled it, and, led by Capt. Reynolds and Major Craddock (whose absence from Headquarters was thus accounted for), delivered a smashing assault on an enemy strong-point, killing several of the garrison and capturing the remainder. " A " Company on the left was not called upon to go into the fight.

By 4 p.m. the whole of the Kauwukah System had fallen, and a large number of prisoners and a quantity of booty had been captured. An hour later the Rushdi System, a continuation of Kauwukah westwards, was officially reported to be in the hands of the 10th (Irish) Division, and the way was clear for the advance to Sheria, with its badly-needed water supplies.

On reaching their objectives, the 180th Brigade had been ordered to throw out outposts on high ground on the northern slope of Kauwukah Redoubt, overlooking the railway station and water-tanks of Sheria and the plain on which they lay. Tel es Sheria, a huge chalk mound, towered up behind the water-tanks and the little group of buildings which formed the railway station. Between lay the broad, deep Wadi Sheria.

Unsupported and unprotected on either flank, and exposed to heavy fire, " D " Company had followed up their successful assault by pressing on with great vigour, and establishing a position on a small hill about 600 yards south-east of the station, and completely overlooking it. In their advance they had captured prisoners and a machine gun, and had inflicted casualties on the enemy. Pte. A. R. Greenaway, who was subsequently awarded the Military Medal for his action, under heavy fire took a Lewis gun forward to a railway cutting, and, disregarding the Turkish snipers and machine guns, played on the retreating columns of the enemy until he was severely wounded. The enemy had discovered Capt. Reynolds's position, and registered the fact by inflicting several casualties. Sergt. G. Macdonald, a very popular N.C.O., received wounds from which he died some days later.

At 5 p.m. Capt. Reynolds was able to send Pte. Killow, his groom, back to Headquarters with a report describing his position and giving the first information of his advance. He added that the Turks were still in Sheria in force, but that if more troops could be sent up immediately, an attempt to drive the enemy out of the station before dark would probably be successful. If action were postponed until dawn, the Turks would probably reinforce during the night. Major Craddock immediately reported the situation to the Brigadier, who cancelled the outpost arrangements, and ordered the 2/20th Battalion to move forward without delay to secure Tel es Sheria, and establish a bridgehead covering the railway viaduct over the wadi. By 7 p.m. the Battalion was concentrated near " D " Company's position, and shortly afterwards the advance was made by " A " Company and " B " Company under Capt. Travers, with two platoons of " D " in support. By this time darkness was setting in rapidly. The enemy, by opening a fierce resistance with machine guns and rifle fire, soon proved his strength. An ammunition dump in the station commenced to explode and illumined the whole countryside, showing up the advancing troops and making any approach to the station impossible. In these circumstances the station buildings were left in charge of a small party ; outposts were put out, and the remainder of the Battalion lay in the open in extended order awaiting the further opportunity to go forward. Lieut. H. F. Baker, commanding " B " Company, had been seriously wounded in the advance of " A " and " B " Companies.

The 2/17th Battalion (Lieut.-Col. H. J. Dear) had by this time arrived, with orders to co-operate in the attack, and Lieut.-Col. A. E. Borton (2/22nd London Regiment) had also come to Battalion Headquarters with a view to his battalion assisting. As a result of a conference between the three Commanding Officers, it was decided that, provided the explosions had ceased, the attack should be launched at 3.30 a.m., the 2/22nd Battalion to be on the right, the 2/20th in the centre, with its left on the railway embankment, and the 2/17th on the left.

Little was heard of the Turks during the night. The explosions from the munition dump drowned all other noise, or doubtless we should have heard the enemy destroying the railway viaduct over the Wadi Sheria with dynamite. No doubt, also, the Turks took advantage of the noise to withdraw guns and heavy transport from the neighbourhood of Tel es Sheria. But they still had a considerable force holding the position, and the garrison showed no intention of evacuating the wadi without a struggle.

The railway embankment which marked the left flank of the Battalion frontage was an excellent guide in the dark, as we had found on the previous evening when we deployed on its left. After the midnight conference Col. Dear's battalion remained on the left, and we doubled over the embankment to our jumping-off positions on the right of it. It was decided that there should be no artillery preparation for the attack, though an enterprising battery commander of our own Division had sent a F.O.O. forward to offer the assistance of the guns. It was obvious that the enemy was scattered over a wide frontage, and in these circumstances, reconnaissance being impossible, it was unlikely that our artillery could do him very much damage. A bombardment would merely warn him of our intentions. Suitable positions were found for a few machine guns, to provide overhead covering fire, but otherwise the assault was to be a bayonet charge quickly carried out and delivered with the utmost vigour.

Many of the men must have fallen asleep as they lay in extended order waiting for dawn and the command to advance. The explosions in the station continued incessantly, but with varying intensity, until 2.30 a.m. The 2/22nd Battalion had not arrived in time to commence the attack at 3.30, and the start was postponed until 5.5 a.m.

The 2/20th had a frontage of about 700 yards. " A " Company (Capt. Travers) and " C " Company (Capt. Hearn) formed the leading waves, with " B " Company (2nd-Lieut. M. Lane) in support, and " D " Company in reserve.

Dawn was just breaking as our machine guns opened fire, and the men advanced rapidly over the exposed ground to Sheria Station. The enemy, who was now seen to be in a strong position on some high ground north of the wadi, opened a fierce defence with concentrated machine-gun and rifle fire. The Battalion, led by " A " and " C " Companies, advanced in silence and charged with the bayonet through the station and past the water-tanks to the wadi, where hand-to-hand fighting took place, resulting in our favour. A rush was then made by " C " Company, under the gallant leadership of Capt. Hearn, Sergt. E. G. Oliver, Cpl. C. Dickens, and other officers and N.C.Os., for the Pimple (Tel es Sheria), which was surrounded, and the complete garrison of a Battalion Commander, 3 other officers, and 71 men, and a motor lorry and a quantity of war material, were captured. A large number of Turkish dead found in the position afterwards had in many cases been killed at the point of the bayonet by our men. The Company then took up and consolidated a position north of the Pimple.

Meanwhile "A" Company had worked to the right, and, having crossed the wadi, advanced towards a Turkish bivouac on the north side of it. The bivouac included a large fully-equipped hospital marquee and a group of tumble-down shacks which had served the Turks as a bakehouse, and where bakers at this very moment were making that day's bread. Several enemy snipers had taken up their position here, and had caused the Company numerous casualties in its advance. While leading his men, Capt. Travers was killed by a Turk who stepped out of the hospital marquee, picking up a rifle as he did so. Capt. Travers fired, but unfortunately missed, and before he could fire again the Turk had shot him in the head. The hospital was subsequently found to contain enemy snipers. Their violation of the most elementary law of civilized warfare by firing from the shelter of the Red Cross angered our men, who, seeing Capt. Travers fall, made a rush for the marquee and bakehouse, clearing both in a very short time, and killing or capturing every Turk in the vicinity.

The station, the Wadi Sheria, and the Pimple were now firmly in our hands, and the enemy was in full retreat, though he left a stiff rearguard to delay our advance. Our line was pushed forward to a ridge 1,500 yards north of the station, and here, under artillery, machine-gun, and rifle fire, the Battalion dug in with entrenching tools. The enemy launched several small counter-attacks, but these were repulsed, and the men spent the day lying in the little niches which each had carved for himself on the ground where he lay. The indirect fire of hostile machine guns and rifles made it impossible to move about without casualties. Indeed, several men were wounded without moving, and Pte. H. G. Roberts, a stretcher-bearer belonging to "B" Company, did gallant work in binding up these cases under fire. In the afternoon an attempt was made by the cavalry to charge the Turks, but the latter opened a withering fire, which caused heavy casualties among men and horses, and the attempt failed.

The Turk, who was a past master in the gentle art of bluff, had no intention of prolonging his stay. At dusk the 179th Brigade passed through us, and found the enemy retiring all along the line. Orders were given for a night outpost position to be taken up. This was done by troops of the 179th Brigade, and, with a platoon as local protection, the 2/20th automatically came into support.

The capture of Sheria marked a definite point in the progress of the Palestine offensive. The enemy was now in rout. A considerable portion of his force was still waiting on the Hebron Road, where the 53rd Division had provided gallant and adequate defence. The Turkish army was split in two, the only means of communication between the divisions on the Hebron Road and those fleeing from Sheria being by aeroplane. Moreover, Gen. Bulfin's Corps had assaulted Gaza, the garrison of which, through fear of being cut off by our rapid advance on the right, had evacuated the town, and was now in full retreat across the maritime plain. Our success at Sheria enabled us to link up with the right flank of the 21st Corps and join in the pursuit.

The Turks were given no opportunity of making a stand on the line of the Wadi Hesi, and there was little fear of their offering serious resistance south of Junction Station, some twenty-five miles farther north.

The 2/20th, in its first attack, had covered itself with glory. For many of the men it had been their first time " over the top," but there had been nothing of the novice in the charge which had driven a strong force of the enemy from one of his most highly prized positions, and had repulsed him when he attempted an organized counter-attack. The initiative and gallantry of " D " Company in their advance on the evening of the 6th was specially referred to in Gen. Shea's official account of the battle. Referring to the attacks at Kauwukah and Sheria, the Divisional Commander remarks :—

"The comparative lightness of our casualties was probably largely due to wide extensions, and also to the *élan* displayed by all ranks, who, once they got to close quarters with the enemy, pursued him relentlessly, giving him no time to develop counter-attacks or occupy a fresh line of resistance."

The battle of Sheria was a type of action seldom seen outside the pages of military textbooks. Neither attackers nor defenders were entrenched before the battle. The latter were in a strong position, had ample machine guns, and knew every inch of the ground. The attack, resolutely delivered and rapidly completed, gained the day. No elaborate artillery plan, barrage, or bombardment preceded the assault, nor did a single gun on the attacking side open fire. It was a contest between the metal of the British bayonet and the metal of the Turkish bullet. The British bayonet won.

When the Battalion had its first opportunity of forwarding recommendations for gallantry after the battle, many cases of individual acts of great gallantry were brought to notice—more than could possibly receive recognition. It was with pride and pleasure that the Battalion heard some days later that the Military Medal had been awarded to Lce.-Sergt. J. Graney and Pte. J. Collinson, and after a lapse of some weeks that Capt. Travers, Capt. R. C. Hearn (Military Cross), and Sergt. E. G. Oliver (Distinguished Conduct Medal) had been decorated for their part in the action. Capt. Reynolds received the Military Cross for his leadership in the gallant advance of his company on the previous day.

The following names were entered in the Battalion "Gallantry Book" after the battle :—

Sergt. A. J. L. Smith	Sergt. H. G. Legge
Lce.-Cpl. J. Forbes	Pte. H. W. Gamble
Lce.-Cpl. W. Fuller	Pte. N. McDougall

Pte. G. Dampier
Pte. E. W. Cross
Pte. F. Armstrong
Lce.-Cpl. W. E. Cowell
Pte. J. E. Yare
Lce.-Cpl. J. W. Lamb
Sergt. R. Pallister

Pte. G. J. Shaw
Pte. A. Symons
Sergt. A. J. Spittle
Pte. E. Semaine
Sergt. T. Vickery
Lce.-Cpl. Swinnerton
Pte. W. J. Mitchell

The loss of Capt. Travers was indeed an irreparable one. The writer had lain next to him for some hours when we were waiting for the attack on the night before his death, and it was hard to realize that we should speak to him no more. Serving with the Battalion, as he had, since a very few days after its formation at Blackheath, he had been ever since closely identified with its every interest, and all ranks mourned his death. As machine-gun officer in the old days at home, then as Second-in-Command of " B " Company, and finally, since August, 1916, as O.C. " A " Company, it was obvious to us all that he had earned the confidence and respect of his men in a peculiar degree. His Maxim gun section had had an *esprit de corps* of its own, and to them, even after they had been split up over companies as Lewis gunners, Capt. Travers was always the " Skipper." Largely owing to his sound training, they had become first-class Lewis gunners in no time, when that weapon replaced the Maxim as part of the equipment of the Battalion. Educated at Christ's Hospital, Horsham, Capt. Travers was essentially a sportsman, and he was always to be found in the scrum when the Battalion had a " Rugger " match, or among the leading four when there was a cross-country run. The Battalion had lost a fine soldier and a cheerful comrade. He was laid to rest near the spot where he fell east of Tel es Sheria.

Among the N.C.Os. killed were Sergt. S. B. Bayfield and Cpl. J. H. Walker, both of " A " Company. Sergt. J. Linklater, " B " Company, was badly wounded during the consolidation after the battle, and died in the dressing station.

The wounded included:—

2nd-Lieut. L. E. M. Weatherley	Intelligence Officer
2nd-Lieut. D. F. P. Spurgeon	" A " Company
2nd-Lieut. A. H. Hunt	" C " Company
Sergt. H. W. Watts	" A " Company
Sergt. W. J. Wiles	" B " Company
Lce.-Sergt. W. T. Hemens	" A " Company
Cpl. C. Dickens	" C " Company
Lce.-Cpl. C. F. Bishop	" A" Company
Lce.-Cpl. C. L. Robinson	" D " Company
Lce.-Cpl. E. T. Williams	" D " Company

Total casualties on November 6th and 7th were as follows:—

Killed	Officers		1
	Other ranks		12
Died of wounds	Other ranks		2
Wounded	Officers		4
	Other ranks		71

Capt. R. C. Hearn took over command of " A " Company after the battle of Sheria, and 2nd-Lieut. Lane was the senior officer left with " B " Company, Capt. Watson being still employed at Brigade Headquarters.

CHAPTER IX

THROUGH HUJ TO THE COAST—ACROSS THE PLAIN TO
ENAB—CLIMBING INTO THE JUDEAN HILLS—THE
NEBI SAMWIL FIGHT

NEVER was food so welcome as the " hard tack " which came up by camel convoy on the evening of November 7th. No rations had reached the Battalion for forty-eight hours, and though the excitement and strain of battle had made us forget both hunger and fatigue for a time, yet when the 179th Brigade passed through at 4.30 p.m., and left us at liberty to rest and take our limited ease, it were hard to say whether food or sleep were most welcome. The camels could not approach before dark. Then, largely through the efforts of the Padre and Capt. Churchouse, the latter of whom under fire and in most difficult conditions had put in a strenuous twenty-four hours attending to the wounded, and sending them back at dusk on cacolets to the casualty clearing station, a quantity of hot cocoa was made in the improvised shelter in use as a dressing station, and this, with " bully " and biscuits, was consumed more eagerly than words can express. It smarted considerably on the following morning to have to leave a case of meat and a case of biscuits behind for the Bedouins because we could not carry them !

The discomforts of an empty water-bottle had already been experienced, and there was no need to insure that the men had filled up before leaving Sheria. With as much in the way of water and rations as could be carried on man and horse, and greatly refreshed by its night's sleep, the Battalion waited at the Brigade starting-point on the morning of November 8th to take its place in the column on the march north-west across ten miles of flat dusty plain to Huj. Gen. Shea and Gen. Watson were both there to congratulate Major Craddock and the Battalion on the "Sheria stunt," and the C.O. was informed that the Division had now temporarily joined the Desert Mounted Corps, the 20th Corps having had to be ordered back to the neighbourhood of Karm on account of supply and water difficulties in the forward area.

As part of the Desert Mounted Corps, then, the whole Division was on the move. It was a hot, thirsty march, and one, moreover, which was very trying to the feet. The 179th Brigade, as advance guard, had set off soon after dawn, and we subsequently heard that the leading battalions had had several encounters with the Turkish rearguard. Gen. Shea himself went forward in a light armoured car, and, acting on his verbal orders, the Warwickshire and Worcestershire Yeomanry made a gallant charge, which rounded up a battery of guns and completely demoralized a large detached force of Turks. The scene of this charge, as we saw it a few hours later, remains as one of the most vivid memories of the campaign. Six field guns and two 5.9's were still standing in their gun positions, the ground all round strewn with dead men and horses, and with equipment that had been hurriedly cast aside. One gun was still swung half left, as it had been to meet the advancing cavalry at point-blank range. The team had fallen a yard in front of the nozzle. One could picture the terror of the animals and, in contrast, the steadiness and subdued excitement of the men as they loaded those last shells and bravely served their guns to the end.

Our bivouac on the night of the 8th was close to this spot. Huj was a mere map-location, a dry waterless area of pathless uncultivated wilderness, with here and there a shallow nullah or a piece of rising ground to break the monotony. But it was comfortable enough when we realized that it had been in the hands of the Turks only a few hours previously, and that the enemy was now fleeing in disorder in front of us. We slept soundly enough, anyway.

On the following day Col. Warde-Aldam took over command from Major Craddock. He had rejoined the Division from leave on the day after the battle of Beersheba, and had been employed on the Divisional Staff since that date. On the 9th, with a goodly number of officers, N.C.Os., and men, he was present on parade when Pte. Collinson was decorated by the Divisional Commander with the ribbon of the Military Medal.

The Division was thoroughly glad of the period of rest which commenced on arrival at Huj. The first " lap " of the offensive had been completed in record time, and a short breather before taking another spurt was much valued. In his official account to higher authority of what the 60th had so far accomplished, Gen. Shea concluded with the following summary :—

" Between 12.30 a.m. on November 6th and 4.30 p.m. on the 8th the Division marched twenty-three and a half miles, in the course of which advance the Kauwukah and Rushdi systems of defensive works were captured, the bridgehead at Sheria stormed, a determined counter-attack repulsed, and the Turkish rearguard driven from Zuheilikah to beyond Huj, entailing attacks on three defensive positions on the way. The total captures by the Division in the whole operations amounted to 12 guns, 26 machine guns, 51 officers, and 907 other ranks."

From the Commander-in-Chief the General received the following letter :—

" The fighting and marching of your Division has been beyond praise. The Turk has been outmanœuvred and outfought, and Von Kress's army is now beaten and demoralized."

Some idea of the extent to which the enemy had been dismayed and disorganized by his succession of defeats was obtained from prisoners captured on the 7th and 8th. On the fall of Kauwukah, they told us, picked troops had been hastily formed into composite units, and ordered to resist our advance at all costs. (This no doubt accounted for the large number of enemy regiments represented among the prisoners captured by the 2/20th at Sheria.) When the fall of Gaza, in face of Gen. Bulfin's determined attack, was seen to be imminent, special orders were issued that at all costs we must be held up at Sheria, in order to secure the left flank of the retreating Gaza garrison. That the enemy had failed to make a stand on the Wadi Hesi, or anywhere else behind Gaza, was partially due to his overwhelming defeat at Tel es Sheria.

The advance—which, on account of water difficulties in the country north of Huj, could not be continued by the 20th Corps—was on November 10th and the following days taken up by Gen. Bulfin's Corps on the coast, and by the Desert Mounted Corps. The 20th Corps, withdrawn to Karm, was able to feed itself from railhead with the aid of very little transport, and units sent a large proportion of their camels to assist the supply columns of the advancing 21st Corps. The enemy was in full retreat across the plain north of Gaza. The situation called for every available man, horse, and camel to be thrown into the scale to make the pursuit as relentless as possible. " The problem," says the Dispatch, " became one of supply rather than manœuvre. The question of water and forage was a very difficult one. Even where water was found in sufficient quantities, it was usually in wells and not on the surface, and consequently, if the machinery for working the wells was damaged, or a sufficient supply of troughs was not available, the process of watering a large number of animals was slow and difficult. In these circumstances our progress on the 10th and 11th was slow ; the troops suffered considerably from thirst—a hot, exhausting wind blew during these two days— and our supply difficulties were great."

The scarcity of water had necessitated whole units being withdrawn to back areas where water was plentiful and supplies could be easily brought up. The Australian Mounted Division had been out of the line for some days, and the cavalry who set off in pursuit of the retreating Turks on the plain found that wadibeds were nearly all dry, and wells sadly needed replenishing. Both horses and men had a bad time in the torrid heat and stiff fighting, but the Turks were given no opportunity to make a real stand, and the infantry of the 21st Corps followed hard on the heels of the cavalry. The 2/20th had to trek some miles westwards, so as to avoid the waterless country north of Huj, before it could take its place ready to join in the pursuit.

Marching for miles on sandy soil with a scorching sun overhead was stiff work, but the Battalion was in splendid condition physically, and in high morale, and the task was carried through light-heartedly. Leaving Huj on the morning of November 11th, we pitched bivouacs in the Wadi Jemmameh for one night, moving to the Wadi Hesi on the 12th. A letter written home by an officer on this date concludes :—" We have moved on again, and here we are to-day in rather a charming spot overlooking the sea. Unfortunately, the sea is about twelve miles away, so there is no chance of a bathe. But still it is a treat to see the beautiful blue after the eternal sand. The country we are now in is hilly, fairly rocky, and blessed with a fair amount of very coarse and dry grass. We get some lovely views from the hills. The flies here are worse than ever, and we cannot eat without eating a few. There is also a plentiful supply of dead horses, which does not add greatly to the charm of the place ! We are doing our best to bury them, though it is very hard work, and sometimes almost calls for the use of gas-helmets.

Apparently the Turks worked their horses to death in their flight, for the country is strewn with dead horses and mules. Water is fairly plentiful now, although it is difficult to get it to the spot where we are at the moment. We are still limited to half a gallon a day. During the past fortnight our water was brought some seventeen to twenty miles by camels, so you may imagine it was scarce. The majority of our horses and mules were three days without a drink, poor beasts! We are giving them plenty of water and a rest now. When the Padre gets home he is going to include water in his Harvest Thanksgiving. Personally, I shall sit in the bathroom and watch the taps run."

On the 13th the Battalion returned for a night to the Wadi Jemmameh, and on the 14th marched due south to Abu Jerrah, close to Abu Hareira. We were at first a little mystified by these moves and at finding ourselves once again south of Sheria, but our withdrawal from the line was another result of the transport and water difficulties in the country north of Huj, and our future advance was to be over a route more circuitous, but more easy of supply—westwards by the Gaza—Beersheba road to the coast at Gaza, and then northwards after the Turks across the maritime plain, behind the 21st Corps, to Deir Sineid and Latron.

It had not been possible to bring up any mails or canteen goods since the offensive opened, and the scarcity of cigarettes was more felt by the men than any other of their troubles. From Hareira, Major Craddock and Capt. Watson proceeded back on horseback to Karm to make an attempt to get up some " smokes." Their efforts were well rewarded. On the following day a good quantity of luxuries, including cigarettes, chocolate, biscuits, and a large tinned ham, arrived. It need hardly be added that the canteen staff (Sergt. F. G. Watts, Sergt. A. B. Crummey, and Pte. W. Oakley) made light work of the selling.

The climate at this time was excessively hot by day

and cold by night, and we were very glad to welcome an issue of serge tunics for wearing after sunset. Drill tunics continued to be worn by day except in " shirtsleeve order." On the 19th the Battalion had a sweltering march to Gaza, passing the formidable Tank and Atawineh Redoubts, now for the first time for two years unoccupied and silent. The innumerable shell-holes which surrounded these miniature fortresses still remained to tell the story of their two years' travail. Our bivouac was half a mile east of Gaza, and in the afternoon some of us had an opportunity of visiting the city. We found it a pile of ruins—such a sight as we had not seen since leaving Mont St. Eloi. Surrounded by a belt of giant cactus hedges to a depth of a mile or more, the pile of ruins had excellent natural protection. The Turks had brought all their ingenuity to bear on its defence, and right stubbornly had they repulsed all previous attacks with machine guns cleverly concealed behind the impenetrable entanglements of cactus growth. The famous mosque in the centre of the city, used by the enemy as an observation post and munition store, as was proved by a carpet of empty cartridge cases six feet deep on the floor, was a mass of wreckage, and the streets had long since been buried under the torrent of bricks and rubble which had fallen from the buildings on either side of them. The enemy had gambled on the strength of his Gaza fortress. But this last staggering blow had left his right flank shattered, and Gaza remained empty, desolate, and— free !

A new factor entered into the situation in the third week of November. This was the commencement of the autumn rains—torrential downpours accompanied by a decided fall in atmospheric temperature. The troops were in summer clothing, without greatcoats or blankets, and the change in the weather, though easing the difficulty of water-supply, had brought another which was equally formidable and unpleasant. Moreover, the rain made the tracks so slippery that many of the camel convoys were immobile. Equal, as always, to the emergency, the " Q " Staff later sent 2,000 donkeys forward as substitutes for camels, and these animals did their work admirably. But during the first few days of rain the conditions were as uncomfortable, and the supply chain was as weak, as at any time during the operations.

In pouring rain the Battalion marched from Gaza up the sandy coastal track to El Rebakbeh, in the wake of Gen. Bulfin's victorious Corps, and on to El Kustine, reaching Junction Station on the 22nd, and Latron one day later. Though encumbered by the immense supply difficulty (our troops were now operating some thirty-five miles in front of railhead), there was no question of halting. The enemy must be allowed no chance to reorganize on any scale that mattered. He had collected as though to make a stand in front of Junction Station and the Jaffa—Jerusalem road, but, in spite of terrible weather and execrable roads, the troops of the 21st Corps had compelled him to evacuate his positions. Defeated once more, he had continued his retreat, his scattered groups making in the direction of north and east. The capture of the railway from Jaffa to Junction Station meant a lot to us, and later enabled a great strain to be removed from the lorry and horse transport services and the camel convoys.

In its march from Huj the Battalion had crossed first the outskirts of the desert, then the sandhills of the coast and the plain of Palestine, and now it was climbing the foothills into the mountains of Judea. From a climate of summer heat it had come to one of bitter cold and pouring rain ; from the bareness of the desert it had come to populated villages, busy monasteries, and hills spread with olive-trees and terraced vineyards. The villagers of the places we passed through were not slow to produce goods which they knew would be marketable, and eggs, oranges, figs, and dates were obtainable in limited quantities. The monastery at Enab had a quite considerable stock of palatable red wine, but the supply was very soon sold out.

In their flight into the hills the Turks were closely followed and harassed by the troops of the 21st Corps, and the enemy, thrown back on to his Jerusalem defences, prepared to make a last attempt to keep us out of the Holy City. At one point in particular he took pains to put up a strong defence. This was on the towering height of Nebi Samwil (" the Prophet Samuel"), north of the Jaffa—Jerusalem road, a position which stands 2,900 feet above sea-level, and commands not only Jerusalem, but also all the broken mountain range stretching far north towards Nablus. No modern army which could hold the heights of Nebi Samwil could be long denied access to the Holy City itself, though it was on this bleak hill-top that Richard the Lion Heart, many centuries before, had buried his face in his casque and exclaimed : " Lord God, I pray that I may never see Thy Holy City, if so be that I may not rescue it from the hands of Thine enemies." To the Turks the loss of Nebi Samwil would inevitably mean the loss of the Holy City, and of much else besides. It was here, at Nebi Samwil, that the Battalion was to have its next contact with the enemy.

A Gurkha battalion of the 75th Division had first captured the place. The Indians had fought their way to the crest of the ridge, where stood an ancient Mohammedan mosque, a landmark for miles. The Turks counter-attacked fiercely, but the Gurkhas held on, and were eventually relieved by Scotsmen of the 52nd (Lowland) Division. The extreme summit of the crest and the mosque changed hands more than once in twenty-four hours, and finally the mosque remained in our hands, whilst the surrounding houses—in some places only twenty yards distant—remained in the hands of the enemy. The Turks concentrated a large force in the village of El Jib, at the bottom of the slope. The Lowlanders had a battalion of the Royal Scots in close support at Biddu, a mile behind them, round the curved shoulder of the steep and rocky wadi-banks.

As part of a Corps relief (the 20th relieving the 21st), the 2/19th Battalion took over the Nebi Samwil defences on November 25th, and on the same day the 2/20th marched from Latron to Biddu by the Latron—Jerusalem metalled road, and became battalion in support. No wheel transport could use the Roman road from Enab winding up into the hills, and as this was the only means of approach, we had to dump reserve ammunition and stores in an olive-grove in the village, and issue the men with blankets (which, thank Heaven! had now arrived), one bandolier of small-arm ammunition per man, and picks and shovels. Except where it first left the main road, there was hardly a trace of the route described on the map as the Roman road. For long stretches it had been blotted out by fallen boulders. The winding track was in no place wider than a narrow goat-path, and camels had great difficulty in picking their way among the boulders, and moving at every few yards over slippery stretches of rock. The battalion of the Royal Scots was on its way back to Latron, and we had to halt to let them pass. They had had a bad time in the matter of rations and sleep, and were battle-worn and tired. Cigarettes were what they pined for most, and it was a fine thing to see our men pressing whole packets into their willing hands—packets which, for the most part, came from the scanty allotment paid for by each man at Hareira. The sacrifice was the more real as there was very little prospect of fresh supplies reaching us in the Judean hills.

The bivouac at Biddu was in a cactus grove neatly cut out of surroundings of rock, and adjoined the village and monastery of Kubeibeh (the Emmaus of the New Testament). Biddu was accurately registered by the enemy's guns, and on November 26th shells fell in the vicinity of the bivouac throughout the day and a few minor casualties were sustained.

That night an urgent wire was received from Brigade ordering a company to be dispatched immediately to Beit Surik, a piece of high ground about a mile south of Biddu, which was being held by the 2/18th Battalion, and against which the Turks had launched an attack. " D " Company was turned out, and within a few minutes had moved off. On learning that a party of the enemy had penetrated our line, Capt. Reynolds decided to counter-attack at once with the bayonet. So effectively was the charge carried out that the Turks were completely routed, and sustained heavy casualties, leaving three prisoners in our hands. The line having been restored, Capt. Reynolds and his company returned to Biddu.

The hostile shelling of the previous day was repeated with greater intensity on the 27th, and the mosque of Nebi Samwil was subjected to a heavy bombardment. At 4.30 p.m. the 2/19th Battalion reported that they were being heavily attacked. Two companies of the 2/20th were ordered to reinforce, and the Commanding Officer led " A " and " C " Companies forward. The enemy was searching all approaches to Nebi Samwil and the surrounding wadis with artillery and machine-gun fire, and he put over a quantity of gas into the Wadi Amir. The companies, however, reached the terraced slope of Nebi Samwil without casualties, and were ordered to stand by in case they might be needed. The attack was driven off by the 2/19th Battalion, and as there were no signs of a second assault, " A " and " C " Companies returned to Biddu just before midnight.

On the following evening the 2/20th took over the Nebi Samwil defences from Col. Sword's battalion. Three companies were set to hold the posts in the mosque and on the summit of the hill. " D " Company was in close support, bivouacked near Headquarters cave on one of the terraces on the near slope.

No better description of Nebi Samwil can be given than the following, which was written on the spot by the Commanding Officer :—

"*November* 30*th*, 1917.

" I am writing from a difficult bit of the line which I took over the night before last—the weirdest sort of ' Grimm's Fairy Tale ' sort of place I've ever imagined. Try to picture to yourself an enormous mosque on a high hill, the sides of which are a succession of stony terraces separated by stone walls. Attached to the mosque is a village built of solid stone and mud roofs. There is a graceful minaret and fine terraces, and an unsurpassed view of the Holy City on one side, and the Shephelah, the Plain of Sharon, and the sea on the other. The mosque itself is built over the tomb of one of the prophets of the Old Testament, and is the scene of much Old Testament history. Now *don't* try to imagine it as I have seen it since. Twice I have seen it just a cloud of dust and smoke, and *that* is my present recollection of it. A roofless mass on the top of a hill standing up in the moonlight. No minaret, and great holes in the walls. Scattered all round are dead Turks, dead Gurkhas, dead English, and dead animals ; rifles and equipment all over the place ; snipers' bullets cracking continually overhead ; soldiers picking their way quietly along the sheltered corners of the débris, and, in places where there is no cover, running the gauntlet for ten, twenty, thirty, or forty yards in the open— silent groups of eager, alert men along a very artificial line in the village watching the windows and corners of houses, in some places only twenty yards away. Sometimes you crawl through the inky darkness of the inside of a ruined house and scramble over you know not what. Sometimes you walk through the mosque, and bits of the crumbling walls fall round you. I just can't describe the uncanniness of it all. . . . Now picture to yourself a large, low-roofed cave with small entrance and a few dim candles. At the back is a crowd of wounded men in various stages of seriousness; they are being looked after by two doctors in shirt-sleeves, one of whom is Churchouse. Most of them are awfully plucky, and happy to feel they have given more than they've got. In the centre of the cave are two groups of telephonists, with probably six operators, all talking at once. On each side a group of officers and men, filthy, strained to the utmost; near each group half-eaten meals or meals waiting to be eaten. Officers often leave the groups to go and talk at the telephone, generally only to return and say, ' D—— ! still " dis " to So-and-so.' (' Dis ' means disconnected.) Through the narrow entrance comes and goes an intermittent stream of bloody, dusty wounded, or breathless messengers. The atmosphere of the place reeks.

* * * *

" Yesterday, after the hell of a bombardment, we beat off two enemy attacks. The Turk has not fired at us to-day, and I am sitting in the sun outside the cave, still dirty, but partially rested. Alongside me is a badly wounded Greek Turk and a semi-' luny ' Arab whom we captured, and who is trembling with funk because he thinks he is going to be shot. Overhead scream *our* shells, and one of our aeroplanes is taking photographs. This is a poor effort, but may give you some idea of one of the strangest scenes and episodes of my life. One of my sergeants (Sergt. T. Vickery) brought me down two very interesting Arabic books, and told me he had found a library in the mosque. It will all be destroyed, and I might go and save some of it, but somehow I don't; it requires energy, which I must apply elsewhere."

To complete the picture of the Nebi Samwil experience, it only remains to give some account of the two attacks to which the Colonel refers.

The position of our posts called for more than normal

alertness on the part of every sentry, as the Turkish force in El Gib was known to be only waiting for a suitable opportunity to launch a new assault. To make matters worse, it was found impossible to get water to some of the " C " Company posts.

Shells began to fall on various parts of the crest and on the mosque at 9 a.m. on the morning of November 29th. The mosque had already lost its minaret. The walls and roof now began to fall in, and Capt. Partridge and Lieut. Lane had to rearrange their dispositions. It was as well they did so. The bombardment increased in fury throughout the morning, and at 1.30 p.m. it became intensive. The enemy, having withdrawn his snipers, was free to make what havoc he could. Soon after 1.30 p.m. a large body of Turks made a rush into the mosque, doubtless expecting to find our posts evacuated after the bombardment. Our men were all ready and waiting, and the attack was doomed by this fact. Met by the full fury of Lewis guns, rifles, bombs, and Stokes mortars, the Turks stood for a moment, drew back, rallied, advanced, and then, in terrified disorder, rushed back and vanished over the brow. Twice that afternoon the enemy came to the assault, assisted by a continuous intensive artillery barrage. He gained not an inch, and soon after 5 p.m., his last attack having failed, his artillery fire died down and ceased. During the attacks it had been impossible for Battalion Headquarters to keep in touch with the situation, owing to repeated breaks in the wire from shelling, and in the middle of the fight an important situation report from Capt. Partridge had to be carried by runner through the thickest of the bombardment. Pte. R. Gatenby volunteered for this duty, though with only a remote chance of getting through, and safely delivered the message at Headquarters. Subsequently, as a result of splendid work under heavy fire in the open by the signallers, the telephone line was repaired, and Lieut. Lane was able to speak to the C.O. At about 4.45 p.m. he said (in effect): "We have driven them off again. I don't think they will make another attempt. Their casualties must be tremendous. I have not been able to see all our posts, but am going round now. From what I have seen, I fear we have suffered pretty heavily." He was right. One post of "C" Company, under Lce.-Cpl. C. Doughty, had been completely wiped out by the enemy barrage, and a platoon of sixteen men had only two survivors. Pte. J. Collinson, M.M., was among the killed.

Capt. Partridge and Lieut. Lane had maintained their headquarters in the hottest parts of the mosque. They afterwards bore eloquent testimony to the devotion with which the posts had stood their ground during the preliminary intensive bombardment, and had fought, to the death in some cases, when the enemy attacked. Lce.-Cpl. H. Bland, Pte. R. Gatenby, Pte. W. Paxton, Pte. N. McDougall, and Pte. J. Greer had done particularly gallant work. The bombardment had been concentrated on the mosque and its immediate vicinity, and the sectors on right and left had been almost untouched. The Turks had no mind to renew their advances, and the night passed quietly.

The Brigadier received the following letter from Divisional Headquarters two days later:—

"The G.O.C. has asked me to write to you about the report of Lieut.-Col. Warde-Aldam on the action at Nebi Samwil on November 29th. He would be glad if you would tell Col. Warde-Aldam with what pride and pleasure the General read his report of the action. He wishes you to convey his congratulations to the 2/20th Battalion on their stubborn resistance and the fine soldierly qualities they displayed on this occasion.

"Believe me,
"Yours sincerely,
(Sgd.) "A. C. TEMPERLEY, *Lieut.-Col.,*
General Staff, 60th Division."

More than 500 enemy dead were afterwards found by our burial parties on the slopes of Nebi Samwil. Many had been killed in the fighting by the 75th and 52nd Divisions, but a large number undoubtedly perished on the afternoon of November 29th.

The 2/22nd Battalion, under Lieut.-Col. A. E. Borton, V.C., D.S.O., relieved the 2/20th on the 30th, and we moved back to a bivouac near Kubeibeh. On the same day Major Craddock proceeded to Cairo for five weeks to attend the Senior Officers' Course at Heliopolis, Capt. Watson acting as Second-in-Command in his absence. Lieut. Jones had gone to Brigade Headquarters for duty earlier in the month, and 2nd-Lieut. Blundell was now Transport Officer.

On December 1st a short march north-east from Kubeibeh brought us to Beit Izza, a quiet spot in the line which we took over from Col. Streatfeild's battalion, the 2/23rd London Regiment. Our stay of four days was characterized by little of interest save some shelling on Tuesday, December 4th.

The enemy seemed to have spotted the Headquarter Officers' Mess—if, indeed, a bare stretch of grass and a score of filled small-arm ammunition boxes can be called a Mess, in the absence of a nicely furnished room and a dining-table. Col. Heywood-Lonsdale and Major Glazebrook, of the 10th K.O.S.L.I., arrived to look round the line just as we were going to seat ourselves at the ammunition boxes for lunch. Their visit fortunately delayed the meal. A few minutes later a heavy shower of shrapnel burst over the lunch table. Lce.-Cpl. Snoad, the Mess Corporal, was slightly wounded, but there was no other damage.

The Adjutant had the satisfactory experience of being introduced by the Commanding Officer to the Adjutant of the Turkish regiment immediately opposite to us. This gentleman had wandered into our lines at 2 a.m., and Col. Warde-Aldam wasted no time in waking Capt. Elliot, so that he might discuss ration strengths and parade states with his " opposite number." Fortunately, the latter, whose father was a schoolmaster in Jerusalem, had his ration indent for the following day in his pocket, and this, with some other documents, gave us all the information we needed about the 1st Battalion of the 2nd Turkish Regiment.

Beit Izza, which is memorable also for the number of dead camels in its vicinity, has one further claim to notoriety so far as the officers of the Battalion are concerned. It was here that a certain officer who shall be nameless gave demonstrations before other officers in a stable, badly lit and somewhat dirty. The demonstrations were not exactly of an impersonal kind so far as the Commanding Officer was concerned, and the officer was naturally horrified at the conclusion of his performance to find the C.O. among his spectators. He was heard to mutter a prayer to the roof to fall on him. Finding this unanswered, he dashed for the entrance and the daylight, and made good his escape.

2nd-Lieut. A. Stone, the Intelligence Officer, with Cpl. Oliver and several men of the Intelligence Section, had been attached to the 179th Brigade for some days to reconnoitre the ground in the neighbourhood of Kulonieh, and on December 7th, in pouring rain, the 2/20th and the remainder of the Brigade concentrated just west of Kustul for the attack which was to deliver Jerusalem.

The 60th Division was to play the most prominent part in this historic battle, as it had done in the arduous fighting in November. The Londoners had undoubtedly made a great name, and in this connection we may quote from an account by Mr. W. T. Massey, the official Press correspondent with the Egyptian Expeditionary Force, who writes thus of the Division in his book, " How Jerusalem was Won " :—

" I was with the Division the night after they had taken Huj. It was their first day of rest for some time, but the men showed few signs of fatigue. No one could move among them without being proud of the Londoners. They were strong, self-reliant, well-disciplined, brave fellows. I well remember what Col. Temperley, the G.S.O. 1 of the Division, told me when sitting out on a hill in the twilight that night. Col. Temperley had been Brigade Major of the first New Zealand Infantry Brigade which came to Egypt, and took a full share in the work on Gallipoli, on its way to France. He had over two years of active service on the Western Front before coming out to Palestine for duty with the 60th Division, and his views on men in action were based on the sound experience of the professional soldier. Of the London County Territorials he said :—' I cannot speak of these warriors without a lump rising in my throat. These Cockneys are the best men in the world. Their spirits are simply wonderful, and I do not think any Division ever went into a big show with higher morale. After three years of war it is refreshing to hear the men's earnestly expressed desire to go into action again. These grand fellows went forward with the full bloom on them ; there never was any hesitation ; their discipline was absolutely perfect, their physique and courage were alike magnificent, and their valour beyond words. The Cockney makes the perfect soldier.'

" I wrote at the time that, whether the men came from Bermondsey, Camberwell, or Kennington, or belonged to what were known as ' class corps,' such as the Civil Service or Kensingtons, before the war, all battalions were equally good. They were trained for months for the big battle till their bodies were brought to such a state of fitness that Spartan fare during the days of ceaseless action caused neither grumble nor fatigue. The men may well be rewarded with the title ' London's Pride,' and London is honoured by having such stalwarts to represent the heart of the British Empire. In eight days the Londoners marched sixty-six miles, and fought a number of hot actions. The march may not seem long, but Palestine is not Salisbury Plain. A leg-weary man was asked by an officer if his feet were blistered, and replied : ' They're rotten sore, but my heart's gay.' That is typical of the spirit of these unconquerable Cockneys. I have just left them. They still have the bloom of freshness, and I do not think it will ever fade. Scorching winds which parched the throat and made everything one wore hot to the touch were enough to oppress the staunchest soldier, but these sterling Territorials—costers and labourers, artisans and tradesmen, professional men and men of independent means, true brothers in arms and good Britons—left their bivouacs and trudged across heavy country, fearless, strong, proud, and with the cheerfulness of good men who fight for right. What I said in those early days of the great advance was more than borne out later, and in the capture of Jerusalem, in taking Jericho and in forcing the passage of the Jordan, this glorious Division of Londoners was always the same—a pride to its Commander, a bulwark of the 20th Corps, and a great asset of the Empire."

CHAPTER X

SURROUNDING JERUSALEM: A DECISIVE ASSAULT AT LIFTA: FALL OF THE HOLY CITY

GEN. ALLENBY'S strangle-hold was tightening round the Holy City, but there was one fierce and final bout to be contested before the enemy could be counted out and the holy places could be secured. This contest was to fall to the lot of the 20th Corps. Gen. Bulfin's Divisions had carried all before them in their difficult advance from Gaza, and they must have been a little disappointed that, having driven the enemy into the hills, they were not allowed to carry on, at least, until they had swept him through Jerusalem. But they had already done more—much more—than is normally expected of troops in such conditions as those in which they had been called upon to operate, and on November 28th, as already reported, they had been relieved by the 20th Corps. To Gen. Chetwode, therefore, fell the task of preparing the details of the final moves which should secure Jerusalem. The Turkish position was undoubtedly a strong one—not, as might have been expected, a hastily improvised series of defences, but a carefully planned and well-dug system of fortifications, prepared before ever we had commenced our march to Beersheba, and sited with peculiar skill on the commanding heights surrounding the Holy City. On the western and south-western sides of the city there is the steep and precipitous Wadi Surar outside a belt of high hills. On these hills the Turks had dug their defence works, Heart Redoubt, Liver Redoubt, and the rest. They were splendid vantage-points, and the wadi, with the Turkish guns on the heights ready to barrage it, formed a magnificent natural obstacle, a moat which the British attacking troops must cross or die.

Such were the positions to be stormed by two Brigades of Londoners, the 179th on the right and the 180th on the left. After taking them the Division was to " change direction left," encircle the western outskirts of the city, and finish on an objective due north of it. (This somewhat difficult operation was dictated by the necessity of avoiding all fighting in the Holy City and its immediate neighbourhood.) The 74th Division was to attack on the left of the 60th, and the 53rd, on the right, was meantime to advance up the Hebron Road from the south, directing its march so as to envelop the eastern and north-eastern outskirts. The combined movements of the three Divisions were designed to force the evacuation of the city without resistance by completely encircling it. The main difficulty of the operation was one to which the Staff had already become accustomed—*i.e.*, the lack of roads for artillery and supply columns. Fortunately, a period of fine weather had set in during the last days of November; new roads connecting Latron with Beit Likia and Enab with Kubeibeh had been begun, and much work had been put in on the improvement of existing roads and tracks, which, when captured from the Turks, had become unserviceable for transport and camels after a few hours' rain.

Meanwhile the Turks in the Jerusalem defences were known to have been reinforced, and there was every sign that they intended to make one last effort to hold the city and the important Nablus and Jericho roads.

The spell of fine weather broke on December 7th, and the five-mile march of the 2/20th from a bivouac just north of Saris to a concentration area at Kulonieh, south of Kustul, on that day was completed in a heavy downpour of rain. Overcoats and blankets had been dumped at Enab, and the absence of these comforts did not make the twelve hours' wait before the attack any more endurable. Bivouacs were pitched in an olive grove at 4 p.m., companies being separated by safe distances as a precaution in case of shelling, and the Battalion rested. What a splendid picture the bivouac would have made for an artist—" Twentieth Century Crusaders assembled for the attack on Jerusalem." It was a cold, dark, wet night. Rain fell in torrents, and a heavy ground mist covered the hills. As always when conditions were abnormally trying, the men were—outwardly, at least—abnormally cheerful. Songs were continued till long after dark. No fires could be lit even had the tactical situation admitted, and the men huddled together as well as they could, and sang till they fell asleep. The one redeeming feature of the evening was the unexpected arrival of a rum ration, which the acting Regimental Quartermaster-Sergeant (C.S.M. Dawes) and the warrant officers and sergeants who had been left as " first reinforcements " at the transport lines had man-handled over some miles of rough country. That rum issue will never be forgotten. When companies struck bivouac at 1.30 a.m., and the Battalion advanced over the Kustul Ridge to its position of deployment, most of the men were warm, even if thoroughly wet. By this time the rain had ceased, though the mist remained, and the night was very dark.

The Intelligence Officer and his men had done their work well. The ground leading down into the abyss of the Wadi Surar (which had been assigned to the Brigade as position of deployment) was as difficult for men and mules as could be imagined. From the summit of the Kustul Ridge it continued over a crest, down a thousand feet over terraced slopes covered with vineyards and olive-yards, and up the other side. How in the darkness the muleteers got their fourteen pack-mules per company over such ground is a mystery to this day. The fact remains that they did it. For some nights previously the Turks had patrolled the area in order to discover our intentions. This had complicated the reconnaissance, and the thick ground mist now made the task of guiding doubly difficult. The scouts made no mistake, and the companies were safely concentrated under the terraces of the eastern bank of the wadi long before 5.15 a.m., the hour at which the other three battalions of the Brigade commenced to attack. The 2/20th was in Brigade reserve.

As day dawned we could discern the enemy earthworks on the three heights which towered above us, and the cracking of the Turkish machine guns soon told that the attack had begun. Red flares were to be lit on each work when it was captured, and we very soon saw a red glow on two of the mist-covered hills— a very impressive sight. Hard fighting was required to gain the right-hand hill, which had been allotted to the 2/19th Battalion; but they eventually got it, and the 2/20th moved up so as to be ready for developments. Behind Heart and Liver Redoubts, and lying in a slight depression, was the village of Deir Yesin. The 2/19th fought their way through the scattered buildings into some quarries and houses beyond, where, at noon, they were held up by enemy machine-gun nests and sniping from a ridge in front. In spite of most determined efforts, little progress could be made, and the Brigadier issued orders for one company of the 2/20th to go forward and extend the right flank of the 2/19th for a renewed assault. "B" Company, under Capt. Lane, was sent.

The details of this historic assault and its sequel cannot be better described than in the words of Gen. Watson's official account :—

" Three and a half companies 2/19th Battalion were to make the frontal attack, with two companies 2/17th Battalion and one and a half companies 2/18th Battalion working round the left flank, and one company 2/20th Battalion round the right flank. The charge was made at 15.45 hours, under cover of the fire of the 2|18th and 2/20th Battalions and overhead fire of the guns of the 180th Machine Gun Company. One section Howitzers also assisted.

"In spite of very heavy machine-gun and rifle fire and shrapnel, the ridge was carried in magnificent style under the eyes of the Corps and Divisional Commanders, who have signified their high appreciation. The enemy hastily retired towards Jerusalem. The right flank of the Brigade was, however, somewhat exposed, owing to the deep ravine that separated it from the left of the 179th Brigade. A second company of the 2/20th Battalion ('D' Company, under Capt. Reynolds) was sent as a reserve to the 2/19th Battalion, who had sent their last two platoons to the exposed right flank."

The position was consolidated, and nothing was heard of the enemy throughout the night save an outburst of rapid fire lasting for about fifteen minutes. Battalion Headquarters and "A" and "C" Companies spent the night just behind Deir Yesin; "B" and "D" Companies remained in the line.

"B" Company had a difficult task on the exposed right flank of the Brigade in the afternoon, but their very gallant assault had secured their own position and that of the Brigade. Capt. Lane received the Military Cross, Sergt. R. Pallister the Distinguished Conduct Medal, and Lce.-Cpl. J. F. Yare and Pte. T. Newton the Military Medal. The following N.C.Os. and men distinguished themselves by conspicuous gallantry and initiative under heavy fire :—

> Lce.-Cpl. A. M. Smith
> Lce.-Cpl. J. W. Lamb
> Cpl. H. N. Lunt
> Pte. T. Rowlands
> Pte. H. C. Flynn

Sergt. H. K. Holmes did extremely valuable *liaison* work between the 2/20th and 2/19th Battalions throughout the operation.

The company's casualties totalled three other ranks killed (Lce.-Cpl. W. Pullan, Pte. J. Evans, Pte. E. C. Groves), and fourteen other ranks wounded (including Lce.-Cpl. J. Owens).

That this action was regarded by the Higher Command as the decisive blow which finally forced the capitulation of the Holy City is clearly shown by the Divisional Commander's telegram, which appears at the end of this chapter.

The difficult ground over which we had advanced from Kustul had been out of the question for " wheels " and camels, and the transport was still some miles back on the Enab Road. No rations or water could be got up that night. As usual, the cooks had not waited to be sent for, but, under Cpl. Goreham, were on the scene immediately after dark, and very soon had fires going and cocoa prepared for Battalion Headquarters and the two companies not in the line. The Headquarters and " D " Company's Officers' Mess cooks (Pte. A. E. Church and Pte. R. W. J. Andrews), however, did not arrive, though the Colonel's servant, Pte. Adams, turned up with some eatables. The two mess cooks had left Rear Headquarters with him, but had not been seen since. Hours passed, and still there was no sign of Pte. Church. The men's cooks came to the rescue, and the officers thought no more of their cocoa. Not until 5 a.m. on the following day did the two cooks report at Headquarters, each carrying a small dixie. The whole world now knows, through the newspapers, what had happened. A British officers' mess cook had found his way as part of a conquering army to the gates of Jerusalem, and was the first soldier for centuries to do so. Missing their direction in a search for water (for the cocoa !), the two cooks had found themselves at the very gates of the city, and had been told by a group of civilians who had a white flag that the authorities were waiting to surrender. Not quite knowing what might be required of *them* in such circumstances, they had turned and fled, and finally, after much wandering, had found their way after dawn to Battalion Headquarters. Even then they gave no details of their escapade, and it was many hours later before the facts became known.

Night reconnaissances had confirmed the suspicion of a further withdrawal by the enemy. A " B " Company patrol returned to our lines at 5.30 a.m., and reported that no touch could be gained with the Turks. Meanwhile " B " and " D " Companies had received their rations and water, though the remainder of the Battalion was in the unenviable position of being without both.

About 9 a.m. orders were received from Brigade for the plan of attack to be proceeded with. This meant the 2/20th passing through the 2/19th and taking the lead in the advance to Shafat, a village three miles north of Jerusalem on the Nablus Road. A message was sent to " B " and " D " Companies (the companies with rations) to make immediate preparations to move, and the Commanding Officer and the Adjutant went forward to the Headquarters of the 2/19th in Deir Yesin to get in touch with the situation. If there was any fighting going on, it was a long way ahead, for no sound of machine gun, rifle, or artillery fire, such as had made the previous afternoon hideous, could be heard. Lieut. P. M. Bendall, the acting Adjutant of the 2/19th, was still awaiting information from his front companies. Patrols, it appeared, were now working forward in front of our line to get in touch with the Turks, who had withdrawn in the night. Conversation was interrupted by Gen. Watson, who galloped by on a horse which was easily recognized as from the 2/20th lines, and who was closely followed by Lieut. Jones, also mounted. Hardly tightening his rein to enable him to be heard, the Brigadier shouted that the Mayor of Jerusalem was waiting to surrender the city. The Commanding Officer passed the good news on to " B " and " D " Companies, and, telling Capt. Reynolds and Capt. Lane to follow with their companies at once, he sent a message back to Capt. Partridge (who had been left in charge of Headquarters, " A " and " C ") to bring the remainder of the Battalion on as soon as rations and water had been issued.

Meanwhile the Commanding Officer and the Adjutant went forward. There was not a Turk to be seen. The Holy City lay on our right concealed in mist. All was quiet. Little piles of empty machine-gun cartridge cases and the bodies of the dead which lay strewn over the ground where the enemy had made his last desperate resistance on the previous day were the only signs of the bloody means which had had to be employed to free the city. Seeing our approach, hundreds of joyful inhabitants came out to welcome us ; many spoke English, and all crowded round. Every grade of society was there— Armenian priests in quaint, straight, tall hats, surrounded at the lower edges by masses of thick flowing hair ; " Jerusalem Jews," with long curls hanging over either ear ; women dressed in European hat and blouse and skirt, and others in eastern shawl and flowing mantle ; boys and girls ; Bedouins and Arab policemen— all had turned out to lend a voice for cheering their deliverers.

They presented a strange contrast indeed to the bronzed, robustly fit men of " D " Company, who were the first of the Battalion, and indeed the first British troops, to enter the western portion of the Holy City. " B " Company followed, and then " C " and " A." There could be no halt to stop and talk, though adventurous spirits in the crowd came forward with small flat cakes of new bread, and figs and nuts to sell, which the men, though somewhat amused at this so early advance to business, were only too glad to give piastres for.

We could now see a village (which we identified on the map as Shafat) standing on a high hill about two miles away over a long and winding valley of rocks, and we could pick out the main road northwards from Jerusalem running through it. On the road we could see Turks, some in formed bodies, some singly or in pairs hurrying through the village, and some who stayed there. The Commanding Officer sent " D " Company forward with orders to stop at an intermediate hill for reconnaissance ; but, though without Lewis guns (the mules had had to be sent off to water), Capt. Reynolds made no halt, and advanced rapidly over the extremely difficult ground. The flanks were both exposed, there being no sign of other troops on right or left, so " B " Company was sent forward to support " D." Presently the rest of the Battalion arrived. Col. Dear was behind with three companies of the 2/17th, and troops of the 74th Division could now be seen coming forward on the left, so the whole Battalion advanced across the Jaffa-Jerusalem Road at Lifta into the rocky valley and up the other side to Shafat. In their advance " D " Company captured a 5.9-inch howitzer, eight prisoners, and a large quantity of ammunition ; and a patrol of " B " Company, under Sergt. A. E. White, rounded up three officers and twenty-six men of the enemy.

" B " and " D " Companies pressed on from Shafat and advanced to a very high hill, Tel el Ful, about 1,200 yards in front, on the opposite side of the Nablus Road, and Col. Dear occupied two hills on our right. After Headquarters had arrived in Shafat, fire suddenly opened from our right rear, and a fight developed. Lieut. Lamb, of the 180th Machine Gun Company, who happened to be in the village, immediately off-loaded a gun and got it into action against the enemy, who were firing from Mount Scopus, the northern spur of the Mount of Olives. " C " Company and two platoons of " A," under Lieut. V. Slaughter, were sent to work round the right of the Turks, and the 2/17th Battalion assaulted frontally with the bayonet. By nightfall the opposition had disappeared, and the Battalion had established a very good outpost position on Tel el Ful and two hills south of it.

All four companies were required for outpost duty. It was a very wet night—the third running—and the men had no bivouac sheets nor blankets nor greatcoats, and many were wearing drill shorts. Battalion Headquarters was able to get into a house. Here a fire was made from Turkish shell-boxes, of which there were thousands in the village, and hot tea was brewed for the whole Battalion. The night passed without incident, and early in the morning the outpost force was cut down to two and a half companies, the remainder being able to return to Shafat to get dry. For those remaining on duty a certain number of caves were found for men not on sentry, and in the afternoon the Battalion went into Jerusalem to billets, the first since leaving Yaucourt a year previously.

The Holy City, which in our advance from Lifta we had left some distance on our right, had formally surrendered to Gen. Shea at 1 p.m. For the twenty-third time in its history Jerusalem had fallen. The end of Turkish rule, with all its harshness, injustice, and blight of poverty, had come at last. The holiest city of Christendom had been restored to civilization, and a heavy and, as it proved, a fatal blow had been struck at the mighty and dangerous ambitions of Germany in the East. The whole civilized world saw in a flash the significance of the event. No newspaper at home was allowed to record its happening until the House of Commons had been informed through the lips of a Cabinet Minister. Then the news of the great victory penetrated every corner of the British Empire and of Allied and neutral countries, and the whole of Christendom rejoiced. The unbounded happiness of the inhabitants in receiving their freedom was only paralleled by the intense satisfaction of the victors in so successful and historic a result of all their labours and sacrifices. The thanks of the Corps Commander were received in a telegram addressed to Gen. Shea on the day of the surrender in the following terms :—

"It is a fitting reward for the splendid work of your gallant Division since the commencement of operations that the honour of receiving the surrender of Jerusalem should have fallen to them. My heartiest congratulations, and thanks to you and them."

The Divisional Commander telegraphed to General Watson on the same day :—

"I consider that your gallant charge yesterday afternoon made Jerusalem ours."

Gen. Watson addressed the following letter to "All Ranks of the 180th Infantry Brigade":—

"It gives me intense pride and pleasure to circulate the Divisional Commander's telegram. . . . I want to thank all ranks of my Brigade for their gallant conduct during the last phase of operations. The capture of Jerusalem is an appropriate conclusion to your efforts."

In his Dispatch, dated December 16th, 1917, the Commander-in-Chief writes :—

"All ranks and services in the Force under my command have acquitted themselves in a manner beyond praise. Fatigue, thirst, heat, and cold have been endured uncomplainingly. The co-operation of all arms has been admirable, and has enabled success in battle to be consummated by irresistible and victorious pursuit."

In his official account of the work of the 180th Brigade, Gen. Watson wrote :—

"The co-operation between the various units of the Brigade has been most marked, and has very materially contributed to the success of the operations.

"I cannot speak too highly of the determination and endurance of all ranks over extremely difficult country, and under very severe climatic conditions. For three nights in succession few men had any sleep.

"A great deal is due to the administrative personnel of the Brigade in bringing up rations and water."

The following were published on December 12th and 13th respectively :—

SPECIAL ORDER OF THE DAY

BY MAJOR-GEN. J. S. M. SHEA, C.B., C.M.G., D.S.O., COMMANDING 60TH DIVISION.

The G.O.C. wishes to express to all Leaders, N.C.Os., Men, Staffs, and Departments, his profound admiration and heartfelt thanks for their remarkable achievements.

The enemy was always engaged with eagerness and determination ; great difficulties were overcome ; and weather conditions which must have caused at times intense suffering were cheerfully endured.

History will tell of the spirit of the 60th Division, the Division to which Jerusalem was surrendered.

12/12/17.

SPECIAL ORDER OF THE DAY.

BY LIEUT.-GEN. SIR PHILIP W. CHETWODE, BT., K.C.M.G., C.B., D.S.O., COMMANDING 20TH CORPS.

HEADQUARTERS,
20TH CORPS,
December 13th, 1917.

Now that the efforts of Gen. Sir E. H. H. Allenby's Army have been crowned by the capture of Jerusalem, I wish to express to all ranks, Services, and Departments of the 20th Army Corps my personal thanks and my admiration for the soldierly qualities they have displayed.

I have served as a Regimental Officer in two campaigns, and no one knows better than I do what the shortness of food, the fatigue of operating among high mountains, and the cold and wet has meant to the fighting troops ; but in spite of it all, and at the moment when the weather was at its worst, they responded to my call and drove the enemy in one rush through his last defences and beyond Jerusalem.

A fine performance, and I am intensely proud of having had the honour of commanding such a body of men.

I wish to give special praise to the Divisional Ammunition Columns, Divisional Trains, A.S.C., Supply Services, Mechanical Transport personnel, Camel Transport personnel, and to the Royal Army Medical Corps, and all services whose continuous labour, day and night, almost without rest, alone enabled the fighting troops to do what they did.

The Corps Commander wishes the above communicated to all ranks.

E. EVANS, *Brigadier-General*,
D.A. and Q.M.G., 20th Corps.

HEADQUARTERS,
20TH CORPS.

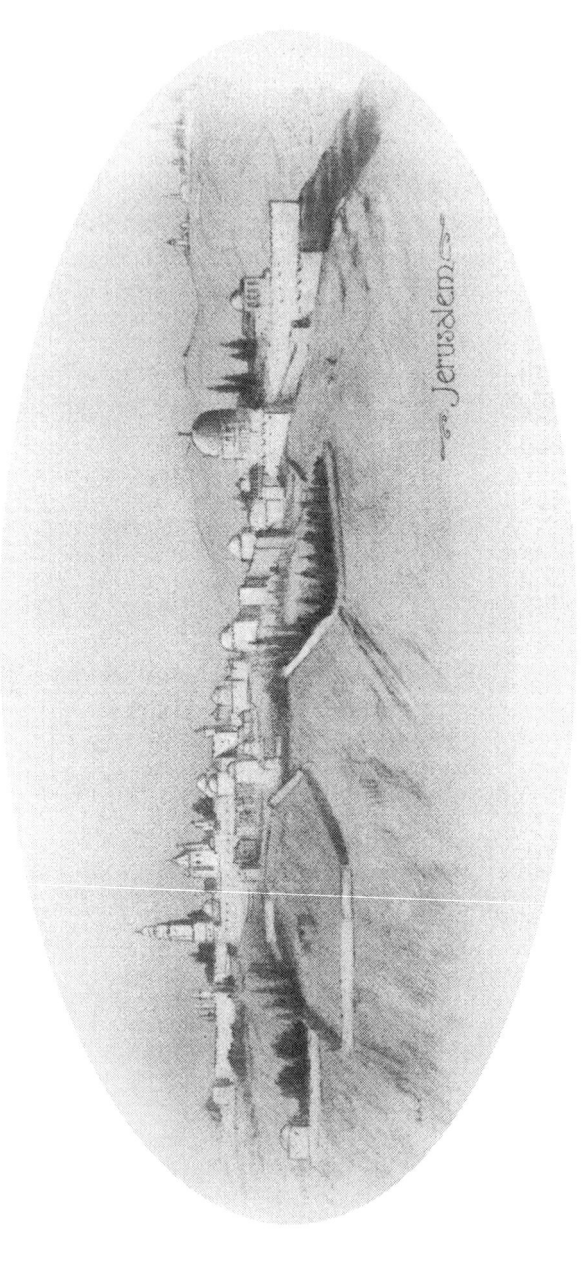

CHAPTER XI

JERUSALEM BEFORE AND AFTER ITS DELIVERANCE

THOUGH it was the military and political significance of the fall of Jerusalem that appealed to the world at large, is it surprising that to the men on the spot more material considerations had first place ? The prospect of billets once more, of a change of clothing, and of baths, was too alluring not to dwarf all else, and it was not until we had actually got into billets and seen the inhabitants and heard their story that the full meaning of it all was brought home to us.

The welcome which we had received from the crowd at Lifta as we had passed through on Sunday morning, December 9th, had been but a foretaste of that which was awaiting every officer and man in the city itself. Surely, never in history were people more glad nor more truly sincere in gratitude to their liberators! Above all else, they were grateful for the careful strategy which in effecting their deliverance had left the buildings of the city undamaged. They told us, when we had settled in billets, that already in the thirty-six hours which had elapsed since its surrender Jerusalem was a changed city. For the last fortnight of Turkish domination many of the women had slept on the doormat with their feet propped against the front door, so that at least they should not be carried off in their sleep. For days they had seemed to hear our guns coming nearer and nearer, and they had prayed that their deliverance might be drawing nigh. The Turkish officers had maintained deception till the previous day, when at last they had been forced to own that British troops were even then fighting round the outskirts of Lifta.

The inhabitants had previously been given definite orders as to their conduct during the street fighting which was sure to develop, in view of the determination of Jemal Pasha to hold on to the city at all costs. The assault on the previous afternoon had suddenly forced a change of plan, and the night of December 8th had witnessed the hurried flight of every Turkish officer and soldier who had legs to carry him. The last of the Turks is said to have left Jerusalem at 7 a.m. on December 9th by the east gate of the city, which is named after St. Stephen; but even later "armed stragglers were still trickling along the road just outside the north wall, requisitioning food and water at the point of the bayonet. This is no grievous crime on the part of defeated troops, uncertain of their next meal, but is recorded as the last kick of the dying Ottoman authority in a city where it had been supreme for four centuries."

A writer has depicted in graphic terms the last hours of Turkish suzerainty in Jerusalem :—

"On the morning of December 8th large numbers of the inhabitants of Jerusalem, with the remaining religious chiefs, were personally warned by the police to be ready to leave at once. The extent to which the Turks were prepared to clear the city is shown by the fact that out of the Armenian community of 1,400 souls, 300 received this notice. Jemal Pasha, when warned that vehicles were unavailable for the transport of the unhappy exiles to Shechem or Jericho, telegraphed curtly that they and theirs must walk. The fate of countless Armenians and many Greeks has shown that a population of all ages suddenly turned out to walk indefinite distances under Turkish escort is exposed to outrage and hardships which prove fatal to most of them; but the delay in telegraphing had saved the population, and the sun had risen for the last time on the Ottoman domination of Jerusalem, and the Turks' power to destroy faded with the day.

" Towards dusk the British troops were reported to have passed Lifta and to be within sight of the city. On this news being received, a sudden panic fell on the Turks west and south-west of the town, and at 5 p.m. civilians were surprised to see a Turkish transport column galloping furiously citywards along the Jaffa Road. In passing they alarmed all units within sight or hearing, and the wearied infantry arose and fled, bootless and without rifles, never pausing to think or to fight. Some were flogged back by their officers, and were compelled to pick up their arms ; others staggered on through the mud, augmenting the confusion of the retreat.

" After four centuries of conquest the Turk was ridding the land of his presence in the bitterness of defeat, and a great enthusiasm arose among the Jews. There was a running to and fro ; daughters called to their fathers and brothers, concealed in outhouses, cellars, and attics from the police, who sought them for arrest and deportation. ' The Turks are running,' they called ; ' the day of deliverance is come.' The nightmare was fast passing away, but the Turk still lingered. In the evening he fired his guns continuously, perhaps heartening himself with the loud noise that comforts the soul of a barbarian, perhaps to cover the sound of his own retreat. Whatever the intention was, the roar of the gunfire persuaded most citizens to remain indoors, and there were few to witness the last act of Osmanli authority.

" Towards midnight the Governor, Izzet Bey, went personally to the telegraph office, discharged the staff, and himself smashed the instruments with a hammer. At 2 a.m. on Sunday tired Turks began to troop through the Jaffa Gate from the west and south-west, and anxious watchers, peering out through the windows of the Grand New Hotel to learn the meaning of the tramping, were cheered by the sullen remark of an officer, ' *Gitmaya mejburuz* ' (' We've got to go ') ; and from 2 a.m. till 7 a.m. that morning the Turks streamed through and out of the city, which echoed for the last time their shuffling tramp. On this same day 2,082 years before, another race of conquerors, equally detested, were looking their last on the city which they could not hold, and inasmuch as the liberation of Jerusalem in 1917 will probably ameliorate the lot of the Jews more than that of any other community in Palestine, it was fitting that the flight of the Turks should have coincided with the national festival of the Hanukah, which commemorates the recapture of the Temple from the heathen Seleucida by Judas Maccabæus in 165 B.C.

"The Governor was the last civil official to depart. He left in a cart belonging to Mr. Vester, an American resident, from whom he had 'borrowed' an hitherto unrequisitioned cart and team. Before the dawn he hastened down the Jericho Road, leaving behind him a letter of surrender, which the Mayor, as the sun rose, set forth to deliver to the British Commander, accompanied by a few frightened policemen holding two tremulous white flags. He walked towards the Lifta Hill, and met the first representative of the British Army on a spot which may be marked in the future with a white stone as the site of an historic episode.

"As the Turkish flood finally ebbed away into the shadowy depths of the Valley of Jehoshaphat, the townsfolk roused themselves from the lethargy into which hunger and the Turkish police had plunged them, and fell upon a variety of buildings, official or requisitioned for official purposes, and looted them, even stripping roofs, doors, and floors from the Ottoman barracks next to the Tower of David for firewood. It must be admitted that, as the Government had furnished and maintained itself almost entirely by uncompensated requisitions, the crowd was only trying to indemnify itself. But this disorder ceased as suddenly as it had arisen on the appearance of the British infantry."

CHAPTER XII

SIGHT-SEEING—BACK IN THE LINE—"D" COMPANY HAS
AN ADVENTURE

THOSE who have not had a similar experience will not readily appreciate how much the billets of Jerusalem meant to us after our twelve months of wandering under the open sky, with hardly a sight of a house. Certainly a change of underclothing and hot water for washing and shaving will never be appreciated as much again by any one of us as they were at that time. We felt as men who had been away from the world. We wanted nothing but to be able to settle down like ordinary mortals, and wash and sleep and eat in decency. Corporal Snoad produced a white tablecloth, and it was astonishing how great a relish it gave to the meals in the Mess. Even the shops and crowded streets had a certain novelty.

The first thing to be done was to bath and disinfect the whole Battalion, and arrangements were made for officers and men to have liberal use of the R.E. baths—a privilege of which the fullest advantage was very soon taken. With many of us the clothing which we had worn during the advance was in every sense unfit for further use, and we were heartily glad to consign it to the flames or bury it. To start again with a complete rig-out of underclothing and khaki was one of the most pleasurable feelings imaginable. The men had not the responsibility of disposing of their discarded garments, as these were collected and returned to Ordnance.

Not the least advantage of being comfortably housed once more, though we knew that we should have to make way for somebody else in a day or two and return out on to the hills, was that we could afford to defy the weather. We laughed at rain, though there had been times quite recently when we could easily have cried at it, and stayed indoors when a bitter east wind was raging. It all seems commonplace enough now, but at the time security from the weather was one of the greatest joys of having a real home of bricks and mortar once more.

In Jerusalem we were able for the first time to gather up and focus all the host of impressions which had been accumulating during the stirring six weeks (it seemed more like six years) since we left Es Shauth. The eternal sand and heat of the desert seemed now like a dream, and the quiet sweltering days in the Wadi Ghuzzee an impossible fantasy. So much had happened, and so greatly had conditions altered. The climb from the Plain of Philistia into the Judean Hills in the last week of November had changed everything. Water, from being almost unobtainable, had suddenly become a nuisance by its abundance in the form of rain. Better and more numerous roads, and the extension of the railway from Gaza, had considerably eased the supply difficulty. The campaign, in fact, from a desert campaign in torrid heat had without any halt become a matter of hill-fighting and skirmishing on heights nearly 3,000 feet above sea-level.

Our billets in Jerusalem consisted of a large empty building in the Russian quarter of the city, the officers being accommodated in houses round. The school—for such it had been—was large enough to hold all four companies and Headquarters, the Orderly Room, and the Quartermaster's Stores. The rooms were all large and had tiled floors, and many of the walls and ceilings were adorned with designs and paintings. There was a small garden, which contained several wells. In one of these there was the dead body of a man, which all our efforts failed to bring to the surface. Only a few of the horses could be accommodated under cover, most of the stabling of the city being infected by either mange or foot-and-mouth disease.

Our stay in billets enabled Battalion records to be brought up to date, and the concentration of all companies in one building brought to light many incidents in the recent fighting which had so far not been told outside the company concerned. One which cannot go unrecorded had occurred on the morning of the 9th in the advance from Lifta to the Nablus Road. A mounted Turkish officer was seen galloping away from Jerusalem northwards, and Capt. Reynolds gave orders to his men to fire. Both horse and horseman came to the ground, and on the men reaching the spot it was found that a large number of Turkish coins, which the rider had been carrying in a bag, lay scattered over the road. Almost every value was represented, and it is most probable that the unfortunate Turk had been sent back at the last moment by his Commanding Officer to make a final " draw " from the Field Cashier, and was probably congratulating himself on his narrow escape at the very moment when he was shot down. With a liberality which was exceedingly gratifying to the recipients, " D " Company presented a set of the coins to several officers in the Battalion. One of these the writer holds, and will always treasure. The remainder of the money was shared among the men.

On the evening of the arrival of the Brigade in billets, all four Battalion Commanders dined with Gen. Watson, to meet Gen. Shea. This was the first occasion on which the King's health was drunk by a British Officers' Mess in Jerusalem. Brandy was the only liquor available to drink it in. The guests later drank Gen. Shea's health, and he theirs as representing " the Brigade which captured Jerusalem."

The Commander-in-Chief made his formal entry into the ancient portion of the city, through the Jaffa Gate, on the following morning. A composite company of the

Battalion—two officers (Capt. Reynolds and Capt. Lane) and fifty other ranks per company—helped to line the route.

The Arab prophecy, that when the waters of the Nile had flowed into Palestine the prophet (El Nebi) from the west would drive the Turks from Jerusalem, had been literally fulfilled, and the inhabitants, who had been forbidden by the Turks to assemble in groups of more than three on pain of blows, fines, imprisonment, and even exile, came in thousands to the Jaffa Gate to hear the British proclamation of liberty, and to see the conqueror himself, without noise or excitement—not even the music of a band—walk on foot into the city, leave it again on foot, mount his horse, and go away to continue his campaign. Those of them who were old enough to be able to make the comparison were doubtless thinking of a certain day in 1898, when a crowned head of Europe—no less a person than the Emperor Wilhelm of Hohenzollern—having ordered a special gap to be made in the ancient wall, rode into the city clad in a white robe and mounted on a white charger. Yet for him who had brought freedom to the citizens by a crushing victory on the battlefield over those who had oppressed them for centuries an entry on foot through the normal entrance of the Jaffa Gate sufficed.

Hitherto only the modern quarters of the city had been accessible to British troops, but after Gen. Allenby's entry the oldest and holiest parts were thrown open. It may be not without interest to refer here to some of the more important of these.

The Church of the Holy Sepulchre, the Via Dolorosa, the Mount of Olives, and the Garden of Gethsemane immediately became objects of interest and veneration to thousands of British and Colonial soldiers, by many of whom it was felt to have been the greatest privilege of a lifetime that they had played a conspicuous part in restoring the Holy City to Christian civilization. Though many of the places in the city which claim to be the site of Biblical incident were felt to be obviously spurious, and many others to be only doubtfully genuine, yet here unquestionably was the actual ground trodden by the Saviour and His Apostles 1900 years before—here the Mount of the Ascension, and here the general habits and native customs known to have changed but little in twenty centuries of time.

The Mohammedan faith, so largely represented in the Arab population of the city, centres round the Mosque of Omar (the Dome of the Rock) and the Mosque of El Aksa, both of which are built on the great platform marked out by Herod the Great on the site of Solomon's Temple. The Dome of the Rock, a magnificent mosaic edifice, enshrines the sacred stone which receives from the Moslem world veneration second only to that given to Mecca. The Jewish population still, as in New Testament days, has its synagogues in Jerusalem, and many devout Jews repair to the Jews' Wailing Place (the tombs of the prophets) on Friday of each week to bewail their national exile. The spot was one of great interest to khaki visitors after the capture of the city.

Jerusalem is encircled by the picturesque city wall erected by Suleiman the Magnificent in the sixteenth century, and standing in many places on the same line as the wall of 2,000 years ago. Its eastern limits are skirted by the precipitous and rocky valley of the Kidron, across which lies the Mount of Olives, with the Garden of Gethsemane nestling on the surface of its western slope. Tucked away unseen over the brow of the southern edge of the Mount lies the little village of El Azirieh (Bethany in the New Testament), and from the summit of the Mount of Olives, looking eastwards, the panorama spreads across to the distant mauve of the Mountains of Moab bounding the horizon. In between lie the peaks of the wilderness of Judea, hiding the city of Jericho, the plain of the Jordan, and the Dead Sea.

An interesting account of an afternoon spent in first visits to the ancient parts of the Holy City was sent home by one of the officers of the Battalion :—

" After getting a permit from the Military Governor, we rode to the Jaffa Gate. Here we found an Armenian priest who spoke French, and volunteered to show us round. We first visited the Church of the Holy Sepulchre. Not having had time to read up anything, and not being very good at French, I did not absorb very much knowledge, but I was really only out for first impressions. The church is much bigger, finer, and more artistic than I expected. Apparently the old church was burned down in 1810, and this new one built, every inch of which is the jealously-guarded possession of either the Greek or the Latin or the Armenian Church. There are always *three* altars, or *three* candlesticks, or *three* pictures. We were pointed out Golgotha, and actually went into the supposed Sepulchre. Outside we were shown the places where the two angels knelt, one being nowadays a Coptic shrine. We were also shown the place where the Cross is supposed to have been found. A small bit of the original church remains, and is very curious. It belongs to the Armenian Church, but the Armenians cannot even put a nail into the wall without permission of all the Churches. The church is guarded by British soldiers. Next, along the Via Dolorosa, where we saw the place where St. Veronica gave Christ the handkerchief, and the place where Pilate handed over Christ to the Jews, each marked by a Latin inscription. We also passed the huge church built by the German Emperor recently. We went through the Golden Gate, and got the most perfect view in the afternoon sun of the Mount of Olives and the Garden of Gethsemane on its slope. Then back to the Temple, which covers a much bigger area than I expected. The courts, which are all flagged, but are on different levels, are very spacious. There are some fine arches. We only saw two things—one, the Dome of the

Rock, a most lovely and magnificent Oriental dome, built by Omar, with wonderful Oriental work outside and mosaic work and stained-glass inside. In the centre, to our surprise, was a bare surface of rock—the very place, apparently, where the Jews used to sacrifice; it was the highest point of Mount Moriah. Underneath is a cave, and here you see a ledge on which Elijah is said to have prayed. We also saw the Mosque of El Aksa, originally and obviously a Christian church, built by Justinian. These mosques are guarded by Indian Mohammedan soldiers. We met the Brigadier with an American resident, who said he regarded to-day as the day when the down-treading heel with which Jerusalem had been cursed was to be removed. We then hurried back to tea. Jerusalem, in its streets and shops, is more Oriental than Cairo. The streets are generally on slopes, and are very much covered in. The natives are very mixed; they are mostly very dirty, and the men wear a long curl over each ear. I am just (9.30 p.m.) beginning to be able to focus my impressions, but this afternoon I was bewildered. The sudden change from cold and wet and danger to interest and beauty and comfort was enough in itself to upset one's balance. And then to think one is in Jerusalem—a sensation quite like the first day in Rome or Athens. Then the excitement of victory, and the pride of being marked out as the particular victors, and to think one had helped to do what thousands have longed to do for countless years! It all appeals to me in so many ways—as a Christian, as a historian, as a soldier."

The men had little time to see the wonders of Jerusalem during their first period in billets. "Cleaning up" was a long process, not a matter of half a day as in the old comfortable times at Mont St. Eloi, and only the latter part of the afternoons was free for sight-seeing. Nevertheless, most of them managed a tour, however short. One of the most popular resorts was the American Store, kept by Mr. Vester, an American, who had carried on his business throughout the Turkish occupation. Mr. Vester had converted his house into a hospital, and here we found several wounded Turkish officers and men, including the Commanding Officer of the battalion which had made the stand at Lifta, besides some British prisoners, all of whom had been too ill to be moved by the enemy when he left. The store sold English books, Eastern embroidery, native olive-wood work, photographs, postage stamps, and a multitude of other articles which appealed to the men at once as valuable souvenirs. The other shops had little except native wine, fruit, and some very doughy bread to sell, though the writer bought a packet of blackcurrant lozenges, made by a well-known London firm, from a chemist who had had them since 1913. They were none the worse for keeping, though the price was exorbitant. Fast's Hotel had been emptied by German officers before they left, and beyond a certain quantity of wine had no stock. The children of the city were miserably underclad, and lost no opportunity of soliciting "backsheesh" from British officers and men in the streets.

Gen. Shea addressed the Battalion on parade on the 14th, congratulating all ranks on the work they had accomplished. On the following day, leaving Rear Headquarters and the transport in Jerusalem, we took over the Tel el Ful sector again from the Civil Service Rifles.

The line north of the city was only three miles from Jerusalem, and it was clear that a move forward would have to be made before we could settle down to permanent consolidation. On the first night after taking over the Battalion was ordered to advance the line on the right to a hill, Ras et Tawil, and on the left about 300 yards to some quarries, with the object of gaining a better command of the country ahead, and the advance was to be accompanied by as thorough a reconnaissance as possible of the ground as far north as Er Ram.

The advance by "C" Company on the left to the quarries was unopposed. "D" Company, on the right, had quite an adventure. The men moved forward in extended order by bright moonlight, making as little noise as possible. Leaving two platoons at the foot of the hill, Capt. Reynolds took half the company forward, and spotted three Turkish sentries near the summit of the crest. Having waited for the moon to set, the party advanced up the hill, and when within twenty yards of them rushed the sentries, one of whom was shot from close range. The remainder of the garrison, two officers and twenty-three other ranks, who were found in a cave adjoining, were taken completely by surprise, and surrendered without resistance. The officers were " armed " with whips, and kept themselves separate from the men, though the Turk who had been wounded, and who was now obviously dying, made repeated requests in his own language, which our men could not interpret. His own officers refused to speak to him. Our casualties were one other rank killed and one other rank wounded.

The 2/17th relieved us on December 19th, and we had five days in support in a tomb behind Shafat, moving into Jerusalem on Christmas Eve. On arrival in billets we found the following order awaiting us from the Brigade :—

" 1. Reliable information has been received from G.H.Q. that the enemy intend to attack either to-night or to-morrow, one attack on the Jericho Road, one on the left of the Corps front, with a main attack down the Nablus Road.

" 2. Units still in the line will maintain the greatest vigilance.

" 3. Units on arrival in billets will remain in a state of readiness, prepared to march off at half an hour's notice."

CHAPTER XIII

CHRISTMAS DAY IN JERUSALEM—A TURKISH COUNTER-ATTACK DEFEATED—THE ADVANCE CONTINUED NORTHWARDS—THE BATTLE OF SHAB SALAH—TRANSFER TO THE ANATA FRONT—HEBRON

THE mere fact of being able to spend Christmas in Jerusalem was in itself a privilege for which we had good reason to be grateful, but, as at Gerbazel the previous year, Christmas Day was somewhat dismal. The weather was bitterly cold, rain fell for some hours, and the possibility of an "alarm" kept everybody close to billets. It is unnatural to take any great pleasure in making a bed comfortable when the chances are that it will never be slept in, and in arranging and preparing an elaborate meal—even though it be a Christmas dinner —which may never be eaten. In the circumstances we were content to eat cold bully beef and risk spending the night on bare boards rather than chance the waste of food and energy. The officers, with water-bottles filled and equipment handy, had their evening meal together, and the occasion suited admirably for a mild celebration in honour of Capt. Lane, the announcement of the award of his Military Cross having arrived earlier in the day. Sergt. Pallister was sent for, and the two heroes of the Battle of Lifta were hurried off to Sergt. Barnard's billet to have their new ribbons sewn on. Later they both returned to the Mess, and were "toasted" and cheered. The Brigadier came in for a few minutes, and had with him Capt. G. R. V. Hume-Gore, M.C., the Brigade Major, who from G.S.O.3 Division had recently succeeded Capt. Willcox. The latter had replaced Capt. Crockatt when he had been severely wounded at Sheria. (On that occasion Gen. Watson himself had narrowly escaped, and Major Gray, commanding the 2/19th, had been killed.)

Probably the severe weather which had set in on Christmas Eve was responsible for the absence of any counter-attack by the enemy, a development which most of us expected hourly on Christmas Day. But nothing materialized, and we who had the good fortune to be in billets slept in our clothes, so as to be ready for instant concentration if the blow came before dawn. We were, however, not disturbed. On the 26th we were beginning to congratulate ourselves as late afternoon arrived and no alarm had sounded, when the Brigadier himself came to Headquarters and told the Commanding Officer that the Battalion must be ready to move within an hour.

Our short Christmas holiday was over. The Battalion was to proceed as soon as possible to a position in the Wadi Beit Hannina, north of the city, to be in reserve to the 181st Brigade, which was holding the line north of Shafat and immediately west of the Nablus Road. Rear Headquarters and the transport lines were to remain in Jerusalem.

Companies, with pack-mules loaded, were on the road outside the Battalion billet within half an hour, and the column was on the move immediately afterwards. Leaving the road on our right, and taking the new track which sappers had constructed east of Lifta, we crossed the very ground which we had covered on December 9th when advancing from Lifta to Shafat. The new bivouac site was in the depths of the Wadi Beit Hannina, but some good paths had been made, and the position was fairly easy of approach from Jerusalem, while the route to the line—a matter which concerned us more closely—was neither too difficult to use nor too intricate to find.

The 179th and 181st Brigades in the line were still only something rather more than three miles from the outskirts of the city—an uncomfortably short distance, considering the strength of the enemy and his intimate knowledge of the country. It had been no surprise to us in Jerusalem before Christmas to note the preparations which were being made to advance the line, " in order," as the Commander-in-Chief explains, " to provide more effectively for the security of Jerusalem and Jaffa." But the severe weather conditions at that time had greatly hampered work on the roads, and had delayed the other preparations necessary for the new advance. As a preliminary operation, the 2/18th Battalion had attempted to carry the line forward in front of Shafat to a piece of commanding ground called Khurbet Adaseh ; but owing to the delay in launching the general offensive, the attempt had been abandoned, though not before the London Irish had sustained very heavy casualties. The new advance was subsequently ordered to commence along the whole front at dawn on December 27th, and when the 2/20th arrived in the Wadi Beit Hannina on the evening of the 26th everything was in readiness.

Before midnight all plans, so far as the 60th Division was concerned, had to be revised. At 11.30 p.m. the enemy drove in the outposts of the 179th Brigade on Ras et Tawil, the hill which " D " Company had captured on December 16th. This was the prelude of a strong enemy assault, delivered on a wide front and developed with particular strength against the two Brigades of the 60th Division astride the Nablus Road. *Storm-Truppen* had been brought up in motor-lorries to carry out this last great effort of the Turks to regain Jerusalem, and very gallantly did they acquit themselves. Time after time they threw their weight against Tel el Ful and the village of Beit Hannina. Eight main assaults were launched in six and a half hours on the morning of the 27th, and the ground was left strewn with dead. At one or two points in the line the enemy gained ground, but only temporarily. He was speedily counter-attacked and driven back by the troops on the spot, and the 2/20th Battalion was not called upon to reinforce.

Though this desperate blow by the enemy on the front of the 60th Division had forestalled the launching of our own offensive in that part of the line, the advance by the 10th and 74th Divisions on the left of the Corps had proceeded at dawn " according to plan." As a result of this advance the enemy was reported by the Royal Flying Corps at 2 p.m. to be moving his reserve division from Bireh westwards to meet the threat levelled at his right flank, thus proving that he had been forced to abandon the initiative on the Nablus Road. His attempt to regain Jerusalem had failed, and the attack petered out before dark.

" Seeing that the Turkish attack was spent," writes the Commander-in-Chief, " I ordered the 20th Corps to make a general advance northwards on December 28th." In this renewed advance the 60th Division was to play the principal part, and the task of leading was entrusted to the 180th Brigade.

After having spent forty-eight hours in the Wadi Beit Hannina, the Battalion concentrated in a wadi north of Shafat on the afternoon of December 28th, in readiness to attack the village of Er Ram at dusk. The 2/19th was to be on our left (west of the road), and the 53rd Division was to move up and protect our right.

As soon as it was sufficiently dark companies moved on to the road and advanced northwards. Having in mind the heavy fighting of the previous day, we had hardly expected to be able to move rapidly, but even the enemy's machine guns were silent, and we made good headway. The road was white under the full moon, and, as a precaution, soon after leaving Tel el Ful we moved on to the safer and less visible ground which lay beside it. " D " Company branched off in the direction of the hill Khurbet Erha, and " A " and " C " Companies assumed attack formations. " B " Company remained in rear in reserve, and Battalion Headquarters was temporarily established near a culvert just south of Er Ram. There had been some suspicion of the road having been mined at this point, but a sapper officer who was attached to Headquarters tested it and reported it safe. A party of Brigade signallers accompanied the Battalion, and ran out a reel of cable along the line of the road. The village of Er Ram, outlined against the horizon, could be clearly seen on some high ground a short distance ahead. " D " Company (Capt. Reynolds) was to approach the village from the southeast, and " A " Company (Capt. Hearn) from the south and south-west.

At 6 p.m. the two companies advanced to the attack in face of intermittent machine-gun fire from the enemy. Our artillery put down a bombardment from 6.20 to 6.30 p.m., and a few minutes later " A " and " D " Companies, closely followed by " C " (Capt. Hasslacher), entered the village to find that the Turks had hastily bolted, leaving their fires burning. The dead bodies of several of the enemy were found, one officer and four other ranks were taken prisoners, and a new pattern machine gun was captured. The Battalion took up an outpost position for the night north of the village.

The Brigadier came forward to Battalion Headquarters early next morning, and at 8 o'clock the advance was resumed. The country was undoubtedly the most difficult we had encountered. It consisted of a succession of steep rocky hills, separated by sheer precipitate wadis. The mere tasks of climbing the former and crossing the latter were in themselves hard physical labour for men in " marching order," quite apart from any fighting that had to be done. Fortunately, in the early stages of the advance no determined resistance was met, and successive ridges were occupied, and a few odd prisoners captured. The village of Kefr Akab was in our hands at 10.30 a.m. So far little had been seen of any large formed bodies of the enemy, but considerable movement could now be observed on the next ridge, Shab Salah, which rose high above neighbouring peaks from the depths of a narrow wadi some 1,000 yards ahead of us.

One of the many points about the Turk for which we had come to have a healthy respect was his choice of ground. It was seldom at fault. On this occasion he had fallen back from Er Ram on to a position which at first sight seemed almost impregnable. From Shab Salah he could watch our every movement. The hill was gigantic in height, and in order to approach it the attacking troops had to descend into the wadi and—what was more difficult—climb out the other side. Having got so far, they would have to pick their way among the rock-boulders in making their steep ascent, and the enemy probably reasoned that the few who were likely to have survived his artillery barrage would be so exhausted as to be unable to launch any serious attack when they reached the top. The reasoning was sound enough, but it made no allowance for the quality of the attacking troops—a factor which, as it happened, was destined to determine the result of the fight.

After carefully considering the situation, Col. Warde-Aldam decided that an organized assault, covered by artillery, was necessary if the position was to be taken without very heavy casualties. " A " Company was sent forward to occupy a small hill on the left of Shab Salah, in order to direct fire on to the Turks on the ridge. " As the Battalion was ahead of the 2/19th London Regiment on the left," writes the Commanding Officer afterwards, in his account of the action, " and there were no signs of the 53rd Division on the right, and our own guns had not come up, I did not consider I could advance farther at the moment. Eventually I was joined by Lieut.-Col. D. C. Sword, and, in conjunction with Col. Thatcher, commanding the artillery group, and a representative of the 5th Royal Welsh Fusiliers, arrangements were made for an organized attack to take place at 14.30 hours."

Punctually at this time, "B" Company (Capt. Lane) on the right and "C" Company (Capt. Hasslacher) on the left commenced to advance. "A" Company, from their position, already described, provided covering fire for the advance of the 2/19th, and protected the left flank of that battalion. "D" Company was in support close to Battalion Headquarters. The attack was covered by a heavy artillery bombardment and by the fire of twelve machine guns.

The two assaulting companies were soon exposed to the full fury of the enemy's artillery. Under a heavy barrage the men climbed down several hundred feet into the depths of the wadi, and while still exposed to the fire of the guns made their way up the steep and difficult terraced slope on the opposite side to the crest of Shab Salah, more than a thousand feet above. The climb was something of an achievement, but the men made light work of it all. Though the Lewis gunners were carrying guns and filled magazines " on the man," they joined in the race, and a member of one of the " B " Company teams was first through the enemy barrage to the top of the hill. Reorganizing just under the brow, the two companies, led by their two gallant Commanders, went over the crest with a rush on to the flat summit, and charged the Turks who were sheltering behind stone sangars. The enemy at first opened heavy fire with machine guns and rifles from a position in rear, and his line withdrew. Later it advanced again. Finally the Turks were driven off the ridge at the point of the bayonet. Our men commenced to dig in behind sangars composed of big rock-boulders, and the enemy heavily barraged the position for a while. The Commanding Officer sent " D " Company up to be ready for a counter-attack, and to assist in the consolidation, but the Turks had lost too heavily to be at all anxious to attempt an assault. Before dark our line was firmly established on the northern slope of the hill, and from here the Turks could be seen in full retreat.

The 2/18th Battalion passed through before dawn, and carried the line forward to Beitin, where it was consolidated. Meanwhile on our left the important villages of Bireh and Ram Allah, which, like Shab Salah, had held out to the last, had been captured by the 181st Brigade and the 74th Division respectively.

During the afternoon twenty prisoners were taken and at least thirty Turks killed, but the Battalion paid a heavy price and sustained a great loss, for the list of the killed included Capt. Lane, Capt. Hasslacher, and Lce.-Sergt. A. Crossley (of " C " Company). The wounded included Sergt. H. G. Legg, of " C " Company.

The battalion had undoubtedly achieved a notable success in face of great difficulties. An examination of the ground afterwards, coupled with the accounts of the action given by officers and N.C.Os. who took part, proved that the attack had been a severe test. The charge on the top of the ridge had been carried out with singular gallantry. 2nd-Lieut. C. R. Salter, the only officer left in " B " Company after Capt. Lane had been killed, subsequently received the Military Cross for his gallantry and initiative in the advance and during the consolidation under the enemy barrage. The following behaved with great gallantry during the attack. The first five were Lewis gunners :—

> Lce.-Cpl. J. W. Lamb
> Pte. J. W. Johnstone
> Pte. A. Jarvis
> Pte. J. McRobie
> Pte. T. Marrison
> Pte. T. J. Goulden
> Pte. C. J. Scouller

Early in the afternoon Lieut. Carey, the Brigade Intelligence Officer, who was standing within a yard or two of both Col. Warde-Aldam and Col. Sword at the time, was killed by a shell.

On the afternoon of December 30th, in the presence of a large gathering of all ranks, the bodies of Capt. Lane, Capt. Hasslacher, Lce.-Sergt. Crossley, Pte. R. H. Hart, Pte. J. H. Tolhurst, and Pte. F. Bates, were laid to rest on Shab Salah in one grave, looking across to the Holy City over the ground of our advance. A large cross, clearly marked, covers the site of the grave. The burial service was conducted by Chaplain the Rev. H. C. McKinley.

In two days the line north of Jerusalem had been advanced six miles, and the city was now virtually secure from recapture from that direction. North of Ram Allah the road to Nablus peters out into a mountain-track, and the country through which it runs is of the roughest. Moreover, it was apparent that months of work on roads and communications behind the line would be necessary before any considerable further advance could be made northwards, and the troops on this part of the front were able to settle down to the first real rest they had had since the last days of October.

On the right of the line, where the battalion was destined to spend most of the next four months, the position was still undergoing changes. From Beitin the line turned sharply south, almost at right angles, and from this point to the right flank it faced east, passing close to the villages of Mukhmas, Jeba, Hizmeh, and Anata, and stretching north and south across the Jericho Road, which it crossed not far east of El Azirieh (Bethany). So long as we held the Mount of Olives there was little to be feared from the enemy east of Jerusalem, though the line at Anata was within three miles of the Jaffa Gate. But there were other reasons which made an advance at this point desirable—almost essential.

In its flight from Jerusalem the Turkish Army had split into two, the main body taking the road north to Nablus and the remainder making east down the

Jericho Road. The force which had used the Jericho Road was now, at the end of the year, holding a strong line of peaks in the Wilderness of Judea, and was thus barring our way to the city of Jericho and the plain of the Jordan, and denying to Gen. Allenby the security and excellent natural protection of that river and of the Dead Sea for his right flank. In addition, so long as the enemy could confine us to the country west of the Jordan, he could prevent our linking up with the Arab forces under the King of the Hedjaz, who were fighting for the Allies east of the river and along the eastern shores of the Dead Sea. The Turks had every reason, therefore, to oppose any advance which was attempted from that part of our line which lay immediately east and north-east of the Holy City.

Handing over the positions astride the Nablus Road to the 53rd Division on January 3rd, the 60th Division took over the defences in the Wilderness east of Jerusalem facing Jericho and stretching from Mukhmas to a point south of the Jericho Road.

The battle of Shab Salah had been followed by two days of pouring rain, during which the Battalion, in its open position on the hills, had got thoroughly drenched. On the last day of the year the Commanding Officer and the Adjutant had proceeded to Anata to reconnoitre the line there, and three days later, with a halt for dinner near Tel el Ful, the Battalion had marched from Shab Salah via Bireh to the Anata sector. By the night of the 3rd the relief by the whole Division was complete.

Owing to the length of the Battalion frontage and to the extreme difficulty of communications, the Commanding Officer decided to decentralize his command, and placed half the Battalion under Capt. Watson with headquarters at Hizmeh, and half under Capt. Reynolds with headquarters at Anata. " A " Company (Lieut. A. W. Pilbeam) and " B " Company (Lieut. Weatherley) went to the left of the line, and " C " Company (Lieut.

Willson) and " D " Company (Lieut. H. L. Goldby) were under Capt. Reynolds on the right. Col. Warde-Aldam also had his Headquarters in Anata. The enemy was known to be some distance away, secreted among the jumbled hills, and our dispositions were largely outpost dispositions. " A " Company held a strong point on high ground (Khurbet Almit), and the other companies occupied the crests of hills in front of the villages. " C " Company for the first few days was kept in reserve at Anata. Lateral communications were very difficult, there being no completed road or track in the sector, though a broad track from Hizmeh to Anata had been started by the 1/1st Herefords (from whom we had taken over), and work on this was continued by a company of the 2/17th from Brigade reserve. Though active operations were not in immediate prospect, every opportunity was taken to reconnoitre the maze of hills and wadis which lay in front of our line, and which, in the event of a further advance, would have to be made good.

The battalion was relieved by the 2/22nd Battalion on January 16th, and marched to the Mount of Olives (a very short distance) to billets in Sir John Gray Hill's house, an empty private residence, " B " Company being accommodated in tents in the grounds.

The Mount of Olives runs almost due north and south, and, as has already been explained, forms a sort of natural border for the Holy City on its eastern side. Standing on the road which covers the entire length of the summit of the Mount from the " Hair Pin Bend " to Bethany, the traveller can look west over the valley of the Kidron immediately below, through the pile of white buildings of " the city that is set upon an hill," away to the country round Lifta, Deir Yesin, Ain Karim, and, by one glance north-west, to Nebi Samwil. The view is absorbing by its very historical interest, but it bears no comparison in beauty to that which lies behind him. Turning round and looking east, he stands amazed at the panorama unfolded at his feet and stretching as far as the eye can see. The colouring is drab, but the vastness of the wilderness, the sharp, clear-cut contours of line after line of hills, intersected at many angles by the deep, long clefts and chasms of the wadis, hold him entranced. Away through the wilderness can be seen the faint line of the plain of the Jordan and the Dead Sea, and, behind all, the great long mountain-range of Moab on the horizon. The buildings on the Mount of Olives are few. No less than three are large, ugly national hospices (respectively Greek, Russian, and German), where pilgrims to the Holy City may find shelter. The huge towers of the German and Russian hospices in particular are veritable eyesores. The former (the Kaiserin Augusta Victoria Hospice, to give it its full title), where Gen. Chetwode had made his Headquarters, was erected by the Emperor Wilhelm after his visit to Palestine in 1898. It contains the famous chapel in which the Kaiser appears in sculpture as a crusader, and in painting (on the ceiling) as a saint occupying the Throne of Heaven, with the Kaiserin at his side, and surrounded by saints and angels. It is, perhaps, some consolation to know that, in spite of several ugly modern buildings, the Mount of Olives and the Garden of Gethsemane stand substantially the same as in the days of old—spots of sacred memory and historic interest for all time.

Sir John Gray Hill's house is the most northerly building on the Mount, and is charmingly situated a few hundred yards from the German Hospice.

On the 22nd orders were received to prepare to move to Hebron for special duty, and on the following day the Battalion left Jerusalem. Companies marched down the metalled Hebron Road, passed close to Bethlehem, and bivouacked for the night at El Burak. The following night was spent at Wadi El Arab (Solomon's Pools), and at midday on the 25th the Battalion arrived in billets at Hebron. Some armoured cars and a squadron of Westminster Dragoons arrived later, and these units, with the 2/20th Battalion, formed the Hebron Detached Force, under Major Craddock (who had returned from the Senior Officers' Course at Heliopolis on the 23rd).

The "special duty" of the force was the collection of a large number of rifles which were known to be in possession of the inhabitants, many of whom were thought to be sheltering deserters from the Turkish Army. Special disciplinary orders were issued to the civilians, strong piquets were posted, and a proclamation was read ordering the people to bring their firearms to the office of the Military Governor, Lieut.-Col. A. E. Parker. " B " Company (under Lieut. Weatherley) was sent to Dura and to Beni Naim, outlying villages, to search for rifles, and " A " Company to Dhareriy. In all 2,400 rifles were collected, of which 470 were modern. The work was completed on Saturday, February 2nd. On Sunday the Battalion returned to Sir John Gray Hill's house, and a thoroughly enjoyable " rest " period on the Mount of Olives followed.

Col. Warde-Aldam, who had been temporarily in command of the Brigade while Gen. Watson was on leave in Cairo, rejoined the Battalion in the first week in February, and on the return of the Battalion from Hebron Major Craddock left to take temporary command of the 2/19th. Capt. Watson acted as Second-in-Command of the 2/20th in his absence. 2nd-Lieut. J. S. Pritchard, Lieut. K. J. Malcolm (who had served with the Battalion on the Vimy Ridge in July and August, 1916), and Lieut. H. W. Wilson joined about this time as reinforcements from home, and Sergt. H. K. Holmes was promoted to commissioned rank in the Battalion.

On the 11th the 2/20th relieved the 2/22nd in tents in the Anata sector, with the same dispositions as those previously taken up. In view of the forthcoming advance on Jericho, an observation post was established on Khurbet Maseirah in front of Hizmeh, and placed in charge of Corporal W. H. Oliver. Panorama sketches of the country were prepared from here by the Intelligence Section, and the movements of the Turks (from whose fires smoke could be seen at dawn and dusk rising from behind the hills) were constantly watched for throughout the day. The Corps Commander, the Divisional Commander, and the Brigadier visited Khurbet Maseirah at different times to obtain a view of the country ahead. The difficulty of the advance was likely to be one of supply and water rather than tactics. On one occasion the Commanding Officer, accompanied by 2nd-Lieut. Stone, made a personal reconnaissance of the Wadi Farah in front of our line, to examine the springs and to bring back samples of the water. The reconnaissance was covered by a party under the Adjutant, posted on some neighbouring high ground. The Turks opened fire on the covering party, but meanwhile Col. Warde-Aldam obtained his sample. The Medical Officer, after testing it, declared the water to be unfit for drinking or cooking.

Leave to Cairo and Alexandria had reopened early in January, and small parties of officers and men continued to be sent twice a week for the next few months. Meanwhile the days in the line were spent in reconnaissances and preparations for the coming attack.

CHAPTER XIV

THE BATTLE OF ARAK IBRAHIM—THE FALL OF JERICHO

THE Palestine Campaign, to be clearly studied, may be conveniently regarded as a story which has three chapters. The first may be said to commence with the operations at Beersheba and to end with the defeat of the Turkish counter-attack on Jerusalem and the battle of Shab Salah; the second to open with the advance on Jericho and to close with the second raid across the Jordan; while the third would tell of the break-through on the coast in the autumn of 1918, and of the events which followed and brought the campaign to a glorious conclusion. It is with the second chapter that we are now concerned.

The main energies of the Egyptian Expeditionary Force, which had been so victoriously at work in the firing-line during two months of strenuous campaigning, had been directed into new channels at the end of the year, and the month of January had witnessed diminished offensive movement, but greatly increased activity behind the line in the construction of roads, the repair and extension of the railway, and the improvement of every means of communication and supply. In the line the month passed quietly and without any of those dramatic events which had made November and December historic. February opened the new chapter with an attack on the enemy's positions across the Jericho Road.

The road runs almost due east and west. Its western limit leaves the Mount of Olives at Bethany, and in a winding course of fifteen miles it descends all the time until finally opening on to the Jordan Plain, more than

1,200 feet below the level of the Mediterranean. There is no more wild and inaccessible tract of country in Palestine than the wilderness of hills and wadis through the heart of which it passes on its way. Many times during the next three months, in full pack and under a scorching sun, the Battalion marched either " down to Jericho " or " up to Jerusalem." Our whole time for many weeks was to be spent either on the Jericho Road or near it. The Cistern Bend, the Good Samaritan Inn (the reputed scene of the New Testament parable), Talat ed Dumm (" The Mound of Blood "), Jebel Ekteif, and the Wadi Kelt became familiar landmarks, as welcome as milestones to tired marchers. But that was later. At the time of which we write—the beginning of February—the inn, with all the country which lies east of it, was in enemy hands.

The main line of Turkish defences crossed the Jericho Road at Talat ed Dumm, which is some eight miles east of Jerusalem as the crow flies, and extended across the hill-tops north and south of the road. The main wadis run from west to east, and, like the road, slope in sinuous courses down towards the Jordan Plain. Their banks are in many cases 150 feet high, and are in all cases rocky and precipitous. Many have layer upon layer of ledges of rock, on which innumerable pigeons have made their homes. The gap between the tops of the cliffs is always too broad to be jumped, and any crossing from one bank to the other is impossible. When walking down the shingle bed of the wadi, the foot passenger is shut in by the giant cliffs on either side, and he can see only a very short distance ahead owing to frequent sharp corners and awkward twists as the wadi winds first to right and then to left. In a few cases there is a trickling stream down the lowest part of the bed. The main wadis, of which the Wadi Farah and the Wadi Kelt are the chief, are joined by numerous tributaries from all directions, breaking up the ridges into a jumbled patchwork of separated hills.

Such is the country which, more than any strength of the enemy, opposed the advance of the 60th Division to Jericho. Any difficulties of ground we had experienced in previous fighting were, with the possible exception of those at Shab Salah, small compared to those which confronted us now in the Wilderness of Judea.

The Turks had, as usual, made the best use of the ground, and from their trenches they could enfilade all approaches. On Talat ed Dumm itself the works had been very cunningly sited, and a line had been pushed forward to the Arak Ibrahim Ridge and other commanding ground. On the south side of the road the gigantic heights of Jebel Ekteif and El Muntar were strongly held.

Orders for the attack were issued by the Brigade on February 16th. The 2/20th was to carry out the preliminary attack by assaulting Arak Ibrahim and the high ground east of it, so making the way clear for the attack on Talat ed Dumm by the 2/18th, under Col. Norton, and the 2/19th, under Major Craddock, on the following day. After capturing the formidable Talat ed Dumm position, the whole Brigade was to advance astride the Jericho Road and occupy the hill Khurbet Kakun, overlooking the Jordan Valley. The 179th Brigade on our right, and the 181st on our left, were to attack simultaneously with us; and on the right of the 179th cavalry were to move on to the plain through a narrow gorge, encircling the Turks' left flank, and making a bee-line for Jericho. February 19th was fixed as " Z day."

The Battalion left Anata at 1 a.m. on that day, and moved under cover of darkness to an assembly position in the Wadi Suleim. Two platoons of " D " Company, under 2nd-Lieut. S. P. Pattisson, and one platoon under 2nd-Lieut. Stone, were sent to positions on high ground from which they could protect the left flank of the attack. Owing to the difficult nature of the country, a preliminary ground reconnaissance had been impossible. In order to insure that the deployment of the two assaulting companies would not be overlooked or interrupted by the enemy, one platoon of " C " Company, under 2nd-Lieut. F. D. Parker, was sent forward to seize and occupy the Twin Hills, west of Arak Ibrahim. This was done without opposition.

At 4.25 a.m., without artillery bombardment, " A " Company (Capt. Hearn), with " B " Company (Lieut. Weatherley) in close support, moved forward from their deployment positions. " C " Company (Capt. Willson) remained with Battalion Headquarters in the Wadi Suleim. As anticipated, the country was found to be extremely difficult, and there was some delay in the opening stages of the advance. But at 6.10 a.m. red " success flares " were burning on the summit of Arak Ibrahim, and two prisoners had been taken. The advance was continued rapidly after dawn along a high and narrow ridge running north-east from Arak Ibrahim until the leading lines suddenly found themselves on open ground, and exposed to a withering fire from enemy artillery, machine guns, and rifles from a dominating ridge in front. Small further advances were made, at considerable cost in casualties, and it was soon apparent that without an organized preliminary bombardment it would be impossible for any large number of men to cross the 1,000 yards of undulating ground which still separated the front wave from the commanding position occupied by the enemy. " A " Company had forged ahead, and now formed the first wave. One platoon of " B " Company had come up on the right flank, but was separated from " A " Company by a razor-backed hill which was heavily enfiladed by enemy machine guns. Any advance by " A " Company or by this platoon of " B " was met by an annihilating fire from the enemy.

By this time Battalion Headquarters and " C " Company had moved up to Arak Ibrahim, and the Commanding Officer came forward to confer with Capt. Watson (who was already on the spot) and with the

Forward Observation Officers of the heavy battery and 18-pounder battery who were attached to the Battalion for the operation.

"At 09.30 hours," he wrote afterwards, "I sent Capt. Watson forward to organize an assault. I could not get telephonic communication forward or backward from here, and so shortly afterwards went back to the neighbourhood of Arak Ibrahim Cave (a distance of about 800 yards over the brow of the hill), where my Headquarters had now been established. From there I arranged with the Forward Observation Officers that the artillery should bombard 'F11' (the Turkish position) for half an hour to knock out the enemy's machine guns. Further artillery assistance was provided through the 180th Brigade Headquarters by the addition of one heavy battery and one 18-pounder battery.

"Captain Watson made a careful reconnaissance of the ground from 'F10.' The reconnaissance was extremely difficult owing to the fact that the ground to be covered in the assault consisted of two deep wadis separated by a long narrow ridge parallel with the advance. At 11.00 hours Captain Watson reported that another company would be necessary. 'C' Company was sent, Capt. Willson going on in advance to see the ground."

At 1.30 p.m. the attack was continued, three platoons of "B" Company, with "C" Company in close support, advancing towards the Turkish position. The assault was covered by the artillery already mentioned, by three machine guns (under Lieut. Kirby), and on the right by the covering fire of "A" Company and the one platoon of "B" Company who had been unable to move. Enemy artillery barraged each wadi and hill as the troops crossed it. The line was soon thinned by casualties, as the ground was too difficult to allow rapid headway, and the advance was met by heavy rifle and machine-gun fire on the part of the enemy. Excellent observation of our own artillery fire was possible, and it was concentrated on the two main enemy trenches. Capt. Willson led "C" Company forward until he was severely wounded. Though only semi-conscious, he managed to scrawl a few disjointed words on a piece of paper before he lapsed into unconsciousness. This message was brought to Headquarters, and was only deciphered with great difficulty. It contained almost the first news received that the attack was going well.

During the advance somewhat unexpected opposition was experienced from the enemy's left flank, so Lieut. D. F. P. Spurgeon, of "B" Company, who was in charge of a platoon on our right flank, immediately changed direction to meet it. By this time our leading line was at the foot of the final objective. The enemy, seeing Lieut. Spurgeon's platoon threatening his left flank, did not wait for the men of "B" and "C" Companies to climb the slope, but commenced to retire, and at 2.15 p.m. the whole of the hill was in our hands. Consolidation commenced immediately.

The enemy continued to shell the hill for about two hours, and the consolidating parties were subjected to continuous sniping from the flanks. "B" and "C" Companies remained on the objective, and carried on consolidation throughout the night. "A" Company was withdrawn into close support, and "D" Company, two platoons of which had been recalled from their position on the left flank at 4 p.m., was in reserve at Battalion Headquarters.

The Battalion had every reason to be proud of its day's work. An advance of more than three miles had been made over extremely difficult country, and at the end a strong enemy position had been carried in face of fierce resistance. The Turks had chosen their own ground, and had been driven off it. Three prisoners were captured and after the action thirteen enemy dead were buried The Commanding Officer's report concludes :—

"I should like to call attention to the magnificent spirit of the men of the Battalion, who carried out their difficult task with great courage. The success of the operation was largely due to the initiative and leadership of the young officers and N.C.Os. ; after most of the former had become casualties, the latter grasped the situation and took over control with extraordinary promptness and determination."

The following warrant officer, N.C.Os. and men displayed great gallantry in this operation :—

> C.S.M. J. T. Hills
> Sergt. T. E. Davies
> Lce.-Sergt. J. Graney, M.M.
> Pte. J. McRobie
> Pte. A. Barron
> Pte. M. Drawater

Sergt. Davies was specially recommended for a commission in the Battalion in recognition of his work as Acting Company Sergeant-Major of "C" Company. After Capt. Willson had been wounded and Lieut. Malcolm had been killed, he took charge of the company and led the men on.

The toll of casualties, though light compared to what it seemed likely at one time to become, was fairly heavy. A number of the wounded lay out all night on the hill where they had fallen, and Capt. Churchouse, Pte. Bean, and the company stretcher-bearers did splendid work, spending the whole night attending to cases on the battlefield, and collecting them at points where they could be most easily picked up and evacuated by the Field Ambulance camels after dawn. The dead included Lieut. Weatherley, an irreparable loss to the Battalion ; Lieut. Malcolm, who had returned from home only just in time to take part in this action, and who was likewise a most valuable officer ; Lce.-Cpl. N. McDougall (the Battalion barber), Cpl. L. Waring ("C" Company), and Pte. W. Paxton, M.M. ("B" Company). Lce.-

Sergt. W. Hoffman (" B " Company) died of wounds.
Among the wounded were :—
>Capt. Willson (seriously)
>Lieut. A. W. Pilbeam
>Sergt. F. W. Cook
>Sergt. R. Pallister, D.C.M.
>Sergt. T. E. Davies
>Lce.-Sergt. G. Buckmaster
>Lce.-Sergt. H. Cannon
>Lce.-Sergt. A. Jones
>Cpl. A. Lenzberg
>Cpl. W. E. Cowell
>Cpl. P. E. May
>Cpl. R. Bell
>Lce.-Cpl. A. J. Pridgeon
>Lce.-Cpl. E. J. Wood

The night passed without incident. At dawn " D " Company, under Lieut. Stone, took part in the further advance of the Brigade by working forward on the left of the 2/19th Battalion during the successful assault on Talat ed Dumm, and the company continued to guard the left flank of the Brigade throughout the day. By nightfall the line had been considerably further advanced.

At 8 a.m. Battalion Headquarters, " A " and " B " Companies had moved down from " F11 " on to the Jericho Road, where assistance was given to the R.Es. in making good a track for the guns, many of the bridges and culverts having been destroyed by the Turks in their retreat. Later " C " Company rejoined Headquarters, and in the afternoon the Battalion, less " D " Company, moved along the road to Talat ed Dumm, and bivouacked for the night some 400 yards east of the Good Samaritan Inn, and close to the ruins of a medieval castle, " Le Castel Rouge." " D " Company remained on the left of the Brigade for the night, and the other three companies took up outpost positions and put them in a state of defence.

Meanwhile, farther east the attack was making good headway. The 1st Australian Light Horse Brigade, on the right flank of our line, had passed through the gorge of the Wadi Kumran and reached the plain on the north-western shores of the Dead Sea. Early on the 21st they started across the slimy marl plain, and entered Jericho at 8.20 a.m. Two hours previously the London Scottish had advanced and occupied the monastery of Nebi Musa, four and a half miles south-east of Talat ed Dumm, in the hills on the southern side of the Jericho Road, and it now became apparent that the Turks had retired during the night along the whole line. There was no further opposition as the Division advanced to its final objective, and the 180th Brigade occupied the heights of Khurbet Kakun, on the line of steep cliffs which mark the eastern edge of the Judean hills, and from the foot of which the plain spreads for miles—east to the Jordan, south to the Dead Sea, and north to the Wadi Aujah.

The line was soon divided into sectors, and on February 23rd the Battalion took over a long stretch from the Jericho Road on the left, across the mountain Jebel Ekteif to the Nebi Musa Monastery (held by " B " Company) on the right. Nebi Musa is interesting as the place to which a Mohammedan pilgrimage is made once a year, the tomb of Moses being located there by Mohammedan tradition. The pilgrimages frequently result in feuds between the Jews and the Mohammedans in Jerusalem. The Turks had withdrawn eight miles across the plain, and it was known that their nearest troops were those occupying the bridgehead on the west bank of the Jordan at Ghoraniyeh. The task of holding the line at Jebel Ekteif was not, therefore, a very arduous one, and the rest which it brought was more than welcome. Many parts of Jebel Ekteif were carpeted with flowers. The weather was gloriously fine and cool on the hills where we had our bivouacs, though oppressively hot for the company in the valley at Nebi Musa.

A draft of officers—2nd-Lieut. F. Barnes, 2nd-Lieut. P. S. R. Marshall, 2nd-Lieut. S. G. Cumner, 2nd-Lieut. E. R. Spice, 2nd-Lieut. W. H. Bright, and 2nd-Lieut. J. Hirst, M.M.—joined the Battalion on February 25th, and Lieut. A. H. Hunt returned from hospital. Lieut. Jones, who had been doing duty as Brigade Intelligence Officer for some months, returned and took over command of " B " Company.

The month of March opened with a series of tactical reconnaissances of the River Jordan.

CHAPTER XV

RAIDS ACROSS THE JORDAN

THE traveller from Jerusalem to the Jordan, on entering the plain by the Jericho Road, will find the city of Jericho away on his left. It nestles rather closely under the towering cliffs of Jebel Kuruntul (" The Mount of Temptation "). He need not go far to get a full view of the whole flat expanse, from the Wadi Aujah away on his left to the blue waters of the Dead Sea on his right front. Then he will note that the cluster of mud buildings called Jericho, showing through the pleasant shade of olive and almond trees, is the only oasis on this barren, sterile waste of the Jordan Plain. Everywhere else only the shimmering mirage, the scrub, and the clay soil of the open plain for miles, as far as the foot of the Moab Hills in front of him. If he is attracted and follows the road into the city, he will be disappointed by the squalor and dirt and stench of the place. Far better to stand at a distance and gaze from there on this one bright jewel in a setting of hard granite.

Our stay at Jebel Ekteif enabled us to explore the country around. The sense of freedom afforded by the open plain, after the confinement of the hills, acted like a tonic. It was a delight to gallop over flat country once more, to explore its wadis, and to ride up into the secluded corners of the Wilderness. The sheer drop of the cliffs overlooking the plain reminded of nothing so much as the cliffs of Dover. Every now and again there is a break in the cliffs where a wadi comes to a sudden end, and this is the explorer's opportunity. He will find much that is strange and fascinating. The Wadi Kelt is perhaps the most romantic and awe-inspiring

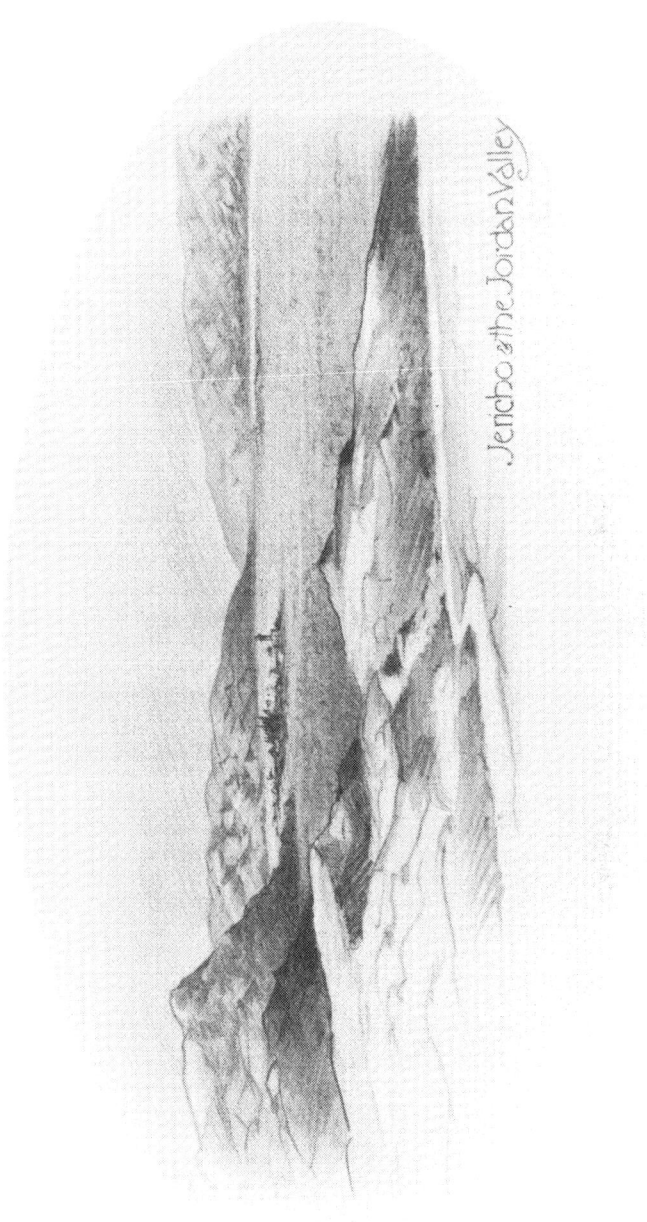

of all the sights in this wild country. Its narrowness, its height, its exceeding fertility of vegetation, and its bed watered by a running stream, attract and lead the explorer on and on. In one place a monastery, dedicated to St. George, has been marvellously carved out of the red-brick bank, and in the bed of the wadi a well-kept garden, a bridge, and an artificial waterfall pay tribute to the labour of the monks in time past. During the war they seem to have left their home, for we found it deserted save by pariah dogs, and there were evident signs of jackals. The Kelt does not stop on reaching the plain, but continues on for eight miles to the banks of the Jordan. No great imagination is required to picture it as the home of Elijah at the time when he was fed by the ravens, and to this day the wadi is the haunt of thousands of birds. The Wilderness has always since New Testament times been the special delight of hermits, anchorites, and monks, mainly because of its historic associations (it was the scene of Our Lord's Temptation), but also, no doubt, because of its weird seclusion from the eyes of the world.

The Jordan Plain has been described as the home of malaria, and it is considered barely habitable for Europeans during the summer months for this reason. It says much for the precautions and measures taken by the Army medical authorities that the number of cases reported from the troops who had to live on it during the worst season of the year was very small. A special mosquito squad was later formed in each battalion of the 60th Division to act under the Battalion Medical Officer to remove scrub and vegetation where it acted as a breeding-place for mosquitoes, and to take other precautions against malaria. Quinine parades came in again, too, if the writer remembers rightly.

The Jordan Valley harbours the mosquito in the marshes and vegetation of its wadis, and its enervating heat lowers human vitality and prepares the way for disease. Most of the soil is sand, or cotton soil, or clay, and near the Dead Sea the clay is covered with strata of salt and gypsum, and is very soft after rain. The sea itself is so salt that the human body floats without exertion on the surface, and can be submerged only with difficulty; but swimming is unpleasant, as the feet have too great a tendency to rise to the surface. Fresh eggs float in it with a third of their volume above water. On the northern shore we found a group of wooden huts and workshops, which had formed the Turkish Base upon the Dead Sea. A party of " B " Company, under 2nd-Lieut. Spurgeon, spent some days in the neighbourhood of this spot, acting as guard over a hydroplane.

The reconnaissance of the Jordan, orders for which were received on March 1st, soon monopolized interest and attention. The river from the Wadi Aujah to the Dead Sea was divided by the Brigadier into four sectors, one sector being given to each battalion to reconnoitre. The two points on which information was specifically required were the location of fords at which infantry and cavalry could cross, and the position of the enemy force holding the eastern bank. The sector allotted to the 2/20th included the ford of El Henu, and extended from Makhadet Hajlah to the Dead Sea. The 2/19th had the next sector on our left, including Makhadet Hajlah ford, and farther north still the 2/17th were responsible for El Ghoraniyeh.

For reconnaissance of El Henu Ford, a convenient base for operations was provided by the monastery of Kasr Hajlah, two and a half miles west of the Jordan. Such a base was necessary as a " lying-up " place by day, it being found impossible to carry out reconnaissances or move at all in the neighbourhood of the Jordan except at night, and the distance back to the hills of the Wilderness being too great to cover between the completion of the reconnaissance and the return of daylight.

The monastery was still inhabited by Greek monks, whose integrity as far as espionage was concerned was by no means above suspicion. They certainly lost no opportunity of assuring us, in French, that they wished the Turks no good, but after we had returned to Jebel Ekteif there was nothing to prevent their giving valuable information to the enemy. The monastery was of white plaster, and had a nice chapel, two towers, and a spacious courtyard with many passages.

The first reconnoitring party from the 2/20th, consisting of the Commanding Officer, Capt. Watson, Capt. Jones, and the Adjutant, crossed the plain on horseback in daylight on the morning of March 2nd, and at Kasr Hajlah Monastery joined a patrol of a troop of the Auckland Mounted Rifles. The whole party moved forward from the monastery at 8.30 a.m., and proceeded eastwards down a sheltered wadi, and then across a belt of low scrub to a ridge of small sandhills. Here the horses were left, and the advance was continued on foot. After leaving the scrub the ground was found to be flat and totally devoid of cover. It consists of cotton soil, and this means very heavy going even in dry weather. It is quite impassable by any type of vehicle. The patrol was shelled and sniped at while crossing the last 300 yards to the Jordan. Close to the west bank of the river there was found to be a good deal of marsh, with a considerable number of trees (willows and tamarisks mostly) on both banks. On the east bank a ledge of rocks overlooks the river. The Turks were scattered among the trees and along the ledge of rocks on the east bank. On this ledge two or three shelters made of brushwood could be seen, which were evidently in use. One of the tracks on the western bank leading down to the river showed signs of considerable—though not recent—use. The enemy on the opposite bank kept up a running fire for some time, and the patrol was well peppered with bullets on returning across the open to the horses at noon. Later the party made its way back to Jebel Ekteif. The reconnaissance, if it had done nothing else, had proved the hopelessness of attempting a detailed and careful reconnaissance of the river in daylight.

The second and final reconnaissance was on a much larger scale, two companies being engaged. On the evening of March 4th the Battalion (less " C " and " D " Companies, who remained at Jebel Ekteif and Nebi Musa) moved to Kasr Hajlah, under Capt. Watson, and established a combined Headquarters with the 2/19th Battalion, who were reconnoitring Makhadet Hajlah the same night. The two battalions reached the monastery simultaneously about 9.30 p.m. A signalling station was established by the Signalling Officer (Lieut. Salter) at the monastery, and two platoons of " A " Company were left here under Lieut. H. C. Lovell. The remainder of " A " Company left the monastery at 8.30 p.m., followed later by Headquarters and " B " Company.

Over the same ground as the officers' daylight patrol had covered two days previously, the six platoons and Headquarters moved first down a wide and rather shallow wadi, and eventually came to a point where a line of low cliffs ended the sheltered ground, and from here onwards there was no cover. The ford was extremely difficult to locate, owing to the undergrowth and thick trees on the western banks. The river was found to be broad and very rapid. The suspicions of the enemy were not aroused, and the patrol withdrew to Kasr Hajlah before dawn. The day was spent in the monastery. A further reconnaissance was carried out by " B " Company under Capt. Jones in the evening, but no new information was gained. The whole party returned to Jebel Ekteif after dark on the 6th, leaving two platoons of " A " Company, under Lieut. Lovell, at the monastery. These platoons were relieved by " D " Company (less one platoon) on the evening of the 7th. On the following morning Lce.-Cpl. J. W. Lamb, of " B " Company, a very gallant N.C.O., was killed while standing in the open in daylight close to the banks of the Jordan. At the time he was sniped, Lce.-Cpl. Lamb, who had repeatedly distinguished himself in action as a Lewis gunner, was talking to Sergt. Mould, and though urged to get under cover he refused, and at great personal risk insisted on pointing out the features of the river, exposed as he was to enemy snipers at short range.

The whole battalion was back in the Jebel Ekteif sector on March 19th, and baths, disinfection, and a light programme of training filled the next few days.

On March 14th all officers, except six, attended a Brigade dinner, at which 115 officers of the Brigade were present.

Orders were received two days later for the crossing of the Jordan by the whole Brigade on a night to be notified, the object being a raid on the enemy's communications east of the Jordan with a view to assisting the Arab forces under the King of the Hedjaz, who were working northwards on the hills bordering the eastern shores of the Dead Sea. The enemy's railway line on the Moab Hills was to be destroyed for some miles in the neighbourhood of Amman.

The reconnaissances of the Jordan had established that at this time of the year the river was unfordable at any available point, and it had therefore been decided to throw bridges across at the two most suitable places —Makhadet Hajlah and Ghoraniyeh. It was hoped that the thick undergrowth at these two points would afford ample concealment to the first crossings. The force taking part in the raid—officially termed " Shea's Group," from the name of its commander—consisted of a mounted division, an infantry division (the 60th), the Imperial Camel Brigade, a Heavy Battery R.G.A., a Mountain Artillery Brigade, a Light Armoured Car Brigade, and two Bridging Trains. The first crossings were to be made by swimmers with cable ropes. Rafts were then to be used to carry troops across for the establishment of a bridgehead on the east bank. Meanwhile the bridges were to be constructed under cover of the trees. Light rafts had been made by the R.Es. for the preliminary crossings. The instructions for boarding the rafts issued with Battalion Operation Orders may not be without interest, though the 2/20th, as events turned out, had no reason to use the rafts.

INSTRUCTIONS *re* BOARDING RAFTS.

1. Twelve to a raft.
2. Form up in threes.
3. Lewis gunners in the four centre positions.
4. Men must not step on wire netting, but only on the footboards provided.
5. Sit facing the enemy.
6. Hold rifle in one hand and equipment in the other.
7. Absolute silence.
8. Keep clear of the cable.
9. Do not interfere in any way with the work of the Sappers.

The crossing at Makhadet Hajlah was to be made by the 2/19th, and that at Ghoraniyeh by the 2/17th. The 2/20th was to cross behind the 2/17th at Ghoraniyeh, and, owing to information at the last moment that the Turks had been heavily reinforced, the 2/18th were sent to be in support to the 2/19th at Makhadet Hajlah. The Battalion moved down to Kh. Kakun on the afternoon of the 20th, and bivouacked for the night there. At dusk on the following day companies moved through Jericho across the plain to the Wadi Nueiameh, where a concentration position had already been reconnoitred by Capt. Watson, Capt. Reynolds, and Lieut. Parker. The Battalion was in position by 10.30 p.m.

A quantity of rafting material had been accumulated on the west bank of the river, and at midnight the 2/17th launched two small punts, one north and one south of Ghoraniyeh. The enemy was quickly alarmed, and opened intermittent rifle and machine-gun fire from the

The advance to the Jordan
on 22.1.18
(A W.G.Carter)

east bank. The current was found to be far stronger than had been anticipated, and crossing by punts was found to be impracticable. Swimmers were tried, but they were immediately carried away by the current or swept back to the bank. Repeated gallant attempts were made, but these had no result except the loss of two small punts and one raft. By 12.35 a.m. the Turks had scented serious trouble. Green lights sent up by them resulted in a commencement of artillery fire, while to make matters more difficult the R.E. officer and the officer of the 2/17th working north of Ghoraniyeh had been dangerously wounded.

The 2/20th received frequent information of the situation owing to Brigade Headquarters being close to us in the Wadi Nueiameh.

Meanwhile the 2/19th Battalion at Makhadet Hajlah had been more successful, and, without hostile observation, had effected a crossing by swimmers. This news, received at 1.3 a.m., was followed fifteen minutes later by a report that the first raft of the 2/19th had crossed, and twenty-seven men were east of the Jordan. The Brigadier quickly decided to abandon the crossing at Ghoraniyeh for a time, and to concentrate all efforts on forcing the crossing at Makhadet Hajlah. At 1.40 a.m. the 2/20th was ordered to proceed at once to Makhadet Hajlah, and Brigade Headquarters moved to Kasr Hajlah Monastery.

The Battalion set out immediately, and had to march eight miles back to Jericho before joining the Wadi Kelt and moving east again six miles to Kasr Hajlah. The thick vegetation of the wadi made progress very slow and very tiring, and it was 11 a.m. before the whole of the Battalion arrived at the Headquarters of the 2/19th. By that time the men had been on the move practically since 6 p.m. on the previous day. The advance to the Jordan from the Wadi Kelt was exposed in places to enemy machine-gun and rifle fire, but the Battalion reached cover without casualties.

On our arrival Major Craddock informed us that the situation had developed considerably. The first complete company of the 2/19th had been across the Jordan at 2.10 a.m., and by 5.30 a.m. 300 men had crossed. A bridge had meanwhile been got under way by the Anzac Bridging Train. Shortly after dawn the Turks had opened heavy enfilade fire on the rafts as they had been pulled across. It had only been possible to send eight men over at a time, and these had had to be at the bottom ot the raft. One load had had seven men hit. By 7.45 a.m. the whole of the 2/19th had crossed the river, and soon afterwards the 2/18th had begun to cross. Meanwhile the first pontoon bridge had been thrown across, and the 2/18th had been able to use it instead of rafts. The bridge was in a splendid position, being well sheltered by overhanging trees.

After crossing, the 2/19th had found it impossible to advance beyond a dense, almost impenetrable jungle, and here the line was placed at 11 a.m., when the 2/20th arrived. Several unsuccessful attempts were made by the 2/18th and 2/19th Battalions to advance the bridgehead, in order to enable mounted troops to cross and deploy, and at 6.30 p.m. the Brigadier held a conference of Commanding Officers at the 2/20th Headquarters near the bridge. It was arranged to make an advance on a broad front at midnight, with the object of securing a line of foot-hills. The 2/20th was to be in the centre, with the 2/19th on our right, the 2/18th on our left, and the 2/17th in Brigade reserve.

"At midnight," says the Brigade account, "this operation was carried out successfully. The 2/20th, getting forward with considerable *élan*, stormed and put out a sniping post on one of the lower foot-hills, which was harassing the 2/19th. This action enabled the 2/19th—who had been compelled to skirt a very swampy marsh on their right, and, further, to advance partially to the rear of the 2/20th—to come into line again with that battalion, and deploy to the right. The lower foot-

The River Jordan

hills were then carried with little opposition, the enemy leaving two prisoners in our hands. Moonlight, which had been of some use to hostile snipers at the start of this advance, was now of the greatest assistance to us. We were able to establish a very firm bridgehead on the furthest foot-hills, an excellent field of fire being obtained over the plateau beyond, which enabled machine guns the next morning to disperse small enemy groups, and a good line of advance up to our positions, through the small wadis which intersected the foot-hills in our rear, being secured for the cavalry."

One bridge was not sufficient to get the whole of " Shea's Group " across the river without considerable congestion and delay. Very soon after the 2/20th crossed at Makhadet Hajlah, the Auckland Mounted Rifles used the bridge and moved along the east bank of the river towards Ghoraniyeh, where the Turks were still in possession of the bridgehead. The enemy thus found himself threatened from the rear, and quickly evacuated his position, though not without sustaining considerable casualties. The Mounted Rifles took possession, and in a very short time a bridge had been thrown across by the R.Es.

Soon after noon on the 23rd H.R.H. the Duke of Connaught crossed the Jordan at Makhadet Hajlah, and, with a number of Staff officers, remained on the east bank for a considerable time. He showed great interest in finding London troops east of the river, and talked to several of the men.

The situation by the end of the day was that the cavalry had thoroughly scoured the plain ; infantry, artillery, and transport were making the crossing behind our bridgehead, and everything was getting into readiness for the advance into the Moab Hills next morning. The Battalion had had no sleep for forty-eight hours, and all ranks were thoroughly tired. The heat of the plain during the day was intense.

When the advance was resumed at 6 a.m. on the

24th, the 180th Brigade came into Divisional reserve. The 2/20th marched north to just east of Ghoraniyeh Bridge, where it lay up until the afternoon, and then moved two miles east to bivouac. One platoon, under Lieut. Slaughter, was sent to Ghoraniyeh as bridge guard; the remainder of the Battalion moved eastwards with the other battalions of the Brigade, made a prolonged halt under cover of the foot-hills at 8.15 a.m. for some hours, and bivouacked for the night some miles farther east. Next morning at 7 o'clock the Brigade moved forward in rain, and pitched bivouacs in the neighbourhood of Shunet Nimrin at the foot of the Moab Hills on the Es Salt Road. Here the 2/20th remained for some days, and put in a lot of hard work on the roads, which were in a very bad state. The other battalions of the Brigade were sent forward to assist the 181st Brigade in the hills in its pursuit of the enemy to Es Salt.

March 25th was very wet, and the advance of the 179th and 181st Brigades and the cavalry was much hampered by the appalling condition of the roads, which were soon knee-deep in mud in many places. Es Salt itself was occupied by cavalry at 6 p.m., and during the night of March 26th-27th a raiding party of the Mounted Division blew up a considerable stretch of the railway at a point seven miles south of Amman. Considerable further damage was done on the 27th by demolition parties, and during the night the 2nd Australian Light Horse Brigade succeeded in destroying a two-arch bridge on the railway seven miles north of Amman. On the 28th a park of twenty-two Turkish lorries was completely destroyed by the Armoured Car Brigade on the road between Es Salt and Sweileh.

At 5.15 p.m. on the 28th enemy 'planes bombed the 180th Brigade bivouac, and caused heavy casualties among the camels of the 2/5th Advanced Dressing Station. Only one man was wounded.

At 6.45 p.m. the 2/20th was ordered to proceed to the left flank, to support the 1st Australian Light Horse Brigade (Brig.-Gen. C. F. Cox). On arrival " A " and " B " Companies took over a portion of the line without any noteworthy incident. On the afternoon of the 29th (Good Friday) we returned to our previous bivouac in the neighbourhood of Shunet Nimrin.

Meanwhile Amman had been the centre of a stiff fight, in which the 2/18th had played a conspicuously gallant part. Refugees from Es Salt, carrying all their worldly belongings, poured down the Es Salt Road past Shunet Nimrin, obviously in a hurry to cross the Jordan and to claim Christian protection. Large numbers of Turkish prisoners also passed on their way back to the collecting stations.

The fighting in and around Amman had succeeded in its object of drawing heavy Turkish reinforcements, and during the night of March 30th-31st the withdrawal of the raiding party began. The 2/20th took up defensive positions on El Haud and Tel Bileibil, to cover the withdrawal of troops down the Salt—Nimrin road. On the following day, when the troops had passed through, the Battalion, in conjunction with the 2/18th on Jeria Hill, on the south side of the road, withdrew to the western slopes of El Haud. Two parties of enemy cavalry were seen to approach down the road, but these quickly withdrew on sustaining casualties from two armoured cars which were sent after them. There was no further pressure from the enemy, and by 8 p.m. the Battalion and the rest of the Brigade was in the Ghoraniyeh bridgehead position.

At noon on April 3rd the whole Brigade was relieved by the 1st Australian Light Horse Brigade, and marched back to bivouac areas in the neighbourhood of Khurbet Kakun.

Gen. Watson thus concludes his account of this first Jordan raid :—

" I cannot speak too highly of the keenness and spirit

displayed by all ranks throughout these operations, which included a river crossing, mountain warfare, and rearguard work. A great deal of credit is due to the ration parties, whose work over execrable roads was beyond praise."

On April 7th we were on the Jordan Plain once more, and on this occasion pitched bivouacs about a mile and a half north of Jericho. The few days spent here were occupied in training and sport, and some reconnaissances of the line were made. On April 14th the whole Brigade moved back along the Jericho Road to Talat ed Dumm, where training was continued. In four days the Battalion again moved down to the neighbourhood of Ghoraniyeh for a period of thirty-six hours. This move, however, was only made to deceive the enemy, and camp fires were lit. " C " Company had a merry sing-song round their fire, and hot rum punch was served by Pte. Crane and the other company cooks. The Battalion subsequently returned to Talat ed Dumm, where the announcement was made that Major Craddock had been awarded the Military Cross. He had so frequently distinguished himself by gallantry in action that it was good to hear that his work was at last receiving recognition.

The Battalion had recently received several drafts of reinforcements, the officers who had joined being 2nd-Lieut. E. B. Jones, 2nd-Lieut. V. C. W. Sutton, and 2nd-Lieut. J. Priest.

The Brigade had an early morning march "up" to Jerusalem on April 21st, and the 2/20th arrived at Sir John Gray Hill's house at 10 a.m. Battalion training, with disinfecting and bathing, filled the time until April 27th, when the Brigade left Jerusalem to make its second raid across the Jordan. Col. Warde-Aldam has supplied the following account of this operation :—

The Battalion only received a very short warning of this new and totally unexpected expedition. The

Adjutant had just departed for a week's well-earned leave, his place being filled by Lieut. F. D. Parker. Little did he think that on his return ten days later he would find the Battalion already returned from a brief but strenuous expedition, during which it had fought probably the stiffest action that it was destined to experience. During April the Turks had concentrated a considerable force east of the Jordan, and had made good use of the time at their disposal in organizing a system of defence consisting of good trenches and sangars along the line running roughly north and south through Shunet Nimrin, where the hills begin to rise from the plain ; these defences were held by well and newly equipped troops, with a useful proportion of machine and mountain guns.

The object of this Es Salt raid was to harass and, if possible, cut off these troops. The 179th and 180th Brigades were to make a frontal attack, while the Australian Mounted Division was to recapture Es Salt and take the Turks in rear. The attack was organized to co-operate with an attack on Es Salt from the south by Sherifian Arabs and a rising of the Beni Sakhr tribe in the Wadi Es Sir. These two movements should have completed the isolation of the Turks.

During the night of April 28th-29th the 179th and 180th Brigades were concentrated in the jungle east of the Jordan, and within the Ghoraniyeh bridgehead. The next day was spent in conferences and final preparations. It was a trying day for all ranks. Movement was reduced to a minimum so as to avoid observation ; there was intermittent shelling, and the heat was already becoming reminiscent of the parching days at Es Shauth.

At 10 p.m. on the 29th the Battalion, to which were attached " D " Company 2/18th London Regiment (Capt. Manning) and No. 4 Section, 180th Machine Gun Company (Lieut. Lamb, M.C.), left its bivouac, and marched in column to a position of assembly about one mile east of the wire guarding the bridgehead. From this point the advance to the line of deployment began. " C " Company (Capt. Goldby) proceeded along the right bank of the Wadi Nimrin. " B " Company (Capt. Wilson), followed by " D " (Capt. Reynolds), proceeded through the scrub directly towards their objectives on Tel Bileibel. Battalion Headquarters, with the remainder of the column, followed slowly behind " C " Company. The Battalion had been allotted this particular sector in the attack as being the same ground over which it had acted as rearguard during the final withdrawal from Amman. It had therefore been possible to give " B," " C," and " D " Companies for their primary objectives the identical final positions they had held as a rearguard three weeks before. This arrangement had a unique advantage, in that all ranks had a previous thorough knowledge of the ground, and also that it greatly facilitated giving clear orders, which would otherwise have been a difficult matter at such short notice in a semi-surveyed country. The only outstanding feature in the area was a white shed at the foot of the hills opposite the angle at which they curved back to form the Wadi Nimrin. The scrub extended across the plain to a line about 400 yards west of the foot of the hills, and then there was a bare belt of stony ground to the actual foot of the hills. The edge of the scrub was the position of deployment, at which the companies were able to deploy unobserved, and where also touch was obtained with the 2nd London Scottish on their left.

At 2 a.m. on the 30th the advance began, and met with little opposition until near the edge of the first crest. Here the enemy was found in strength, but his trenches were captured by an immediate bayonet charge, and the advance then continued, till it was checked by a strong enemy counter-attack from the left. " D " Company, however, who had been following hitherto in close support, came straight on, and the three companies completely smashed up the counter-attack, killing in all 40 Turks, capturing over 100 prisoners, and carrying our line still farther forwards. At 3.12 a.m. red flares were lighted to show that the first objectives had been taken. At 4 a.m. Battalion Headquarters, with the two remaining companies and the Machine Gun Section, arrived. As it became light, it was apparent how completely the Turks had been surprised : their bivouacs stood intact behind our line, much commotion could be seen in the Wadi Nimrin, and away to the right stood an officer's white tent with his horse tethered outside ; several Turks were seen to run into this tent, and one of our machine guns did quick work in ranging on this exceptional target. By 5 a.m. the Battalion was reorganized and was holding a definite line—" C " Company and two platoons of " A " Company on the right, " B " Company in the centre, and " D " on the left, " D " Company of the London Irish building a reserve line of sangars slightly in rear. It was now seen that the London Scottish on our left and the 2/19th on our right (from whom we were separated by the Wadi Nimrin and its stream) were both held up. Two platoons of " A " Company made a gallant but abortive attempt to cross the Nimrin and help the 2/19th, while two machine guns tried to help the London Scottish, and one the 2/19th. The enemy were now able to organize a new position, which was soon bristling with machine guns ; these enfiladed our line from both flanks, inflicting heavy casualties, and completely stopped the repeated attempts to continue the advance. Unfortunately, there was no telephone wire and no sun for the " helio," so that, although a mounted officer was sent back to explain the situation, no artillery help was forthcoming till much later in the day.

Meanwhile the Turks brought up a light gun on our left front which enfiladed our positions at point-blank range, making them completely untenable, and the line had to be withdrawn to the first crest above the plain under cover of the supporting company of the London Irish. This movement was begun soon after 8 a.m. and completed by 12 noon, when " B " Company of the London Irish and No. 3 Section of the Machine Gun Company arrived as a new reserve. The position was maintained thus till the end of the day. During the early part of the night the new line was partially extended and fresh defences were dug. Later the Battalion was relieved by the London Irish, but remained in close support under the crest. All along the line the Turks had proved themselves too strong, and the whole frontal attack was held up. Meanwhile the Australian Light Horse had captured Es Salt, but had failed to capture the Turkish bridgehead over the Jordan at El Damie. This failure, together with that of the Beni Sakhr tribe to function at all, were the decisive factors which stopped the success of this expedition. On May 1st the Turks brought up large reinforcements from west of the Jordan, and drove back the Australian Light Horse on our left flank; they thus threatened to cut off the Brigade in Es Salt, and made any further frontal attack useless.

On May 2nd a last effort was made to retrieve the situation with a joint attempt to advance along the Shunet Nimrin—Es Salt road by the Light Horse from the north and the infantry from the south; the cavalry, however, were held up at Howeij, and though the two forces were thus only five miles apart, the Wadi Es Sir was still open, and final orders for the withdrawal of the cavalry were given. This was accomplished on May 3rd.

As far as the Battalion was concerned, it remained in close support to the London Irish and spent the four days in burial work, salvage, sniping, patrolling, and guarding the Wadi Nimrin itself. It was during this period that one of Lieut. Lamb's machine guns brought down an enemy aeroplane, which crashed in the middle of a company bivouac of the London Irish.

On the night of May 4th the 179th and 180th Brigades were withdrawn west of the Jordan. The Battalion relieved the London Irish in the line, and for the second time acted as rearguard to a retirement from Bileibil. On May 5th it arrived at its old bivouac area at Tel es Sultan, near Jericho, and in the afternoon, to the joy of those who had so often " gone up to Jerusalem," " embussed " at Jericho and " debussed " at Sir John Gray Hill's house. These words—almost irreverent, and certainly slang—are typical of the contrast between the first and twentieth century—a contrast which was brought out almost every day during " the last crusade."

The losses of the Battalion during this last ten days had been :—2 officers, 36 other ranks killed ; 5 officers, 151 other ranks wounded ; 10 other ranks missing. Amongst the killed were Capt. Hearn, 2nd-Lieut. E. R. Spice, Sergt. S. G. Giles, Sergt. J. G. Rennie, and Sergt. E. Strachan. It was a heavy toll, but not without result. There is no doubt that the expedition " finally convinced the enemy that future British operations would be in this area," and so led to that dispersal of the enemy forces which materially assisted the final September victory in Palestine.

C.S.M. J. T. Hills and Sergt. S. N. Seager were awarded the D.C.M., and Sergt. J. Tyler, Lce.-Cpl. L. A. Pearson, and Pte. A. H. Kent the Military Medal, for gallant conduct during this operation.

The long list of wounded included Capt. Reynolds, Lieut. D. F. Spurgeon, 2nd-Lieut. W. L. Sutton, 2nd-Lieut. P. W. Robinson, 2nd-Lieut. P. S. R. Marshall, R.S.M. Skeer, C.S.M. Hills (twice), Sergt. Chappell, Sergt. S. J. Lucas, Sergt. W. Narraway, Sergt. C. P. Oakshott, Sergt. A. E. White, Sergt. R. J. Milton, Sergt. J. Graney, M.M., Sergt. L. Walters, Cpl. A. C. Crate, Cpl. A. R. Greenaway, M.M., Cpl. W. H. Oliver, Cpl. T. Smith, Cpl. A. Lewis, Lce.-Cpl. T. C. Brown, Lce.-Cpl. T. Broxup, Lce.-Cpl. G. D. Draycott, Lce.-Cpl. H. E. Dillow, Lce.-Cpl. A. J. Deuters, Lce.-Cpl. G.

Giddings, Lce.-Cpl. W. Greenaway, Lce.-Cpl. G. Jackson, Lce.-Cpl. W. J. Mitchell, Lce.-Cpl. L. A. Pearson, Lce.-Cpl. E. H. Wallis, Lce.-Cpl. C. W. Wright, Lce.-Cpl. A. Young, Lce.-Cpl. C. E. Swinnerton, and Lce.-Cpl. F. J. Paris.

The Adjutant, on returning from leave in Cairo, found the Battalion very cheerful, but somewhat tired after its trying experience. The exhausting heat of the Jordan Plain had told its tale, and the men were thoroughly glad to reach Sir John Gray Hill's house. It was our last sojourn there. After two days of rest and re-organization, we marched up the Nablus Road to Ramallah, and went under canvas in a standing camp. Capt. Bacon had now taken over " A " Company, and Lieut. Woolfe " D " Company.

It was the wish of the Divisional Commander that the men should have a period of thorough rest, and for the next few days training was reduced to a minimum. Col. Warde-Aldam took over temporary command of the Brigade on May 9th, and left Capt. Elliot in charge of the Battalion. Capt. Watson was away at Heliopolis on the Senior Officers' Course.

In the absence of work and fighting it was necessary to provide amusement and occupation for the men, and this was done in the form of Brigade and Battalion competitions and concerts. The Brigade Horse Show on May 12th was a very splendid affair. Gen. Chetwode and Gen. Shea attended, together with practically every officer and man in the Brigade. The 2/20th took a fair share of the prizes. " Nancy " (Capt. Reynolds's mare) won the competition for the best officer's charger with owner up, and " Aeroplane," the " D " Company Mess donkey, went far in the contest for that branch of the transport. The Battalion did well in the Brigade Athletic Sports Meeting two days later. The details of the results are, unfortunately, not on record.

The evenings were filled with concerts, regimental and divisional. " The Roosters " supplied the programme of the latter, but the men seemed to enjoy " local " talent quite as much as semi-professional, and the Battalion concerts arranged by Chaplain the Rev. H. M. Gilliatt, who had succeeded the Rev. C. Jenkins with the 2/20th, and Capt. Jones were admirable examples of impromptu effort. The Padre himself was no mean comedian, and his song, " With Stiffy between the Sticks," became well known throughout the Brigade, and earned for him the affectionate sobriquet of " Stiffy." At one of the concerts a prize was offered for the best comb band. Many excellent combinations of " combists " came forward, but there was no doubt about the winner of the competition after " Blundell's Celebrated Transport Band," under Pte. Turner, had performed. The successful musicians, who were all transport men, had practised assiduously, and their effort was as near perfection as could be expected. In such ways did the Battalion amuse itself at Ramallah !

Col. Warde-Aldam rejoined on May 21st, the day after the Battalion had moved to Ain Yebrud for road repair work. There had been rumours for some days among those " in the know " that some battalions of the Division would be sent to France in the near future, and when it was announced that companies would parade at full strength at 1 p.m. on May 22nd for a " few words " from the Brigadier, most—of the officers, anyway—guessed what was coming. Gen. Watson told the Battalion that the 60th Division was being broken up. Some battalions, among them the 2/20th, would very shortly proceed to France, some would be disbanded, and some would remain in Palestine to form the nucleus of the new 60th Division. He thanked the Battalion for all it had done for the 180th Brigade, assured the men of his conviction that the 2/20th would do great things in France, and wished all ranks " Godspeed."

The men were, on the whole, delighted at the prospect. Its principal attraction was, of course, the possibility of home leave once they had reached France. But those who had the guiding and administration of the Battalion were a little sorrowful at the prospect of parting with so many friends. We realized our loss in leaving the 60th Division, and the uncertainty of the future as regards our brigade and division was depressing. Still there was leave ahead, and that compensated for everything.

The Divisional Commander came to say good-bye on the 26th. After presenting the Order of the Nile to the Adjutant, and decorating Sergt. Seager and Pte. Kent with the ribbons of their newly-won decorations, he addressed the parade.

It was soon established that the 2/17th was to proceed with us to France, the 2/18th was to be disbanded, and the 2/19th was to remain in Palestine. There was very little time to say good-bye to those who were being left behind. Early on May 27th the Battalion was on the move to Ramallah. Here a short halt was made, and we were able to have a few words with the officers and men of Brigade Headquarters, the 2/18th and 2/19th Battalions, the 180th Machine Gun Company, and the Trench Mortar Battery, as we passed their bivouacs. Our last view of the 180th Brigade was of officers and men of these units standing on the side of the road cheering. In reply they received somewhat pathetic shouts of "Last time, 180!" (a favourite Brigade call) from our men.

The journey by march route to Ludd, via Ain Arik, Beit Nuba, Latron, and Surafend, was for the most part uneventful. From Ludd we entrained for Kantara on May 31st, and after a three weeks' stay moved on again to Alexandria, which was reached on June 22nd.

Many farewell messages were received, and Gen. Watson and his Brigade Major, Capt. R. V. Read, came to the platform at Kantara to say a final good-bye.

The Brigadier had previously sent the following letter to Col. Warde-Aldam :—

" I cannot allow you, the officers, N.C.Os., or men of the 2/20th Battalion London Regiment to leave the Brigade without saying how proud I am to have been associated with you all, and how deeply I feel your departure. You have one and all been ever loyal to me, and it has been the greatest pleasure to serve with such a magnificent Battalion.

" Whatever task the 2/20th Battalion London Regiment has had to do has been carried out thoroughly and well. Your battle record is second to none, and in bidding you 'God-speed,' I know that you will carry high the honours that you have won, and will increase your already great reputation."

Gen. Chetwode wired :—

" I much regret that I was unable to see you and your Battalion before your departure, and wish you good-bye and ' God-speed ' personally. Please convey to your men how deeply and sincerely I thank you all for the magnificent work done by you all while in my Corps. I wish you all good fortune in your new theatre, where I am confident you will fully maintain the reputation you have won in this country."

To this the Commanding Officer replied :—

" All ranks 2/20th Battalion London Regiment thank you for your kind message of good-bye and 'God-speed.' They will always remember with pride and pleasure the months they have served under your orders. They are confident that the valuable experience gained under your command will materially help them to do their duty in another theatre of war."

The following letter was received from Gen. Shea :—

" The Commander-in-Chief has asked me to express to the 60th (London) Division his thanks and his admiration for their work up to now, and his good wishes for the future.

" ' The Battalions going to another theatre will carry with them a proud record. The Battalions staying here will be the same fine fighters as ever.'

" It affords me the keenest satisfaction to communicate the Commander-in-Chief's message to the Division."

The total of casualties sustained by the Battalion whilst serving in the E.E.F. was as follows :—

	Officers.	O.R.
Killed in action	7	87
Died of wounds	—	22
Accidentally killed (drowned) ...	—	1
Died of disease	—	4
Wounded	12	316
Totals	19	430

CHAPTER XVI

BACK TO FRANCE—THE BATTLE OF VRAUCOURT

OUR departure from Egypt, though it gave birth to many pleasurable anticipations of leave and an early peace, was in itself certainly painful. Most of us had developed more than a passing affection for the country, and in this sense, quite apart from all the glorious and happy memories which it now held for us, we were sorry to leave. An altogether deeper source of regret lay in the severance of our long relationship with the 60th Division—a relationship which had been nurtured in the days of France and of Macedonia, but which had lately become more and more intimate by reason of all the strange experiences through which we had been guided by Division and Brigade Headquarters since the opening of the Palestine offensive. After the Battalion itself, our Brigade and Division meant almost everything to us in a military sense. They had been our pride—yes, and our comfort too—for more than a score of momentous months, and now that the time had come to part company, the parting could not be without more than ordinary regret—on our side, at least. That the Battalion had made many friends we knew, but that they were so numerous and so loyal we only came to realize fully as we said good-bye to them. Some, like Col. McCall (the A.A. and Q.M.G. of the Division) and Capt. Lane (late Adjutant of the 2/18th, and now G.S.O.3 of the Division), knew the 2/20th before ever its fighting days began. Many others—among them Major Courtauld (the D.A.A.G.), Col. Lunn (commanding 2/5th Field Ambulance), Major Nell (commanding 519th Company R.E.), the Rev. J. C. Fitzgerald (Senior Chaplain), Capt. Gilbert and the men of the 180th

Company of the Divisional Machine Gun Battalion, Capt. Osborne (commanding 180th Trench Mortar Battery) and his men, and many officers and men of the Divisional Artillery, had worked for us and with us, both in the fighting line and out of it, during the most strenuous years of our existence. To all these and many more the 2/20th owed a deep debt—a much deeper one, by the way, than the majority of officers and men in the Battalion had any opportunity of realizing. To Gen. Shea and Gen. Watson, " *our* Generals," we owed even more, and much also to Col. Dear, Col. Norton, Col. Sword, and Major Craddock and their battalions for frequent loyal assistance and cooperation. Finally, to the Brigade Staff, Capt. Read, and Capt. Cooper-Willis, the Battalion was indebted in a very special degree. They and their predecessors (the writer would like particularly to mention Capt. Ash among these) had often made our path easy when it might have been most difficult, and had shown consideration when the lack of it might have seriously prejudiced our success. Now that we were returning to France to join a new Brigade and a new Division— the Fates alone knew which—we felt more than ever grateful for the privilege of having been allowed to serve in the 180th Brigade of the historic 60th (London) Division. Every officer and man who survived them will carry the memory of those glorious days as long as he lives.

We had to leave several officers and a number of men behind in Egypt and Palestine. The men had for the most part been casualties in the second Jordan raid, and they were greatly disappointed to find themselves still in hospital when the Battalion was setting out homewards. Some of the officers had been away for a considerable time. Among those left behind were Capt. Partridge, Capt. Willson, Capt. Goldby, the Rev. H. M. Gilliatt (who, though a *Brigade* Chaplain, had come to be considered as " one of us "), Lieut. Stone, and Lieut. Spurgeon. It was with very sincere regret that we parted with these old fighting companions. On the other hand, it was a real pleasure to have Major Craddock in the Battalion again. He rejoined at Kantara. His period of three months in command of the 2/19th had been attended by the most obvious and remarkable success, though, as Col. Sword was still nominally in command, it was impossible for Major Craddock to receive promotion to Acting Lieutenant-Colonel. The part played by the 2/19th under his leadership in the attack on Talat ed Dumm, and in the very difficult operations in the Jordan Valley, had been heralded on all sides. Tangible recognition by higher authority was long delayed, but it came many months afterwards in the form of the D.S.O. By that time it had been earned again, and some will learn for the first time when they read these lines that the D.S.O. awarded to Col. Craddock (as he then was) in January, 1919 was won, not in France, but in Palestine. The fact that Major Craddock received no promotion while he was away reacted on the 2/20th, as it meant that Capt. Watson, who carried on as Second-in-Command in his absence, could not receive his long-deserved Majority.

The Battalion was split into four detachments for the "voyage home," as it was generally called. The largest, under Col. Warde-Aldam, travelled on the *Rose* ; a smaller party went with the 2/23rd London Regiment in the same convoy as the *Rose* ; and a third detachment, under Major Craddock, remained at Kantara for some days after the rest of the Battalion had left, and subsequently came on by the *Malwa*. The personnel and animals of the Transport Section formed a detachment of their own under Lieut. Blundell. Besides the officers and men of the Battalion, the *Rose* carried a number of unattached officers who were proceeding home from India, Mesopotamia, and Egypt. The voyage proved to be of greater interest than either of our previous journeys in the Mediterranean. This was partly owing to the historic places which the *Rose* passed on her course, and partly owing to her having to put into harbour suddenly on two occasions so as to avoid enemy submarines. Further, several incidents occurred which served to break the monotony of the journey.

The ship was almost deserted when Col. Warde-Aldam, as O.C. Ship, the Adjutant, and the orderly-room staff went on board. The greater part of the crew had gone ashore overnight, and the decks were almost deserted. Some parts of them were dirty, and had obviously been left so by the last troops on board. The C.O. refused to allow the men to pass up the gangways until the ship was thoroughly clean, and two interviews with the Embarkation Staff and a stormy scene with the captain were necessary before matters were put right. We were not due to leave until the following day, so in the afternoon a large party went off to bathe. Capt. Willson arrived in a yacht while the *Rose* was still in harbour, and he came on board to say good-bye. His visit was opportune. The supply of beer in hand for the voyage was very small, and as all ranks were confined to the ship it had been impossible to remedy the deficiency. Capt. Willson disappeared soon and returned with many bottles—a characteristic action for which he was subsequently much blessed during the voyage.

The *Rose* put out into outer harbour at mid-day on June 24th, and in the evening, as part of a convoy of three transports and escorted by five French torpedo-boats, we steamed in a north-westerly course from Alexandria. While still within gunshot of the town, we passed the hulk of a ship recently wrecked. It was an ominous reminder of the perils of our journey The submarine menace was now a factor in the war which none could disregard. In earlier months it had taken a heavy toll, but its position as a *decisive* influence had been overlooked. Gradually the list of victims had mounted up until the sinking of the *Lusitania* had produced a crisis. Now, in June, 1918, the U-boat was recognized throughout the world as one of the most deadly weapons in the armoury of Germany. British troops returning from the East were for the most part landed at Taranto, on the south coast of Italy, whence they continued their journey on into France by rail. The opportunity of seeing Italy—though it was only from the train—was one to which we looked forward with some pleasure.

Daily routine on board the *Rose* was laid down in Ship's Standing Orders, which were drawn up as soon as the Battalion embarked. Each morning, after breakfast, hammocks were stowed away and troop-decks were thoroughly scrubbed before the ship's captain made his morning inspection. The men were paraded on deck, and the captain was accompanied on his rounds by the O.C. Ship, the Adjutant, the Quartermaster, the Medical Officer, and the Captain of the Day. Sergt.-Major Skeer went ahead and sounded a whistle, which acted as a warning to the troops to stand " to attention." On the completion of his rounds, the captain returned to the bridge, and the submarine guards and duties for the next twenty-four hours were mounted. The men not detailed for guard paraded for rifle inspection and one hour of physical training. Several practice alarms were held, and each company was allotted part of the deck as an alarm-post. On the " hooter " being sounded three times, the men immediately " doubled " to this spot. Each officer and man was also detailed off to a position in one of the boats as a precaution in case of the boat being torpedoed. Life-belts were worn throughout the voyage except at meals, when they were kept within reach.

Crete was safely passed on the morning of the 26th, but the same evening, on account of wireless information of enemy submarines ahead, the captain put in to the island of Milos, and cast anchor. The opportunity of a bathe was too good to resist, and several of the men had a dip from the boat-side; but the water was full of coaldust and refuse, and they hardly enjoyed their swim. After a peaceful stay of twenty-four hours, during which, to the joy of all concerned, submarine guards were considerably reduced, we resumed our journey, and passed through the wondrous Corinth Canal into the Gulf of Corinth. At the time it was nearly midnight. There was a bright moon which cast eerie shadows on the narrow vein of water and the white concrete banks of the canal on either side. The passage was narrow, and often it seemed as though the sides of the ship, as it glided forward, would strike one bank or the other. There was a towing path on one side, but we saw no sign of human life save the men on duty at either end, the entrance and the exit, of the Canal. Long before dawn we were once again on the high seas. We passed through the Ionian Islands, and came within a short distance of the coast of Ithea. Enemy submarines called another halt on June 28th. On this occasion our anchorage lay between the island of Oxia and the coast of Greece, and we were there for twelve hours. At Oxia there was a soldiers' boat-race between a boat from the *Rose* and one from the *Hazel*, another ship in the convoy. The *Rose* was beaten. The weather was now anything but favourable, and we were glad to sight Taranto early on Sunday morning, June 30th. The Italian Battle Fleet was in harbour, and presented a wonderful sight as, in a coat of new paint, it lay in its deep blue setting glittering in the sunshine. On many of the ships Divine Service was in progress, and there was a mass of white uniforms and bared heads on deck.

The Battalion disembarked in the early afternoon, and repaired to a large rest-camp to await entrainment. A bulky mail had been held up by the Army postal authorities pending our arrival; and as Cpl. Read lost no time in sorting and distributing it, there were many letters and parcels to cheer the seven days' train journey which lay immediately ahead. Entrainment began in the evening. The first party left under Capt. Watson at 9 p.m. ; " D " Company and the greater part of Battalion Headquarters followed with the 2/23rd London Regiment four hours later ; and a final party, under Capt. Jones, came on on the following day.

The journey up the east coast of Italy was thoroughly enjoyable. The trucks were not uncomfortably full, there were frequent *haltes repas* to break the monotony, the scenery was interesting, and the weather all that could be desired. The men seemed to enjoy the experience thoroughly, especially when the inhabitants of the Italian villages turned out and cheered. For long periods on end the rattle of the train was accompanied— almost drowned—by popular choruses which were taken up enthusiastically, whether it were during the day or in the middle of the night, by truck after truck.

Halts were made at Brindisi, Bari, Foggia, Castellmare, Ancona, Faenza, Bologna, Piacenza, Voghera, and Savona. Eventually, after passing through many long tunnels, we reached San Remo and the Riviera, and stopped at Ventimiglia, Bordighera, Monaco, Monte Carlo, Nice, and Cannes. At the last-named place the train drew up by the side of the sea, and a halt was made while the whole Battalion undressed on the beach and bathed *en masse*. Soon after leaving San Remo we crossed the frontier and were once more in *la belle France*.

We were still in the dark as to our destination, and could only base guesses on the number of days we still had in hand to complete seven. At mid-day on Sunday, July 7th, we came to a sudden stop, and received orders, through the R.T.O., to detrain. The station was Forges-les-Eaux. In accordance with instructions, the Battalion marched to Serqueux, remained there for the night, and moved on again by train next morning to Arques-les-Batailles. From Arques we marched to camp at Martin Eglise, two miles south of Dieppe, where we found Capt. Watson and his party awaiting us.

Our lot was cast in a delightful part of France. The country was for the most part rich pasture-land and thick woods. Martin Eglise was a small hamlet of half a dozen houses. Its green fields were very pleasant camping ground after the sandy desert, and the contrast was further emphasized by a rippling trout stream which flowed through the village. The estaminet served an excellent dinner, which included fish freshly taken from the stream.

The British troops in the neighbourhood were almost exclusively " malaria battalions " from the East, and from the first it was obvious that the 2/20th would not have a long stay. The Battalion was, practically speaking, free from malaria, and certainly had no need of restricted training and limited physical activities— the treatment prescribed for malaria troops. While at Martin Eglise the Battalion was under the orders of the 50th Division (Major-Gen. Jackson).

The detachment under Capt. Jones proceeded by train from Taranto direct to Abancourt, and here it was joined by Col. Warde-Aldam's party. It was something of a coincidence that the Area Staff Captain of Abancourt was Major F. C. Bentley. Simultaneously with coming into the Abancourt area, the Battalion joined the 198th Brigade (Brig.-Gen. Hunter) of the 66th Division. Major Craddock and his party arrived on July 19th, in company with the 2/24th London Regiment (Lieut.-Col. J. P. Crosbie, D.S.O.). The 2/24th went into a camp adjoining that of the 2/20th. The Transport, which had gone all the way to Marseilles by sea, put in an appearance about a week later, having had a long train journey through Belgium.

Regular allotments of leave to " Blighty " were already established. A party of four had left each day from Martin Eglise, and within a short time this number was substantially increased. Officers, N.C.Os., and men took their turn on the roster. Major Craddock was in command in the absence of Col. Warde-Aldam, and when Major Craddock was away Capt. Watson remained and took charge. When the allotments increased so that more than 200 all ranks were away at one time the Battalion was reduced to a skeleton of specialists and employed men. Serious training was then out of the question, and the leave-roster was arranged so as to cause a minimum of dislocation to specialist training. On one occasion forty-five signallers were sent as one party.

The organization of the Battalion in accordance with the official tables laid down in " O.B. 1919 " was, in the meantime, carefully watched. In this connection everything was so arranged that when all ranks had had leave, the Battalion was prepared to take its place in the line without any further delay. 2nd-Lieut. Rogers was appointed Battalion Intelligence Officer, 2nd-Lieut. F. D. Parker Assistant Adjutant, and Capt. H. C. Lovell took over the Quartermaster's duties when it was found that Capt. Dark had been detained in the United Kingdom by a Medical Board.

The situation on the Western Front at the beginning of July, 1918, needs some slight reference here. It has been the subject of countless books, pamphlets, and newspaper articles since the war. All are agreed that the position of the Allies was desperately critical. The line was in many places behind that which had been occupied in 1914. All the profligate sacrifice of human life, the wholesale destruction of property, and the gigantic daily expenditure on armaments during nearly four years of ghastly conflict, had produced no victory of any permanence. The great enemy offensive which had begun in March had carried all before it, and was now pushing forward the German line, and at the same time driving the armies of England and of France before it. Paris was once again in imminent danger, and the Germans were fighting with deadly success on the banks of the Marne. To the pessimist the war seemed as good as lost. Yet, in spite of much that was alarming, the situation was not altogether as desperate as it seemed. The main sources of confidence lay in Marshal Foch, who was now in supreme command of the whole Allied front from Switzerland to the sea, in the vast numbers of American troops which were pouring into France to assist the Allies, in the immense casualties which his offensive was known to be costing the enemy, and in the increasing discontent of the civilian population of Germany.

The first fortnight in July brought no relief to the harassed forces of the Allies. The enemy continued his attacks, and though he suffered heavily, his advances gained ground. Suddenly, on the 18th of that month, the position underwent a dramatic change. Foch delivered his first staggering blow. The French-American line, preceded by tanks, went forward on a frontage of nearly 30 miles against the German divisions between the Oise and the Marne. From this date the fate of Germany was sealed. The advance had begun which was to break the German battle-line and plant the armies of the Allies on the banks of the Rhine.

The first British troops to join the fray were, curiously enough, our old friends the 51st (Highland) Division, and our new friends (as will be explained presently) the 62nd (West Riding) Division (Major-Gen. W. P. Braithwaite). These two Divisions were hurried into the line beside the French, north of the Marne. During ten days of desperate fighting on the Ardre, Highlanders and Yorkshiremen covered themselves with glory. Both Divisions sustained more than 50 per cent. casualties. One battalion of the 62nd—the 8th West Yorkshires—received the Croix de Guerre from the French Government in recognition of a brilliant victory at the Montagne de Bligny. After the fighting, Gen. Braithwaite's Division was withdrawn from the line.

Early in August it moved up to Thievres in the 4th Corps area to reorganize and refit ; and here, on August 9th, it was joined by the 2/20th Battalion, which then became part of the 185th Infantry Brigade (under Brig.-Gen. Viscount Hampden, C.B., C.M.G.), in place of the 5th West Yorkshire Regiment, which had been disbanded.

The Battalion, still temporarily depleted by big leave allotments, entrained from Abancourt to Doullens, under Capt. Watson, and found the band of the 5th West Yorkshires waiting at the station to lead the march to Thievres. The band was attached to the Battalion for some days. It was hoped to secure it permanently, but other influences were at work, and orders soon arrived for men and instruments to report to another unit.

The Battalion soon had cause to congratulate itself on its new Brigade and Division. Naturally enough, there were many points on which assistance and advice were required. The Brigadier himself and each member of his staff had had a lengthy fighting experience on the Western Front, and it was a real benefit to be able to rely on their support. The Brigade-Major (Capt. H. S. Kreyer, D.S.O.) and the Staff Captain (Capt. C. C. Harland, M.C.) thoroughly entered into our difficulties, and the work of the Commanding Officer and the Adjutant was appreciably lightened in consequence. Lord Hampden was on leave when the Battalion joined the Brigade at Thievres, and Col. Waddy, lately commanding the 5th West Yorkshires, was acting as Brigadier. The 1/5th Devon Regiment (Lieut.-Col. H. V. Bastow) and the 8th West Yorkshire Regt. (Lieut.-Col. N. A. England) were the other battalions of the 185th Brigade.

As a divisional sign the 62nd Division had a pelican with one foot raised. It was Lord Hampden, if memory serves right, who circulated the rumour that when the pelican put his foot down there would be an end to the war. (If the words " 62nd Division " are substituted for " pelican," there will be found to have been considerable truth in this rumour.) Battalions of the 185th Brigade wore a circle (respectively yellow, blue, and red) on the steel helmet, and on the sleeves of the jacket just below the shoulder.

Reinforcements for the Battalion began to arrive in large numbers in August. One draft of men was 160 strong. Several officers joined, including 2nd-Lieut. G. J. P. Holton and 2nd-Lieut. P. Smout. When the greater part of the Battalion had had its leave, training became really strenuous, and the War Diary records a Battalion parade as part of each day's work at Thievres. Gas drill assumed a new importance, and attack formations were practised assiduously.

Though the Commanding Officer was still away, the signallers were all on leave and companies were somewhat thin in numbers, the Battalion was inspected on parade by Gen. Braithwaite on August 12th. Everything passed off happily, and the General seemed pleased. Two evenings later he inspected the Transport (now under Lieut. D. R. Blundell). The Battalion had marched from Thievres to Vauchelles in the afternoon, and in the circumstances it was highly creditable to Lieut. Blundell and his men that the turn-out received " a good chit."

A series of moves commenced on August 18th, consequent on the Division being in Corps Reserve for certain operations. After church parade on Sunday, the 18th, a warning order was received that the Brigade would move in the evening. The Battalion marched to Louvencourt. The village was too small to accommodate the whole Battalion, so the Colonel took Headquarters and " D " Company on to Bus-les-Artois. On the 19th the head of the Brigade passed Louvencourt Windmill at 8.30 p.m., and the 2/20th arrived in billets at Pommera at 1.30 a.m. the next day. The same night the march was continued to La Cauchie, and on the night of the 21st, after passing through St. Amand, Henu, and Authie, the Battalion found itself back in

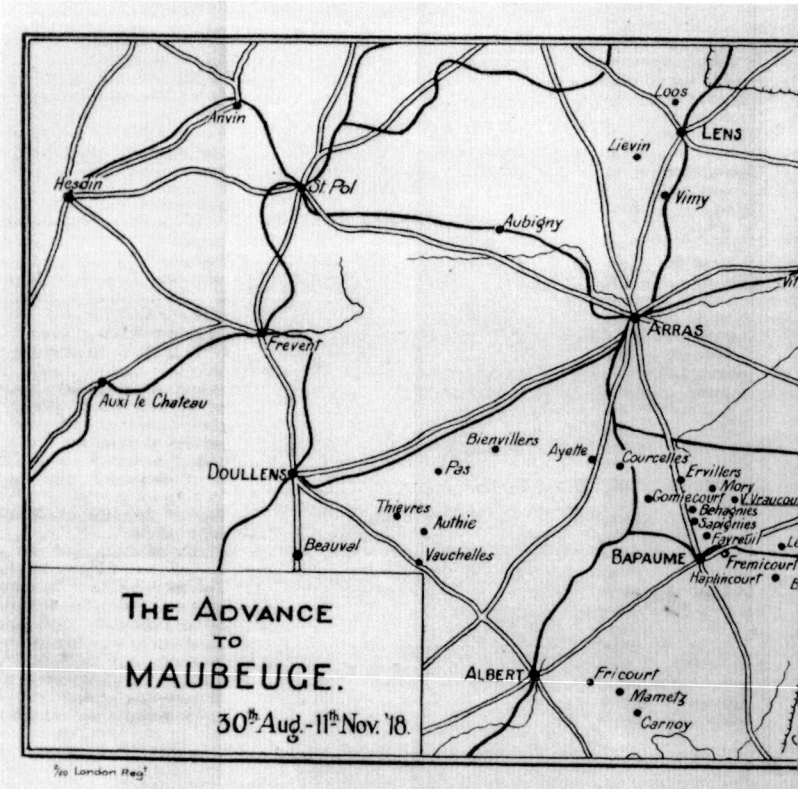

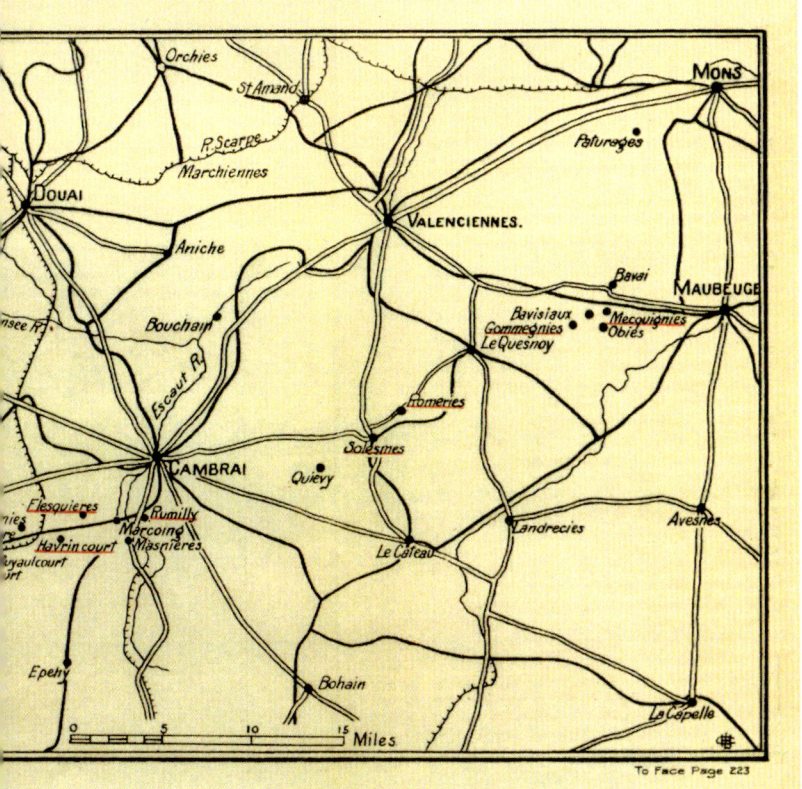

Vauchelles. On the 23rd, after a day's rest, the Division, which had been attached to the 4th Corps, returned to the 6th Corps, and orders arrived for a relief of the 3rd Division in the line about the railway east of Courcelles during the next day.

The War Diary account of the 23rd and 24th is of interest as showing the complete activities of the Battalion during two strenuous days :—

August 23rd.

0730 ...	Battalion parade.
0800 to 1200 ...	" A," " B " and " D " Companies did field training. " C " Company had use of range.
1400 ...	Warning order received, " Battalion will move this evening."
1945 ...	Battalion left Vauchelles.
2000 ...	Passed Brigade starting point.
Midnight	Arrived in billets at Bienvillers.

August 24th.

0200 ...	Orders received by the Battalion that 62nd Division would relieve 3rd Division about the railway east of Courcelles (6 miles north-west of Bapaume) in daylight on the 24th.
0430 ...	Orders received for Battalion to be ready to move at 0730.
0905 ...	Battalion left Bienvillers via Monchy, Douchy, Ayette.
1230 ...	Battalion arrived just west of Courcelles.
1945 ...	Battalion moved forward to railway embankment east of Courcelles, and spent the night there. Rear Headquarters are in some trenches west of Courcelles.

The sector which the Division was about to take over was opposite the most northerly part of the old Somme battlefield. Cambrai and a strongly fortified stretch of the Hindenburg Line lay ahead. The 3rd Division had captured Courcelles three days before the Battalion arrived there, and had gone forward over the high ground on which the village stands down to the railway embankment in the valley east of it. The line had been carried as far as Gommecourt on the following night. The 2nd Division had then taken over, and had secured Ervillers on the 23rd. Here the advance had been held up by very heavy fire from the high ground to the north-east and from Mory Copse, a patch of trees which lay almost directly ahead. The Copse, which was found to be full of machine-gun emplacements and dug-outs, was brilliantly carried on the 24th. Meanwhile the Guards had made splendid progress north of Mory, and had captured St. Leger, and the 52nd (Lowland) Division and the 56th (London) Division on their left had reached the old Hindenburg Line. This substantial advance was followed on the right of the 6th Corps front by the capture of Behagnies and Sapignies by the 2nd Division soon after dawn on the 25th. A few hours later the 2nd Division was relieved by the 62nd, and the 186th and 187th Brigades passed through and advanced towards the village of Vraucourt.

As already stated, the 2/20th spent the night of August 24th—25th on the railway embankment east of Courcelles, where we were the victims of an unpleasant bombing experience at the hands of a squadron of the enemy's airmen. Officers and men dug themselves into the bank, and were thankful for the cover it afforded. The night would have been pleasant enough but for the incessant firing of one of our own batteries. Some of the guns were but 20 yards to our rear. Soon after dawn the Colonel took some officers ahead to reconnoitre the ground as far forward as Ervillers, and in the evening, in anticipation of an enemy counter-attack against the front held by the 187th Brigade, the Battalion was ordered to move forward. Companies took up positions in trenches in the south and south-east corners of the village, while Headquarters and two platoons occupied some old trenches between Courcelles and Ervillers for the night. On the 26th Headquarters moved into some shelters in a quarry on the western side of Ervillers and Brigade Headquarters came into a dug-out in the same neighbourhood.

Though they had made considerable headway, the 186th and 187th Brigades were held up in front of Vraucourt. The enemy had a strong position in a sugar factory in the village, and, as the flanks were not up, it had been found impossible to advance farther. At dawn on August 28th the 185th Brigade relieved the 187th Brigade, and the 1/5th Devons and 8th West Yorkshires took over in the line. During the day the C.O., the Adjutant, and the Company Commanders visited the Headquarters of the 1/5th Devons. Before nightfall some slight advance was made, but Vraucourt was thickly garrisoned, and was strongly defended by machine guns, and no appreciable gain resulted

At 2000 hours on the 29th the Commanding Officer was sent for by the Brigadier and told verbally that the Battalion would attack Vraucourt at dawn. Six tanks were to co-operate in the attack, which was to be made under a creeping barrage. The 186th Brigade was to advance on the right of the 2/20th, and the 3rd Division on the left. Written orders were received half an hour after midnight. A combination of circumstances made the operation a difficult one. The attack had to be made without reconnaissance ; the Battalion had never previously advanced under a creeping barrage, and many of the men had never seen a tank. The only guides to the line were the officers who had visited Col. Bastow's Headquarters on the previous day.

Immediately on receiving verbal orders, the Commanding Officer called a conference of Company Commanders, and explained the position and his plan of attack. The final objective was a ridge overlooking Vaulx and Vraucourt from the east. The Germans were holding both villages. The Battalion frontage included part of Vaulx on the right, and the whole of Vraucourt as far as Vraucourt Trench on the left. Vraucourt Trench ran at right angles to the advance, and in order to prevent the attack being enfiladed from here a company of the 8th West Yorkshires was to work down the trench from the west, clear it, and establish a chain of posts along it. The enemy was known to be in great strength round the sugar factory, which was the meeting-place of four cross-roads, so our artillery had orders to put a specially heavy barrage round this area. One of the cross-roads ran straight across the Battalion frontage parallel with the advance, and it was anticipated that some opposition would be experienced from it by the right company. On the left there was a light railway running parallel with Vraucourt Trench at right angles to the advance. These three features—the sunken road on the right, the sugar factory near the centre, and the light railway on the left—were respectively the main points given to the companies to advance on. The attack was to be made by " A " Company (2nd-Lieut. P. S. R. Marshall) on the right, with orders to ' mop up " part of Vaulx ; by " C " Company (Capt. Hunt) in the centre, with orders to " mop up " Vraucourt ; and by " B " Company (Capt. Jones) on the left, having its left on Vraucourt Trench and its right on the light railway, with orders to move straight through to the objective. " D " Company (Capt. Reynolds) was to be in reserve, and had orders to leapfrog through " A " and " C " Companies when those two companies gained Vaulx and Vraucourt respectively, and to join with " B " Company in consolidating the final objective.

There was no time to lose, and after the conference the Company Commanders hurried off and gave orders to their platoon commanders, who in turn passed on the orders and the plan of attack to their subordinates.

At 0130 hours the Battalion, guided by those officers

who knew the way, moved by companies to a position of assembly in the sunken Mory-Beugnatre Road, and here the men were quickly organized in waves under cover of the steep bank. Battalion Headquarters went to a quarry on the same road just south of Mory, and shared a dug-out with the Headquarters of the 5th Devons. At 0410, in thick darkness, companies moved forward a distance of about a thousand yards to their jumping-off positions, which had been taped out by Lieut. C. Friend, the Brigade Intelligence Officer. These positions had to be approached by a trench, and in consequence progress was slow. To add to the difficulties, enemy gas shells began to fall somewhat thickly just before " zero," and the men had to put on their box-respirators. Our barrage opened immediately afterwards, so respirators were hastily put away, and the line advanced. The tanks had not yet arrived.

" A " Company advanced with considerable spirit. Some opposition was experienced from the sunken road already mentioned, but this was overcome, and several prisoners were secured. After a time the company found itself up against a thick belt of enemy wire which was raked in enfilade by machine guns from both flanks. The men lay in shell-holes while parties were sent out to deal with this opposition. These parties did excellent work. The danger points were dealt with, 30 prisoners were captured, and the advance of the company was then resumed. Very heavy shelling and machine-gun fire now opened from the direction of Vaulx. The line crept gallantly forward to a point about 400 yards from the village, and was there held up. Nothing had been seen of the 186th Brigade on the right, so the right flank of the Battalion was somewhat dangerously exposed.

" C " Company, on the left of " A," also made rapid headway from the start. The men rushed the sugar factory in most determined style, and pressed on through Vraucourt close up to the barrage. The company had to lie down and wait until " the crash " on Vraucourt finished and the barrage lifted. Then the leading wave went straight through the village and occupied a sunken road leading into it from the north. The advance had been so rapid that there were still many Germans in the scattered buildings on the outskirts of Vraucourt. These now started firing rifles and machine guns into the rear of the company apparently from some hutments north of the village. " D " Company, who had come up to within a short distance of " C," so as to be able to pass through immediately Vraucourt was secured, had had Capt. Reynolds wounded early in the advance, and 2nd-Lieut. J. S. Pritchard was the only officer left in the company. Capt. Hunt now arranged with 2nd-Lieut. Pritchard for " D " Company to assault the hutments and clear them. This was done in magnificent style, and 2 officers and 70 men were taken prisoners. " D " Company then moved into the line on the left of " C," and occupied a sunken road running north from the railway. The road was easily identified on the map by a cemetery and crucifix which stood at its southern end.

At 0730 hours, except for a gap of 300 yards between " C " and " D " Companies, the line was continuous from " A " Company's right to " D " Company's left. All three companies were in touch, but there was no news of " B " Company nor of the 186th Brigade on the right, nor of the 3rd Division on the left, so " D " Company formed a defensive flank on the left. At 0800 hours " D " Company gained touch with the 4th Gordons, of the 3rd Division, who were found to be occupying Vraucourt Trench 500 yards west of their left flank. The Battalion was thus firmly established on a continuous front, but the right flank was in the air, the Germans were shelling unmercifully, the line was thinly held, there was no news of " B " Company, and the enemy was known to be in considerable force on the ridge east of Vraucourt.

The German gunners concentrated on the new front line, and put down a heavy barrage on the sunken road occupied by " D " Company, on the cross-roads round the sugar factory, and on the line held by " A " Company. This shelling continued to be very violent throughout the day, especially along a road running east from the sugar factory into Vraucourt. It was along this road that 2nd-Lieut. Ellen and his signallers had laid the telephone wire at the commencement of the advance. The enemy's barrage had soon cut the wire in innumerable places, and communication between Battalion Headquarters and the front line had of course been immediately interrupted. Linesmen had gone out at once to repair the breakage, and after having had to spend a considerable time in the inferno of the barrage round the sugar factory, had returned to Headquarters with their mission accomplished. The line became " dis " again and again, but every time, there were volunteers among the signallers to go out and repair it, though every man knew what it meant to linger in such a living hell as the road had become. 2nd-Lieut. Ellen, Sergt. Powell, Lce.-Cpl. G. F. Crawley, and Pte. D. Woolfe especially did magnificent work that day.

At 1000 hours Sergt. F. W. Cook, of " B " Company, reported by a runner to Battalion Headquarters that he was in charge of a party of thirty men of the company in a sunken road which proved to be 1,000 yards behind the road held by " D " Company. It appeared that soon after the opening of the attack the company had been held up by a nest of machine-gun posts which had caused many casualties. Almost the first to be killed had been the O.C. Company, Capt. Jones. The posts had been knocked out, largely as a result of the gallantry and initiative of the Lewis gun section commanders. Ten of the machine guns had been captured, but the delay and casualties had inevitably broken up the company. Sergt. Cook knew nothing of what had happened to 2nd-Lieut. H. W. Dillingham and the rest of the men.

An enemy counter-attack assembled opposite "C" Company in the early afternoon, but our artillery put down a heavy barrage, and the enemy was dispersed.

By nightfall, all companies had sustained considerable casualties, and, as all four had been engaged, there was no fresh company to throw in in the event of the enemy penetrating the line in a counter-attack. "A," "C," and "D" had each attempted to push on, but had met with heavy barrage fire and severe resistance. The enemy's position on the final objective stiffened considerably during the day, and the heavy shelling continued. The Commanding Officer made a thorough tour of the line, and ordered all companies to dig in after dark.

In the evening a message arrived from 2nd-Lieut. Dillingham stating that he and the rest of "B" Company had lost direction in the advance, and were now occupying a position between the right of "A" Company and the left of the 186th Brigade. The Commanding Officer ordered him to remain where he was for the night, and to join the thirty men under Sergt. Cook in the morning in a support position behind the sugar factory.

During the night the line was continually harassed. At dawn "C" Company advanced and "mopped up" some dug-outs and an enemy trench in front of their position. A party of "B" Company under 2nd-Lieut. F. Barnes, the Battalion Lewis gun officer, attempted to clear a stretch of Vraucourt Trench. Considerable sniping fire was experienced from snipers concealed in enemy barbed wire on the top of the trench, and casualties resulted. 2nd-Lieut. Barnes was wounded, and the party had to withdraw.

Heavy shelling again characterized the twenty-four hours which ended at midnight on the 31st. In the evening the position was reorganized. "C" and "D" now held the front line, with "A" and "B" in support. "A" Company was ordered to dig a strong point south of Vraucourt, and was ordered to be prepared to counter-attack at any part of our line should the enemy penetrate it. At dawn, in co-operation with an attack by the 8th West Yorkshires, one platoon of "A" Company advanced the line a short distance. Another platoon, under 2nd-Lieut. J. Batty, M.M., captured a machine-gun position in a trench, and occupied the trench. Two trench mortars were taken.

Early the next morning, September 2nd, the 187th Brigade passed through under a creeping barrage, and the 2/20th came into support. In the afternoon "C" and "D" Companies were sent forward to block the Vaulx-Lagnicourt and Vaulx-Morchies roads as a precaution in case of counter-attack. They were, however, met by the Brigadier personally, and diverted to occupy Vaulx Trench (a continuation of Vraucourt Trench), and another trench south of it. Meanwhile Battalion Headquarters had moved forward to some hutments east of Vraucourt.

Soon after mid-day a warning order had been received that the Division would be relieved by the 2nd Division that night. This relief was subsequently postponed until the early morning of September 3rd, when the 2nd Division advanced through the 62nd, and the 2/20th moved back to breakfasts which had been prepared on open ground east of Ervillers.

As a result of the operations, the Battalion had cleared Vraucourt and part of Vaulx, and had carried the line to the railway 600 yards east of Vraucourt. True, the ridge had not been secured, but a suitable jumping-off line had been gained for any subsequent operation. The advance in the early hours of August 30th had been carried out with remarkable gallantry and determination, but the men had found the hardest part of their task to be the holding of the position under four days of shelling, which for long periods had been intensive. Through all, they had held on grimly and cheerfully. The following officers, N.C.Os., and men were decorated for conspicuous gallantry in the battle :—

Military Cross:
>2nd-Lieut. J. S. Pritchard.
>2nd-Lieut. P. L. Smout.
>2nd-Lieut. H. J. Ellen.

Bar to the Military Medal:
>Pte. A. Barron, M.M.
>Pte. G. Earl, M.M.

Military Medal:
>C.S.M. J. B. Salkeld.
>Sergt. F. Powell.
>Sergt. F. W. Cook.
>Cpl. C. L. Robinson.
>Lce.-Cpl. G. F. Crawley.
>Lce.-Cpl. A. M. Smith.
>Lce.-Cpl. G. Giddings.
>Pte. A. Westall.
>Pte. D. Woolfe.

Captures were as under:—
>Prisoners—5 officers, 255 men.
>Machine guns—18.
>Trench mortars—7.
>Anti-tank rifles—2.
>2 big ammunition dumps,
>600 tons of coal,

and a collection of hutments, used as stores, which were found to contain a large number of new steel helmets and "Tommy's Cookers," and a quantity of machine-gun belts, leather equipment, and clothing.

Casualties were:—

Officers:
>Killed, 1.
>Wounded, 6.

Other Ranks:
>Killed, 30.
>Died of wounds, 2.
>Wounded, 133.

The officers wounded were Capt. Reynolds, 2nd-Lieut. A. F. Dyball, 2nd-Lieut. P. L. Smout, 2nd-Lieut. W. L. Bright, 2nd-Lieut. F. E. Read, and 2nd-Lieut. F. Barnes. Other ranks wounded included :—

>Sergt. A. E. Ludlow.
>Sergt. L. Walters.
>Sergt. G. Kain.
>Lce.-Sergt. G. D. Myers (gassed at Courcelles).
>Lce.-Sergt. P. Herrington.
>Cpl. G. W. Coleman.
>Cpl. W. Akers.
>Lce.-Cpl. E. V. Dearing.
>Lce.-Cpl. A. Mason.
>Lce.-Cpl. J. F. Wilson.
>Lce.-Cpl. L. J. Spenceley.
>Lce.-Cpl. H. Whelan.
>Lce.-Cpl. G. B. Yallup.

By the death of Capt. Jones the Battalion lost a great personality. Everyone loved him for his cheeriness, his great powers of leadership, his courage, and his whole-hearted concern for his men. He had filled many rôles, but he never made any secret of the fact that it was with the Transport Section that he had felt most at home. Capt. Jones was not only a very popular officer, he was a very efficient and a very gallant one. His end, at the head of " B " Company, was gloriously in keeping with his life. He was the living embodiment of the happy warrior of whom the poet Wordsworth wrote :—

>Who is the Happy Warrior ? He
>Who, doomed to go in company with Pain
>And Fear and Bloodshed (miserable train !),
>Turns his necessity to glorious gain ;
>In face of these doth exercise a power
>Which is our human nature's highest dower ;
>Controls them and subdues, transmutes, bereaves
>Of their bad influence, and their good receives.

May he rest in peace !

CHAPTER XVII

THE BATTLES OF HAVRINCOURT AND FLESQUIERES

FORTUNATELY for the Battalion, September 3rd was a lovely summer day. Companies marched out of the line in the early morning sunshine, breakfasts were served in the open at Ervillers, and a mail was distributed. Before noon we were away under a hot sun to Behagnies. The ruined village was already occupied by troops at rest. Our bivouac was in a narrow gully, the only available shelter from enemy aircraft. The site had previously been occupied by the enemy, and did not appear to have provided much protection from the air, as the neighbourhood of it was strewn with dead horses which had evidently been caught on the lines by our airmen. A good deal of work was necessary to make the place even healthy, but when this had been done the rest period passed happily. In view of recent battle-casualties, reorganization was the first desideratum. Capt. Wilson and Capt. Woolfe succeeded to the command of " B " and " D " Companies respectively, and when Capt. Bacon returned from leave he took over from 2nd-Lieut. Marshall. The gaps in the ranks were filled by drafts of reinforcements, and 2nd-Lieut. F. Jackson joined and was posted to " B " Company.

An impressive funeral service was held at Gommecourt Cemetery on September 4th, when the bodies of many who had fallen in the Battle of Vraucourt were laid to rest. The Divisional Commander was present, and the Senior Chaplain, the Rev. C. Chevasse, M.C., officiated.

Two training demonstrations of considerable value were given before the Battalion returned to the line. The first was carried out by a platoon of " A " Company under 2nd-Lieut J. Priest, with the object of showing a platoon using a smoke screen in an attack on a machine-gun nest. The smoke was provided by " P " bombs, fired from rifles in the manner of a rifle grenade, and the demonstration proved that the smoke screen could be of considerable value in masking the movements of the attacking troops. The demonstration was watched by all officers and platoon commanders. On another occasion a demonstration of a platoon in the attack working with tanks was watched with keen interest by the whole Battalion. After the demonstration the men were allowed to examine the tanks and ask questions, and the officers and N.C.Os. of the 15th Tank Battalion gave them " joy-rides."

At the conclusion of a week's rest the Battalion was ordered to be prepared to move forward in readiness for an attack by the Division on the village of Havrincourt. For this attack the 185th Brigade was to be in Divisional reserve. The Brigade marched on September 10th to an old German hut camp at Fremicourt, and on the night of the 11th the Battalion moved to bivouacs in the south-west corner of Havrincourt Wood. The Transport went to Ruyulcourt.

Havrincourt Wood lies south and south-east of Havrincourt village, and is separated from it by a wide ravine. The trees are thick and closely planted, and provide excellent cover. The wood is intersected by timber plank roads. Apart from these it is impenetrable. In the centre, at a point where the trees had been felled by the Germans, was a meeting of the roads. The spot was called Clayton Cross. North of Clayton Cross the ground was covered with brushwood, and had several small ridges and folds.

The attack was duly carried out by the 186th and 187th Brigades at 0525 hours on September 12th. Havrincourt was captured and held under heavy enemy bombardment. On the evening of the first day of the attack the line ran roughly along the north-eastern outskirts of the village. Hostile counter-attacks were delivered from a cemetery against the left flank of the 187th Brigade and from " T " Wood. Both of these were repulsed with heavy losses to the enemy.

When the attack commenced, the Battalion, as part of the 185th Brigade, moved forward to a reserve assembly position near Clayton Cross, and remained there throughout daylight on the 12th. There was intermittent shelling, and four casualties were sustained. In the evening companies returned to the south-west corner of the wood for the night. Heavy rain had fallen during the afternoon, and the men had got very wet. They were now under cover and able to get dry.

Orders were received from the Brigadier for a reconnaissance to be made of the ground east and south-east of Havrincourt, with a view to finding jumping-off places for a possible attack on Kimber Trench east of the village. A valuable reconnaissance was made by the four company commanders—Capt. Bacon, Capt. Wilson, Lieut. F. A. R. Smith, and Capt. Woolfe—under very difficult circumstances occasioned by heavy shelling and pouring rain. On the following afternoon the 185th Brigade was ordered to attack the " Green Line," from the Hindenburg Line on the right, including Triangle Wood and Kimber Trench, to the cemetery and the light railway on the left. The assault, which was to take place under a creeping barrage at dawn the next morning, was entrusted to the 2/20th.

Orders were at once issued to companies. " B " Company, on the left of the attack, was to form up east of Havrincourt, and was to capture the northern half of Kimber Trench. " C " Company, in the centre, was to jump off from the eastern edge of Havrincourt Chateau Wood, and was to capture the southern half of Kimber Trench, including " T " Wood. " D " Company, on the right, was to send two platoons across the open to Triangle Wood and a trench called Keating's Lane, and two platoons down two trenches of the Hindenburg Line to clear them. " A " Company was to be in reserve. There was some doubt about the situation on the left opposite the cemetery, and it was expected that " B " Company would have some difficulty there. A company of the 4th Duke of Wellington's (187th Brigade) was to " mop up " the Hindenburg Line in rear of the two platoons of " D " Company on the right.

A subaltern officer from each of the three attacking companies (2nd-Lieut. J. Hirst, M.M.; 2nd-Lieut. G. J. P. Holton, and 2nd-Lieut. S. W. Prestidge) was sent forward without delay to ascertain the exact situation east of Havrincourt, and to locate and mark out jumping-off places.

Battalion Headquarters moved from the south-west corner of the wood at 2030 hours, and was established two hours later under the sunken fence south of the chateau park. Close to this point a light railway ran forward through a cutting towards the German lines, and a forward report centre was established on the right of the railway on the forward slope of a hill at the junction of Kangaroo Avenue and Swing Trench. Here " A " Company had its headquarters during the attack.

In moving forward to their jumping-off positions, companies advanced up the railway line, called at Battalion Headquarters under the sunken fence for final instructions, and passed on through the cutting, guided by their respective reconnoitring officers. These three officers had brought back most valuable information, particularly 2nd-Lieut. Hirst, of " B " Company, who had discovered that the cemetery was not occupied by the enemy, and who had found a most valuable jumping-off place for " B " Company along a stretch of railway line on the left of the Battalion frontage running south-west from the cemetery. It was fortunate that the companies got off in good time, as at about 0315 hours the enemy put down a barrage which became more and more intense along the two railway lines and along the north-eastern edge of the village where the 186th Brigade was dug in.

At 0520 hours our barrage opened, and it was shortly followed by an enemy barrage in No Man's Land. Companies started punctually to time, and the attack was pressed by all three with great gallantry, spirit, and determination. The leading wave in each case moved close up under our barrage; in fact, in all companies we had casualties from our own guns. By 0600 hours all objectives had been taken. The position of "D" Company was uncertain for a time, but a contact 'plane reported that it had seen our flares east of Triangle Wood. A large number of prisoners and thirty machine guns were captured. Some small parties of our men, notably one party of "B" Company under 2nd-Lieut. Hirst, passed their objective and brought back prisoners from beyond it. These parties experienced very accurate enemy sniping fire, and had several casualties.

The enemy bombarded the captured line, the village of Havrincourt, and all forward approaches for the whole of the day, and there were many periods of intense shelling. The average strength of companies was only about fifty, but they maintained their position. 2nd-Lieut. W. J. Rogers, the Intelligence Officer, moved about the line freely, and kept Battalion Headquarters constantly informed of the situation. Communication with the line was maintained with "C" Company in "T" Wood by Lucas lamp from the forward report centre. The flashes were observed by the enemy, and he heavily shelled Kangaroo Avenue and Swing Trench in the early afternoon. In this shelling 2nd-Lieut. Ellen, the Signalling Officer, was unfortunately killed, and heavy casualties were caused to No. 4 Platoon of "A" Company.

At 1400 hours the enemy counter-attacked "B" and "C" Companies, who put up a stout defence

MOVING UP FOR THE ATTACK EAST OF HAVRINCOURT.

with rifles and Lewis guns. Second-Lieut. Rogers was in the line at the time, and rendered valuable assistance. He then hurried back to Battalion Headquarters to report. The artillery put down an S.O.S. barrage, and the counter-attacks fizzled out. A few Germans entered Kimber Trench near "T" Wood, but these were dealt with by a bombing section, under Sergt. J. Crimp, which was hurriedly sent up from "A" Company. This section worked south down the trench, and completely cleared it. There was also some trouble from a party of the enemy which had spent the day in a dug-out near "T" Wood, and which had not been mopped up, but this was speedily dealt with.

In the evening, the Colonel received an encouraging message from the Brigadier in the following terms :—

"Your Battalion has done splendidly to-day, and you have every reason to be proud of it. I am afraid you have had losses, and you are poorer by many good fellows, but it was a great success, and such cannot, unfortunately, be gained without paying the price.

"Your companies must have had a very unpleasant time holding the line, but they can comfort themselves with the knowledge that the Boche had a much worse time. Hope all will go well until the relief to-morrow."

A telegram was received from Divisional Headquarters as follows :—

"Major-General wires many congratulations to all concerned in this morning's clever and successful operation."

After dark, a reorganization of the line was ordered. The 186th Brigade took over the sector held by "D" Company, and one company of the 8th West Yorkshires came under the orders of O.C. 2/20th to be in support. "D" Company was ordered to reinforce "B" on the left ; the company of the West Yorkshires was located south of Havrincourt ; "A" Company was ordered to relieve "C," and "C" Company came into reserve near Boggart's Hole, a big chalk-pit west of Havrincourt

Chateau. The enemy maintained a constant bombardment throughout the night and in the early morning of September 15th, and it was not possible to assume the new dispositions until 0900 hours. Capt. Wilson reported that he was so firmly established that he only required one platoon of " D " Company, and the other three platoons were sent to join " C " in reserve near Boggart's Hole. In addition to " B " Company, Capt. Wilson now had under his command twenty men of the 1/5th Devons who had joined him on the previous afternoon, and one platoon of the 8th West Yorkshires had also taken over a portion of his line.

September 15th was a much quieter day, and the line was held until the Battalion was relieved by the 1st Battalion Northumberland Fusiliers (3rd Division) at 2300 hours. On relief, companies marched back to a new bivouac site in the neighbourhood of Hermies. Unfortunately, " B " Company was heavily shelled as it was leaving the line, and sustained about twelve casualties. In approaching Hermies, companies had to cross the Canal du Nord.

As the Commanding Officer points out in his report after the action, the Battalion had captured all the objectives assigned to it, had held them under heavy bombardment for thirty-six hours, and had handed them over intact. The number of prisoners taken was estimated at 250 ; the booty included 30 machine guns and 2 trench mortars.

Our casualties were :—

Officers :
> Killed, 2 (2nd-Lieut. J. Hirst, M.M., and 2nd-Lieut. H. J. Ellen, M.C.).
> Died of wounds, 2 (2nd-Lieut. G. J. P. Holton and 2nd-Lieut. V. C. W. Sutton).

Other Ranks :
> Killed, 32.
> Died of wounds, 3.
> Wounded, 100.

N.C.Os. wounded :
>Sergt. C. H. White.
>Sergt. E. F. Fuller
>Cpl. J. Smith.
>Cpl. W. Mair.
>Cpl. P. E. May.
>Cpl. T. Wright.
>Cpl. A. J. Jones.
>Lce.-Cpl. R. J. Hill.
>Lce.-Cpl. T. Turnbull.
>Lce.-Cpl. R. Bailey.
>Lce.-Cpl. W. S. Robson.

Capt. Woolfe, Capt. Wilson, and 2nd-Lieut. Rogers received the Military Cross ; Sergt. J. Graney, M.M., a bar to his Military Medal, and the following N.C.Os. and men the Military Medal for gallantry :—

>Lce.-Cpl. J. McRobie.
>Pte. S. G. Hales.
>Pte. W. H. Taylor.
>Cpl. H. Challis.
>Sergt. H. F. Cannon
>Pte. W. J. Tapsfield.
>Pte. G. Critchell.
>Pte. H. G. Roberts.
>Pte. W. Mardell.

The award to Pte. Hales, of the Transport Section, was for conspicuous gallantry and initiative when several transport limbers were caught under heavy enemy artillery fire while bringing rations up to the Battalion through Havrincourt Wood.

While out of the line, the Battalion was inspected by the Brigadier, who afterwards wrote the following letter to the Commanding Officer :—

" When addressing your Battalion to-day, I meant to have specially complimented it on its two attacks on Vaulx Vraucourt and on the trenches east of Havrincourt. They were not by any means simple operations, but, in spite of many difficulties, they were extremely well carried out. I regret with you the loss of gallant soldiers, both officers and men, but the price the Battalion paid for these two successes was a small one, if the importance in each case of the ground gained and the severe defeat inflicted on the enemy are borne in mind. I have not the exact figures, but the 2/20th London Regiment, suffering 300 casualties, captured approximately 500 Germans. This speaks for itself, and no account is taken of the enemy's killed and wounded.

" These achievements are proof that the Battalion is not only well officered and well trained, but that there exists a spirit throughout all ranks which will make any further contact with the enemy unpleasant for the latter."

The Battalion, on coming out of the line, only remained at Hermies for one day, and then went into bivouac west of Vraucourt. Maj.-Gen. R. D. Whigham, who had succeeded Maj.-Gen. Braithwaite in command of the Division at the end of August, came round to visit the Battalion, and paid it many compliments on its work at Vraucourt and Kimber Trench.

On September 17th information was issued from the 6th Corps that further offensive operations would shortly take place on the Third Army front.

The whole of the front system of the Hindenburg Line had been captured, and the new offensive was designed to secure the Hindenburg Support Line. The Canadian Corps was to capture Bourlon and Bourlon Wood and advance on Cambrai. The 17th Corps was to advance against the villages of Graincourt and Cantaing, and the 6th Corps was to capture the Hindenburg Support Line, together with the villages of Ribecourt and Flesquieres, and establish a bridgehead across the Canal de St. Quentin, east of Marcoing. On the right of the Army the 4th Corps was to capture two important features—Highland Ridge and Welsh Ridge.

The first stage of the attack of the 6th Corps was to be carried out by the 3rd Division on the right and the Guards Division on the left. The 62nd and 2nd Divisions were to close up on "Z—1" day, and move forward behind the 3rd and Guards Divisions respectively. All preparations for the new advance were to be completed by September 25th.

The task of the 185th Brigade on the left of the 62nd Division was to follow closely in rear of the 76th Brigade (3rd Division), to pass through that Brigade on the capture of the Brown Line east of Flesquieres, and then to advance on Marcoing with the object of securing the crossings over the Canal de St. Quentin. "Z" day was fixed as September 27th. Capt. Watson went to Brigade Headquarters for duty as a *liaison* officer.

The 2/20th moved to Lebucquiere on the 25th, and to a position of readiness in some trenches between Hermies and the Canal du Nord on the following evening. The canal had no bridge, and the troops had to cross by means of ladders. This meant man-handling Lewis guns and S.A.A., and limbers were brought forward to the position of readiness close up to the canal. As luck would have it, while the guns were being "off-loaded," the enemy began to shell the road. The night was very wet and the road was thick with mud. The Lewis gunners carried on their task of "off-loading" under fire with great coolness. Only two casualties were sustained. One of these, unfortunately, was Sergt. G. F. Hannam, "D" Company's Lewis gun sergeant, who was killed. Two horses were knocked out.

In order to maintain close touch with the Battalion of the 76th Brigade (the 2nd Suffolks) which the 2/20th had to follow, Major Craddock went forward to the 2nd Suffolks' Headquarters at the Slag Heap on the western bank of the canal, and remained with that Battalion throughout the operation.

Our barrage went down at 0520 hours, and the 3rd Division advanced. Half an hour later the Battalion moved forward to the canal in the order of companies—"D," "C," "B," "A," Headquarters. The enemy was shelling heavily with 5.9's, and the descent by ladder into the canal and the ascent on the other side was a slow process; but there were no casualties. Companies got across separately, and moved in artillery formation across the open until they could get into Knightsbridge Trench and London Trench. Eventually, at 0930 hours, they were in their jumping-off places as follows:—

"D" Company in Scull Support.
"A" and "C" Companies in Ravine Avenue.
"B" Company—sunken road east of Flesquieres.

The attack of the 3rd and Guards Divisions had made splendid progress, and had secured Flesquieres, but the advance was held up on the Brown Line east of the village. At 0950 hours the Battalion advanced through the leading troops of the 76th Brigade.

The Brown Line was captured with a rush, and companies pushed on some distance down "Scull Trench" and along the ridge running east of Flesquieres to Premy Support Trench, where it was necessary to halt. The 1st Battalion Grenadier Guards was held up on our left, and "A" Company on the left flank of the Battalion were being heavily enfiladed from Premy Chapel and Nine Wood, on the Guards' front. The advance of the Battalion had been uniformly successful, and 520 prisoners, 6 field guns, 34 machine guns, and 6 trench mortars had been captured. Capt. Bacon and his men could see German guns unlimbering and coming into action at Premy Chapel. Though exposed to this deadly enfilade fire, and in spite of heavy casualties, all companies maintained their advanced and isolated position. Two platoons of "C" Company, under Lieut. Slaughter, went forward and actually reached their final objective—the Blue Line—

but they became heavily engaged, and few survivors got back. One section came across a party of the enemy with machine guns. The enemy raised their hands in token that they surrendered, and when Lieut. Slaughter and his men advanced towards them to take them prisoners, they opened fire with a machine gun. As a result, Lieut. Slaughter was killed, and there were several other casualties. Pte. T. L. M. Haynes then at once worked to a flank and rushed the enemy by himself, capturing the entire party and their two machine guns. For this very gallant and resourceful action he received the D.C.M.

The 8th West Yorkshires passed through at 1030 hours, and advanced along Kaiser Trench. Heavy artillery and machine-gun fire from Premy Chapel and Nine Wood was still being experienced by " A " Company on the left of the 2/20th, and this fire was now also directed on the West Yorkshires, the two leading companies of which were drawn off in that direction, and heavy fighting ensued. The third company reached the outskirts of Marcoing, but their left flank was entirely "in the air," they sustained heavy losses from machine-gun fire and field guns firing over open sights, and the survivors were forced to withdraw. Meanwhile the enemy worked round the left flank by Premy Chapel, and inflicted numerous casualties on the two companies which had advanced in this direction, and all their officers were killed or wounded. The left of " A " Company was thus further imperilled. At 2300 hours a line was securely established along Kaiser Trench in conjunction with the 8th West Yorkshires and one company of the Grenadier Guards, and supported by the 1/5th Devons. The night, which was very wet and cold, passed quietly, and companies were able to reorganize. The casualties sustained during the day were :—

Officers :
Killed, 2 (Lieut. Slaughter and 2nd-Lieut. F. Jackson).
Wounded, 1 (2nd-Lieut. S. Herbert).

Other Ranks :
  Killed, 25.
  Wounded, 58.

Companies remained in Kaiser Trench on the 28th. Battalion Headquarters moved forward from Flesquieres to Premy Support.

The attack was continued by the 186th and 187th Brigades, and the line was carried forward to Marcoing, and bridgehead posts were established over the Canal de St. Quentin. On the 29th Masnières was captured by the 187th Brigade, and the 186th reached Rumilly Support Trench. An attempt to capture the village of Rumilly failed. The village was strongly held.

Soon after mid-day on the 29th, instructions were received that the Battalion, under the Second-in-Command, would move to a position of readiness for an attack on Rumilly. The Commanding Officer went to Brigade Headquarters for orders, but found that these could not be issued until 2100 hours. He waited, and it was then explained that the 2/20th would, if possible, clear Rumilly without artillery support at dawn. The Battalion was not to become seriously involved, and a bombardment was to be asked for if it was thought necessary. After clearing Rumilly, the Battalion was to advance eastwards to Seronvillers, with the 5th Devons on its right and the 2nd Division on its left. The night was very wet and dark as pitch, and the Commanding Officer only got back from the conference at 0100 hours on September 30th, by which time the Battalion was concentrated in some dug-outs in a sunken road west of the Canal de St. Quentin.

At 0330 the Battalion marched in the order " D " Company, " C " Company, " B " Company, " A " Company, Headquarters, to an assembly position on the east bank of the canal, guided by runners sent by the 4th King's Own Yorkshire Light Infantry. Here " A " and " B " Companies and Headquarters, with one troop of

Oxford Hussars who had joined the Battalion, remained under Major Craddock, while " C " and " D " Companies, under the Commanding Officer, advanced along the line of the railway towards Rumilly Support Trench. The enemy was shelling heavily, and one platoon of " D " Company had a direct hit. Eventually, just before dawn, the two companies reached Rumilly Support Trench, which was found to be very shallow and isolated. It was not connected with the trenches on right and left, and it had no communication trench approaching it from the rear.

One company of the 5th West Riding Regiment was in occupation. This company, which had been isolated there since noon the previous day, was split in two by German posts which had worked back into the trench, and the West Ridings were not in touch with anybody east of the Masnières—Rumilly Road. The enemy was very strong and active with machine guns, and it was impossible to move without having casualties. Col. Warde-Aldam sent back a message explaining the situation and asking for more troops and artillery support. Pte. A. Barron, M.M., and Pte. W. Mardell volunteered to take the message. During the morning our artillery twice put a barrage on the village, and about midday small parties of " D " Company, under Capt. Woolfe, reached the village, but could not maintain their position in face of a threatened counter-attack. The enemy also brought out a number of fresh machine guns, one of which opened fire from the rear of Rumilly Trench. The artillery bombarded Rumilly again during the afternoon, but no fresh troops could be got up.

Meanwhile Major Craddock, who had been unable to get into touch with Col. Warde-Aldam, had been informed by the Brigadier that on no account was he to move any part of the two companies with him without orders from Divisional Headquarters. Subsequently, at 1500 hours, he received orders to dispatch one company to occupy a trench system running south-east from the

Masnières—Cambrai road, and later to send one company to occupy Plaisir Trench. Battalion Headquarters was to proceed to the catacombs in Masnières. This move was carried out after dark, when Major Craddock was joined by Col. Warde-Aldam and the Adjutant at the catacombs at Masnières. By this time the whole Battalion was in the line, though scattered—" C " and " D " were under 186th Brigade, " B " under 187th Brigade. At 2300 hours orders were received that the 3rd Division would pass through early on October 1st, and that Battalion Headquarters and " A " Company would withdraw forthwith to a trench west of Marcoing, and that the other three companies would follow at 0500 hours.

It was a terribly wet and dark night, and the streets of Masnières were being heavily shelled. The ground between Masnières and the Canal was pitted with deep shell-holes which had been transformed into huge puddles by the rain. The difficulty of keeping the column " closed up," even though it was only a company, was very great, and many were the splashes which followed the headlong fall of some unoffending, weary officer or man into the mud up to his knees. The move was a slow business, and it was not until 0900 hours that the Battalion was all collected west of Marcoing. " C " and " D " Companies had several casualties in withdrawing. All companies were worn out by the strain of battle, and by their tiring march from Masnières.

From the trench west of Marcoing the Battalion passed straight on to Havrincourt, where dug-outs under the village were occupied as rest-billets.

Casualties on the 30th totalled—Other ranks, killed 8, wounded 13. 2nd-Lieut. Cottis wounded.

The official account concludes :—

" Great praise is due to 2nd-Lieut. W. J. Rogers and 2nd-Lieut. E. B. Jones for preliminary reconnaissance work under heavy fire, and for excellent work in guiding troops in this action."

Capt. Bacon received the Military Cross, and Lce.-Cpl. J. A. Gardner, Pte. A. Bates, and Pte. J. D. Clark the Military Medal. Casualties were comparatively light, though " D " Company suffered heavily, and Sergt. A. W. Swinburne was the only sergeant left in the company after the attack east of Flesquieres.

The wounded included :—

        C.S.M. F. W. Cook.
        C.S.M. E. Mullett.
        Sergt. W. W. Linnell.
        Sergt. S. J. Lucas.
        Sergt. J. Fowler.
        Sergt. J. Tyler, M.M.
        Cpl. P. E. Compton.
        Cpl. H. Leach.
        Cpl. F. W. Page.
        Cpl. C. R. King.
        Cpl. R. McIlwrath.
        Lce.-Cpl. R. W. Cartmell.
        Lce.-Cpl. W. Bailey.
        Lce.-Cpl. W. Wray.
        Lce.-Cpl. P. L. Clarke.

CHAPTER XVIII

FROM SOLESMES TO MAUBEUGE

The Battalion completed two months' service with the 62nd Division on October 9th, 1918. In eight weeks the name of the 2/20th was as firmly established in the West Riding Division as it had been in the 60th. Gen. Whigham marked the occasion by sending the following letter to the Chairman of the London Territorial Force Association :—

"I am sure you will like to hear some news of the 2/20th London Regiment, which recently joined the 62nd (West Riding) Division on transfer from Palestine to France.

"The Battalion has taken an important part in the heavy fighting in which the Division has been engaged since August 25th last, and particularly distinguished itself during the Battle of Havrincourt (September 12th to 15th), and again east of Flesquieres and at Masnières between September 27th and October 1st.

"At Havrincourt, on September 14th, the Battalion was given the task of completing the capture of the position by taking the ' Kimber Trench,' which had caused us considerable annoyance after the main position had been occupied.

"On September 27th the Battalion captured a strong section of the Hindenburg Support Line, and captured many prisoners and some field guns.

"The Battalion came to us from the East with a high reputation for fighting qualities which has been nobly upheld by its prowess during the last six weeks, and I am proud to have it under my command."

The Divisional Commander gave further expression to his high opinion of the Battalion by visiting Havrincourt and heartily congratulating the officers on the battles in which the 2/20th had been engaged.

Naturally, the whole British Army in France was elated at the course which the war had recently assumed. Those who had passed through the awful agonies of the March retreat forgot the past in the bright hopes which had dawned in July. Those who, like ourselves, had but recently stepped into this portion of the fight saw a vision of victory clearer and more unmistakable than any hitherto vouchsafed to those who had borne the burden and the heat of the day on the Western Front, The whole conditions of warfare were undergoing a rapid change. The experience of open fighting which the Battalion had had in the East was of immense value to it now that trench fighting was at an end. The Battles of Sheria and Nebi Samwil were splendid training for Solesmes.

At an hour's notice, companies packed up and moved from Havrincourt on October 8th. 2nd-Lieut. Holmes was in advance as billeting officer, and when the Battalion arrived at the location east of Marcoing mentioned in Brigade orders, we found him disconsolately searching the area for some better accommodation than the disused trench which had been allotted him. There was nothing better, so into the shallow trench we went. It contained a dug-out, but this was already packed with snoring troops. Hardly anyone in the Battalion got any sleep that night, and Cpl. Alvin and his fellow-cooks were dispensing mugs of tea to shivering officers and men long before the time of breakfast. Fortunately, there was no further move until the following morning. Then the whole Brigade crossed the Canal de St. Quentin again (on this occasion there was no discomfiting enemy barrage) and went into cosy billets at Masnières. The village had been badly knocked about, but not half so badly as Havrincourt and the other places through which we had passed in the advance. More than half its houses were standing. They were the best billets we had had for many a long day.

The leading Divisions of the Corps were now forging ahead, and the 62nd had nothing to do but to keep close up, ready to help when needed. The Battalion was kept constantly marching forward. Marching in such conditions was almost a pleasure. Who will forget the march from Masnières to Cattenières over the first stretch of unblighted country we had seen for weeks, or the trek from Cattenières across the Cambrai—Le Cateau Road to Bevillers, or that from Bevillers to Quievy? Here was a change indeed! No longer desolation and ruin, but green fields, whole villages intact, roads entirely free from shell-holes. The villages were still uninhabited, but they were habitable, and that was everything.

From Bevillers, Colonel Warde-Aldam went home for a well-deserved three months' rest. He little knew that when he returned, the Battalion would be comfortably established a dozen miles from Cologne. There was something of bitter injustice about the fact of his leaving the Battalion just when he did. More than any man living, he had a right to lead the 2/20th into Germany; but it was not to be. The writer and a few others knew that the Commanding Officer had worn himself out in the service of the Battalion. Every ounce of mental and physical energy he possessed had been thrown into the past two and a half strenuous years. He badly needed a rest. The Battalion had every reason to congratulate itself that his successor was one who had been at his very right hand throughout the thickest of his task. Major Craddock took command, as he had often done before during short periods, and Col. Warde-Aldam was left to rejoice at home over the proud news which he received in letters of the last fighting days of his Battalion.

Large drafts of officers and men joined at Cattenières

and Bevillers. The officers especially were badly needed. Within a short time two of them—Lieut. A. C. Hardie and Lieut. H. P. Cole—were commanding companies.

The Battalion marched to Quievy on the evening of October 19th in preparation for an attack on Solesmes. Zero hour was to be 0200 hours on the 20th. The task of the Division was to capture the town of Solesmes and the high ground one mile east of it, overlooking the village of Romeries. La Selle River, which runs through the adjoining village of St. Python, north-east of Solesmes, presented a formidable obstacle. The river is about 20 feet wide and from 4 to 6 feet deep. The banks in many places reach a height of 10 feet above the water level. With the exception of the ford at St. Python, the bed of the stream is muddy and the banks steep and slippery. All bridges had been destroyed by the enemy.

Both Solesmes and St. Python were full of French civilians, and this put any idea of artillery bombardment of the villages out of the question. It was decided not to attack Solesmes directly from the west, but to pass troops across the river north and south of it, and to capture it by envelopment. This enveloping movement, which was to constitute the first phase of the operation, was entrusted to the 186th Brigade. It was successfully accomplished. The 5th Duke of Wellington's worked through St. Python round the northern outskirts of Solesmes. The 2/4th Hampshires and the 2/4th York and Lancasters skirted its southern limits. After completing their respective encircling movements, these two battalions established a series of posts on the eastern side of the village, and the second phase of the operation, which consisted of an attack by the 2/20th to carry the line forward to the high ground overlooking Romeries, was then embarked upon. The encirclement round the northern flank was strongly opposed by the enemy from Le Pigeon Blanc, a crossroad some 600 yards due north of Solesmes, which commanded the whole of the northern entrances to the town. The Guards attacked on the left of the Division simultaneously with the first phase.

The task of the 2/20th was to move through St. Python and the streets in the northern part of Solesmes, and to pass through the posts of the 186th Brigade. The Battalion's objective was a clearly defined ridge east of Le Pigeon Blanc commanding Romeries. The right flank was secured by the 8th West Yorkshires. The 1/5th Devons were in Brigade reserve west of the railway siding in St. Python.

The 2/20th marched out of Bevillers at 2130 hours on October 19th, having dumped packs. Rain was falling heavily before the column reached Quievy, where billets were occupied for six and a half hours and a hot meal was served. The last battalion of the 186th Brigade had just cleared the village as the head of the column marched in. There was time for a short sleep before the men lined up at the cookers, and at 0400 hours the Battalion was on the road again and was moving forward to its position of assembly along the Solesmes—Valenciennes Road. The enemy was shelling the railway embankment on the outskirts of St. Python, and here Lewis guns, S.A.A., and tools were off-loaded and man-handled forward. St. Python itself was being harassed, but all companies were safely across the river by 0620 without casualties. Battalion Headquarters remained west of the river in a house which adjoined the Headquarters of the 5th Duke of Wellington's (Lieut.-Col. J. Walker, D.S.O.). The crossing of the river was effected by a narrow plank bridge which had been thrown across by the R.Es. This bridge was a source of difficulty to the stretcher-bearers during the battle when bringing the wounded back to the R.A.P.

Col. Walker was able to inform Major Craddock, when he arrived in St. Python with the Battalion, that the 186th Brigade had secured all its objectives. The 2/20th was immediately committed to the advance.

THE SUNKEN ROAD, SOLESMES—DIGGING IN.

By 0830 hours all companies had left their jumping-off positions. Major Craddock and 2nd-Lieut. Holmes were there to see them start.

The attack was a complete success. The line was heavily shelled as it advanced, and the Germans put down a barrage when the companies reached the high ground east of Romeries. In addition to capturing its objective, the Battalion secured 2 field guns, 2 machine guns, 1 trench mortar, and 30 prisoners. As soon as the objective was in their hands, companies commenced to dig in and consolidate. " C " Company (Capt. Hunt) was on the right, with its flank on the railway embankment north-east of Solesmes. " B " Company (Capt. Wilson) was occupying a sunken road west of the Romeries—Solesmes Road in touch with " C " Company's left, and " A " Company (2nd-Lieut. T. E. Davies) was on " B " Company's left and in the same sunken road. " D " Company (Capt. Woolfe) dug in in support at a distance of about 700 yards behind " A." Carrier pigeons were sent out with " B " and " C " Companies at the outset of the attack. These birds proved invaluable in the case of " C " Company. The first message received from Capt. Hunt, advising Headquarters that he had reached his objective, came by pigeon through Corps Headquarters. " B " Company had a telephone line, but unfortunately, owing to lack of cable, this could not be carried farther than Crucifix Corner, on the outskirts of Solesmes. The flanks of the Battalion were safe. " A " Company was in touch with the Guards on the left, and there was a post of the 8th West Yorkshires on the railway embankment close to " C " Company's Headquarters.

A Vickers gun section had been allotted to the Battalion, with orders to take up positions behind the front line when the objective had been gained, and to assist in the consolidation. During the morning information was received from casualties that the section had met with severe machine-gun fire, and that a number of the personnel had become casualties. It subsequently became known that the guns had not got farther than the Crucifix.

Throughout the morning and afternoon there was very heavy shelling on the line which was being consolidated. Communication was rendered difficult. Telephone messages had to be sent forward from the Crucifix, and a great strain was thrown upon the runners and signallers. Both did much excellent work.

Early in the afternoon "B" Company's position was heavily barraged. The shelling was repeated at intervals, and it soon became equally heavy on all parts of the front line and on "D" Company's support position. After a time the enemy was seen to be advancing from Romeries in extended order against "A" and "B" Companies. The artillery S.O.S. was sent up, and the men got to work with rifles and Lewis guns. The attack was completely broken up, and the enemy retired in disorder, having sustained many casualties. There was intermittent shelling until dusk, but none after dark.

During the night "B" Company sent forward a platoon to occupy an orchard, and "C" Company established a post in a small building about 100 yards in advance of the sunken road, and commanding the road leading into Romeries. One machine gun and a wounded German were found in the building. The night passed without other incident save for heavy shelling on Battalion Headquarters and the streets of Solesmes. At dawn, as though to forestall any renewal of our advance, the enemy put down his barrage. This was particularly heavy along the sunken road, on the cross-roads at Le Pigeon Blanc, and the cross-roads by the Crucifix. Patrols had been sent forward frequently through the night, and touch had been maintained with the enemy. Soon after daylight it became apparent that the enemy had moved his field guns back, but the village of Romeries was still occupied, and a reconnaissance along the road leading into the village drew fire at 30 yards' range from a post in a cemetery on the western side of the road. It appeared that the enemy was dribbling forward into the cemetery from Romeries. Later in the morning our artillery harassed the cemetery, but trouble was experienced from this point all day. In addition, Capt. Hunt reported that enemy snipers were established on some high ground on his right flank, and were enfilading his position and causing casualties. There was also an enemy machine gun on the western outskirts of the orchard which was causing trouble to " B " Company's forward platoon.

Communication between Battalion Headquarters and the line was improved during the morning. By the aid of salvaged enemy wire, the telephone was carried forward from Crucifix Corner to " D " Company's Headquarters, and later, by wire specially issued from Brigade, to " B " Company's Headquarters in the line. A second counter-attack was attempted by the enemy during the afternoon, but this was completely broken up before it reached our lines. In the afternoon Battalion Headquarters moved forward to a house in Solesmes.

During the night October 21st-22nd companies sent out frequent patrols. One from " B " Company located a party of the enemy digging in along a hedge about 40 yards in front of the orchard. The patrol was fired on when within 20 yards of the enemy. Retaliation took the form of rifle grenades fired into the middle of the enemy party. At dawn this place was reported clear of the enemy. Hostile aeroplanes, flying at a very low height, came over our lines soon after daybreak and peppered the men in the sunken road. Some of them also, by dropping Véry lights on to the platoon of " B " Company in the orchard, directed very heavy hostile artillery fire on to the orchard and its occupants. As the men scattered, the 'planes followed them and directed fire afresh on to their new positions. Six men were almost completely buried, and three were killed outright. 2nd-Lieut. H. W. Dillingham, the officer in charge, temporarily withdrew the platoon to the sunken road, where there was more cover, and when the enemy aeroplanes left at 0640 hours advanced again with his platoon and re-established the line in the orchard. Throughout the day constant forward movement of the enemy was reported. He was obviously trickling back to his machine gun and snipers' positions.

At 1400 hours a warning order was received that the 3rd Division would attack through our line early on the following morning. Orders followed for the Battalion to withdraw after the 3rd Division had passed through, and proceed to billets at Quievy. The outpost line was to be withdrawn at 0220 hours (zero—1 hour) in order to enable the preliminary barrage to be brought down on the line of the orchard. Commencing before dark and continuing throughout the night, hostile shelling round Le Pigeon Blanc, at Crucifix Cross-roads, on the artillery batteries south of Solesmes, and on Solesmes itself round Battalion Headquarters, was very heavy. The front line escaped. At 0030 hours Battalion Headquarters received an urgent message by telephone from " B " Company that the enemy was advancing on the orchard in strength, and was encircling the platoon in occupation there. The officer in charge withdrew, so that artillery fire might be directed on the orchard. Capt. Wilson was of the opinion that the enemy's advance was in strength, so the Commanding Officer, knowing that there was still three hours before zero, ordered " B " Company to put up the " S.O.S." The enemy retaliated at once with a heavy barrage on all approaches to the front line. A considerable quantity of gas shells was sent over in this retaliation, which was exceedingly awkward in view of the assembling of the troops of the 3rd Division just at that time. 2nd-Lieut. Holmes, the Intelligence Officer, after investigating the situation, reported at 0130 hours that the line was all quiet, and that the platoon of " B " Company was re-established in the orchard. The enemy's artillery fire continued to be very heavy, and the troops of the 3rd Division sustained casualties. Their jumping-off positions had been taped out in the thickest of the enemy barrage by 2nd-Lieut. Holmes. At zero— 1 hour, the attacking troops having arrived in position, the companies of the 2/20th commenced to withdraw. The move was carried out under exceptional difficulties owing to the approaches being heavily barraged by hostile artillery, but by 0830 hours on the 23rd instant all companies had got back to Quievy. The billeting arrangements had had to be made in a great hurry, but, thanks to Lieut. Hardie, the company quartermaster-sergeants and the cooks, the Battalion had nothing to do but eat a hearty breakfast before it turned in for much-needed sleep.

The gallantry list for the three days' fighting was a long one. The advance, the two enemy counter-attacks, and the heavy shelling had made severe demands, but the men, as usual, had come out of the battle with flying colours. Capt. Hunt was awarded the Military Cross. The following N.C.Os. and men received the Military Medal :—

Sergt. C. Dickens.
Lce.-Sergt. C. R. Beckley.
Cpl. C. Smith.
Cpl. T. Smith.
Lce.-Cpl. W. White.
Pte. S. Timms.
Pte. H. J. Meade.
Pte. P. Ross.
Pte. T. R. Marrison.
Sergt. J. Eames.
Cpl. W. H. Feaver.
Cpl. A. C. Crate.
Cpl. H. J. Hadlow.
Lce.-Cpl. G. J. Shaw.
Pte. B. J. Owen.
Pte. C. Allsopp.
Pte. J. T. Barrett.

It is noteworthy that no less than three of the Military Medallists belonged to the Battalion Signal Section and two were company runners.

Casualties, considering the fierceness of the battle, were comparatively light, but the list contained the names of many whom their companies could ill afford to lose. The N.C.Os. wounded were :—

> Sergt. J. B. Lancashire.
> Sergt. S. Denny.
> Cpl. C. Smith.
> Cpl. W. Stephenson.
> Lce.-Cpl. J. C. Brown.
> Lce.-Cpl. A. Young.
> Lce.-Cpl. J. Forbes.
> Sergt. H. Cannon, M.M.
> Cpl. L. F. Gallimore.
> Cpl. G. C. Dawson.
> Cpl. F. C. Aldrich.
> Lce.-Cpl. W. Oakley.
> Lce.-Cpl. W. Mardell, M.M.
> Lce.-Cpl. G. H. Hudson.

Total casualties were :—

Other Ranks—Killed	19
Died of wounds	3
Wounded	87

The Battalion was thoroughly comfortable at Quievy. The whole Brigade was billeted in, or near, the village, and this induced the "Pelicans" to commandeer the local cinema theatre and to give nightly performances there. It was one of the very few opportunities the Battalion ever had of seeing the Divisional Concert Party, and the men were not slow to take advantage of it. Somehow or another the 185th Brigade always came off rather badly in the matter of that concert party. There was plenty of football, and the Battalion team increased its reputation at the expense of several opponents. The "Rugger" side gained a notable victory over the Devons by 12 points to 6. A knockout " Soccer " competition for specialist sections created a large amount of interest, and provided games for those not sufficiently expert for the Battalion side. Best of all, there was some excellent football in inter-company games. " A " Company, in particular, had a very strong side, and Pte. J. Palmer (Capt. Bacon's servant) and Pte. Vines were a tower of strength to the company team, as they were to the Battalion XI. One of the most successful of the sergeants' dinners took place in a barn in Quievy on October 30th. The building was a barn pure and simple, a most unsatisfactory place, one would imagine, for a dinner for sixty people, though it made an admirable store for Capt. Lovell's stock of equipment, rum, bread, and bootlaces, and all the other hundred and one properties of the Quartermaster's department. These were all spirited away by Sergt. Bose and his hard-working storemen during the afternoon. In the evening the barn was furnished with well-lit and well-spread tables, and ample viands, both solid and liquid. At the smoking concert Lord Hampden announced that he hoped at a future date to invite all the warrant officers and sergeants of the Brigade to dine together. The dinner took place two months later in Germany.

The training of Lewis gunners, signallers, scouts, and stretcher-bearers received special attention at Quievy. The casualties in these sections, particularly the Lewis gun sections, had been heavy, very largely as a result of the gallantry and devotion to duty of the N.C.Os. and men composing them. The difficulty of replacing specialists called for special measures during training periods, but steady drill was not neglected. It never was in the 2/20th. Both Col. Warde-Aldam and Col. Craddock emphasized it as the most important part of the discipline-training. At Quievy there were several ceremonial parades. On one of them Gen. Whigham presented medal-ribbons to certain N.C.Os. and men.

Capt. Hunt went to Brigade Headquarters for duty after the battle of Solesmes. Some changes occurred among the officers at Battalion Headquarters. 2nd-Lieut. B. P. O'Dowd, who was acting as Transport Officer, proceeded home on leave. Lieut. Blundell handed back the duties of Quartermaster to Capt. Lovell, and 2nd-Lieut. Rogers, whose work as Intelligence Officer had been absolutely invaluable, succeeded to the charge of the Transport Section. 2nd-Lieut. Holmes was now once again Intelligence Officer. A new Church of England chaplain, the Rev. H. C. Caswall, had joined before Solesmes, and was already exceedingly popular with all ranks. The long-deserved and long-delayed promotion of Capt. Watson to Major came through on October 24th, and later Major Craddock at last received promotion to Lieut.-Colonel after having discharged the duties of the rank for many months.

The inevitable move from Quievy took place in the afternoon of November 2nd. In this, the last, stage of the great advance, the 6th Corps was directed on Maubeuge. The 62nd Division was placed on the right, and the Guards Division on the left.

Prior to taking over the line the 2/20th moved to billets in Romeries, and marched on to Escarmain on the following (Sunday) evening. At 0600 hours on Monday, November 4th, the whole of the 185th Brigade was concentrated in reserve in an area south of Ruesnes. At 0530 the 186th and 187th Brigades launched their assault, and by the early afternoon had captured all objectives, including the village of Frasnoy. A line was consolidated west of Gommegnies.

Just before noon Col. Craddock received verbal orders from the Brigadier for the Battalion to move forward in order that it might be ready to advance to the " red line " which was to be the jumping-off place for an attack by the Battalion on the high ground east of Gommegnies. Three hours later the Battalion was established in a sunken road west of Frasnoy. From here a mounted party, consisting of the Commanding Officer, Capt. Bacon, Capt. Wilson, Lieut. Blundell, and the Adjutant, went forward to reconnoitre the route to Gommegnies, and to find suitable jumping-off places on the " red line." The road into Frasnoy was being continually harassed by an enemy battery which had direct observation, and was enfilading Frasnoy from some high ground north of the village. The reconnoitring party was quickly spotted, and the enemy " bracketed " the road. Capt. Wilson was hit, and in remaining behind to look after him until stretcher-bearers could be obtained, Lieut. Blundell was also wounded. Both horses were hit. Lieut. Blundell, with great gallantry, remained to see Capt. Wilson carried off on a stretcher, and then managed to get back to the Battalion in the sunken road, where he arrived in an exhausted condition, leading his horse. Meanwhile the reconnaissance was carried out. It was discovered that the "red line" was not yet completely captured, but that an advance was to be made by the 186th Brigade immediately after dark, and it was hoped that this would secure it. Suitable jumping-off places were selected close up to the " red line." The party returned to the Battalion to find that the sunken road had been heavily shelled in their absence, and companies had sustained casualties. At 1845 hours definite orders were received that the Battalion would attack Gommegnies and the high ground east of it, at 0600 hours on the following morning.

This attack was carried out entirely according to plan. Companies moved from the sunken road at 0330 hours, and were lined up in their jumping-off positions two hours later. By 0700 hours the Battalion was firmly established on its objective. " B " Company, which had been taken over at short notice by Lieut. A. C. Hardie on Capt. Wilson being wounded, was on the left. " C " Company (Lieut. H. P. Cole) was on the right. These two companies " mopped up " the streets and buildings of Gommegnies, and established a series of posts on the eastern limits of the village. " D " Company (Lieut. Pritchard) and " A " Company (Capt. Bacon) followed at a distance of 500 yards, and passed through the leading companies when the latter reached their objectives. " A " and " D " Companies then dug in on the high ground east of Gommegnies, " C " Company was ordered to consolidate a support position across the whole Battalion frontage, and " B " Company was withdrawn to a large barn in Gommegnies in Battalion reserve. Headquarters moved forward from Frasnoy to Gommegnies, and later from Gommegnies to La Cavee.

Early in the afternoon the 5th King's Own Yorkshire Light Infantry (Lieut.-Col. F. H. Peter, D.S.O., M.C.) advanced through the Battalion across the north-western corner of the Foret de Mormal, which at that point had been almost cleared of timber by the Germans, towards Le Trèchon. The Battalion was ordered to advance in support of the King's Own Yorkshire Light Infantry at a distance of 1,000 yards.

Col. Peter's Battalion met with severe resistance from enemy machine guns in the village, and was momentarily held up. The 2/20th immediately commenced to dig in in support. The rain, which had been falling for eight hours continuously, showed no signs of ceasing. The men were soaked, the ploughed ground on which the line had to be dug was in places little better than a morass, the night was jet black, and shells fell at frequent intervals right in the middle of the diggers and caused casualties. It was an unpleasant task, and apparently a thankless one, but it had to be done. In the event of the enemy counter-attacking, the trenches would have been invaluable. As it proved, they were not needed.

In the evening, while the Battalion was digging in, a conference of Commanding Officers was held at Brigade Headquarters, and Col. Craddock received orders for the 2/20th to continue the advance at dawn to the line of a road running north and south through the village of Mecquignies.

This attack was launched at 0600 hours, when " C " and " D " Companies advanced through Le Trèchon and Bavisiaux, and, going due east, reached the first objective, a sunken road south of Mecquignies. " A " and " B " Companies then moved through them, and occupied a line extending south-east from the crossroads south of Mecquignies Church. Battalion Headquarters moved forward to Bavisiaux, where an unlucky shell put out of action all the Headquarters officers' servants. Pte. A. H. Harrington, of the Intelligence Section, who happened to be among the party, was killed. Lce.-Cpl. A. G. Gibbons, the Mess Corporal, was wounded, as also were Pte. D. J. Mannington, the Mess Cook, Pte. E. E. Smith (the driver of the mess-cart), and the following officers' servants :—Pte. W. V. Adams, Pte. A. Bertram, Pte. F. Staplehurst, Pte. E. H. Ward. The mess-cart was badly damaged, and the horse was killed.

All companies were firmly established on their objectives by 1000 hours. Soon, however, it became apparent that the Guards Division on the left of " A " Company was held up by enemy machine guns from some high ground in the neighbourhood of Mecquignies Chateau. This difficulty had been anticipated by Col. Craddock. Capt. Bacon was well prepared for it, and took all necessary steps to protect his left flank. " B " Company, the left support company, was behind " A," and Lieut. Hardie was ordered so to dispose his command as to give the maximum amount of support to " A " Company in front. One section of machine guns and a trench mortar were placed at Capt. Bacon's disposal.

The enemy was putting up a stiff resistance opposite the Guards. Several British aeroplanes were up, and drew heavy rifle and machine-gun fire from the enemy's line. One pilot hastily scribbled the following message in red chalk on the back of a blank Cox's cheque :—

"Enemy m.g. 50 yds. right of chateau,"

and dropped it on Capt. Bacon's position. The artillery were immediately informed, the machine gun was knocked out, and after other guns had been similarly dealt with by "A" Company's Lewis guns and by the Vickers guns, the Guards were able to come up. Writing afterwards of the gallant conduct of the British airmen on this occasion, Capt. Bacon says :—

"There were four or six flying overhead. I had flares burnt, and one of the airmen seeing these, circled down until he was only 50 feet from the ground, and flew up and down my position. The 'planes then flew over to the left flank, and, flying very low, continually harassed the enemy with machine-gun fire. From time to time the airmen flew very low over my line, and pointed in the direction of enemy positions where rifle fire was most needed. The work of the airmen that morning was splendid, and their *liaison* with the infantry very valuable."

The Guards secured the chateau about noon, and pushed on to the high ground east of it. The Battalion had orders to remain in its present position.

This day, November 6th, was the last day spent by the Battalion in the line. Companies had an uncomfortable time under almost continuous enemy shelling, and Battalion Headquarters in Bavisiaux was also intermittently harassed. The weather was still very wet and cold, and continued so throughout the night, which passed without incident save for a certain amount of artillery and machine-gun fire on both sides. At 1100 hours on the 7th the 187th Brigade continued the advance, and the 2/20th withdrew to billets in Bavisiaux, and remained there under orders to be ready to move at two hours' notice. Next morning we were on the march to La Tomblaine, where the whole Brigade was concentrated in Divisional reserve, and on November 10th all three battalions marched to Mon Plaisir, a south-western suburb of Maubeuge, where they received a great welcome from the inhabitants. A touching incident marked the arrival in billets. An old lady, who had twice been imprisoned by the Germans for refusing to obey them, rushed into the street on seeing the Battalion approaching, and besought the Adjutant to take her house as a billet for the Colonel. Her request was acceded to, and Headquarters Officers' Mess was established in the parlour. The old lady then took the Assistant Adjutant into the garden and told him to dig. Four bottles of champagne which had been hidden from the Germans for four years were dug out, and a solemn ceremony ensued when the lady herself and her two daughters and all the Headquarter officers toasted first Belgium, then England. The old lady was overjoyed, and informed the Colonel, with tears in her eyes, that she had buried the bottles when the Germans arrived in 1914, in full assurance that one day her liberators would arrive. " That day," she said, " is to-day."

With this incident the war history of the 2/20th may be said to close. On the following morning at 10 o'clock the historic news of the Armistice was received in a wire from Brigade Headquarters.

The news was naturally received with joy, but the termination of hostilities came so suddenly in the end that the majority of those most intimately concerned were dazed and unable to realize all that it meant. Fighting and hardships had become so integral a part of our life that it seemed hard to imagine life without them. At first there was a very general feeling in the Battalion that the Armistice meant nothing more than a temporary cease fire, and that fighting would presently recommence. But this feeling was altogether dispelled by Gen. Whigham's address to all available officers of the Division in the theatre at Sous le Bois at noon on

Armistice Day. The General was able to say that a number of Divisions would be required to go forward and occupy Germany, and that the 62nd might very probably be one of these. In the Battalion November 11th was not marked by any great festivities. Almost as soon as we knew that the Armistice was signed, we found ourselves preparing for the new responsibilities of the march to Germany, and the preparations absorbed all our attention.

Between the time of leaving Romeries on November 3rd and the declaration of the Armistice on the 11th the Battalion captured 30 machine guns and sustained the following casualties :—

    Officers : Wounded, 2 (Capt. Wilson and Lieut. Blundell).
    Other Ranks : Killed, 5.
                  Wounded, 42.

Among the wounded were :—

        Lce.-Sergt. K. W. Crimp.
        Lce.-Sergt. W J. Marshman.
        Cpl. E. Semaine.
        Lce.-Cpl. F. A. Denize.
        Lce.-Cpl. F. Longley.

The total casualties of the Battalion during its whole period of two years four months and eighteen days of active service, up to the Armistice, were :—

	Officers.	Other Ranks.
Killed	14	241
Died of wounds	3	72
Died of disease	1	15
Accidentally killed	—	3
Wounded	31	982

    *   *   *   *

Five days was all too short a time to prepare for the long trek into Germany. All equipment and clothing had to be overhauled, and special attention paid to the serviceability of boots. The transport—both animals and vehicles—had to be carefully inspected, and all missing spare parts of cookers and wagons obtained from Ordnance. Men who were not thoroughly fit had to be weeded out, and either evacuated to hospital or left behind at Maubeuge. This last measure proved to be a very wise one. The march to Germany was the most physically exacting task that the Battalion ever undertook. The fact that those who were not fit enough to undertake it were left behind meant that no one fell out on the march, and the Battalion, once it started, was not impeded or delayed.

The Division set out from Maubeuge on November 16th, the 185th Brigade leading. The 2/20th, which was one of only two London Battalions to form part of the Army of Occupation on the Rhine, was in the vanguard, and shared with the 9th Durham Light Infantry (pioneers) and three field companies of Royal Engineers the honour of forming the advance guard to the Division. The daily marches were not as a rule longer than 10 miles. The maximum length was 16 miles; the average was much less. Roads had to be picketed, and each night one company had to sleep with boots on as in-lying piquet. Orders for a move at 0800 hours were frequently not received until well after midnight, and often when the Battalion turned in there was uncertainty about the next day's arrangements. Sometimes, when billets were poor, companies had to be scattered over a wide area, and this meant a very early Réveillé for some of them to reach the starting-point punctually. The weather throughout was cold and often wet.

In spite of all its uncomfortable features, however, the trek was infinitely worth while. Every Belgian village through which we passed was decorated with flags and triumphal arches. The inhabitants turned out *en masse* to cheer and show their gratitude in all sorts of practical ways. In some places, notably at Nalinnes and Ham-sur-Heure, the village band, in top-hats and Sunday clothes, came out to meet the column and lead it in a triumphal march to the Mairie. Col. Craddock and several of the officers would then go in and take wine with the Maire and the councillors, while the men settled into the best quarters that the village afforded. The Battalion was always sorry to have to move on.

Conditions of space prevent any more detailed account of the march into Germany. A whole volume—and it could be a very amusing and a very interesting one—could be written on the subject. Some account must, however, be given of the crossing of the frontier.

The villages of Belgium in which the Battalion was billeted were :—Colloret, Ragnies, Nalinnes, Ham-sur-Heure, Villers Poteries, St. Gerard, Evrehailles, Ciney, Leignon, Pessoux, Mean, My, Harre, and Arbrefontaine. On December 14th, when the Battalion was in the last-named village, the G.S.O.1. of the Division (Col. Gossett) visited the Battalion, and told Col. Craddock that the 2/20th would lead the Division across the frontier into Germany the next day at noon. The following account of the crossing of the little village of Poteau was sent home by one of the officers :—

" We were the Battalion chosen to lead the Division into Germany. We have looked upon it from every point of view, and even I, whom Tosher (the Adjutant) calls the old pessimist, can find no other reason for our leading than that we are, as we always have been, the best of the bunch. As you know, we are the junior Battalion of our Brigade. We have the junior C.O. (Col. Craddock), and we were the farthest from the frontier. However, we received orders last night that we were to lead, and at the same time we received a pretty little diagram of the procession. . . . We marched from Arbrefontaine through Vielsalm (where the rest of the Brigade was billeted) to within half a mile of the frontier. Here we halted, and the procession formed up. Leading was a section of ' A ' Company, then at suitable distances the following :—

"Three sections 'A' Company.
Remainder of 'A' Company (under Capt. Bacon).
Divisional Band.
G.O.C.'s flag-bearer.
The G.O.C. himself (with two A.D.Cs.).
Col. Lee (A.A. and Q.M.G.).
Col. Gossett (G.S.O.1).
Major Bissett (G.S.O.2).
Major Saunders (D.A.A.G.).
Lieut. Robins (Divisional Intelligence Officer).
Major Caulfield (D.A.Q.M.G.).
Lord Hampden (with Capt. Kreyer and Capt. Harland).
The C.O. and Adjutant.
'D' Company (Capt. Woolfe).
'C' Company (Capt. Hunt).
'B' Company (Lieut. Hardie).
The Battalion Transport.

"The original order was that bayonets were to be fixed, but this was washed out for some reason unknown to me. We marched thus until we had crossed the frontier, which was marked by two black-and-white posts, also a sentry-box with 'Gott mit uns' painted on it over the top of the German crest. The head of the procession passed the frontier post at mid-day. The G.O.C. then fell out and took the salute, while we marched past to the tune of the regimental march."

Limitations of space again forbid any detailed account of the march from Recht, just across the frontier, to Sinzenich, 12 miles south-west of Cologne. As in Belgium, the supply service was very difficult during this period of the trek, and rations for men and horses were very short. The inhabitants were hardly gushing in their welcome, but they were always extremely polite, and often went out of their way to be kind. All business was done through the Burgomaster of each village. The wealth of the country in livestock, corn, and vegetables was immediately noticeable in contrast to the sterility of Belgium, and Col. Craddock was quick to take advantage of the fact. Fresh vegetables, chickens, and eggs were in plentiful supply, a fair price being paid to the Burgomasters for them. A policy of sternness combined with justice soon produced a clear understanding on the part of the Germans.

Recht, Heppenbach, Murringen, Blumenthal, and Glehn were occupied in turn. The Battalion marched into Sinzenich on Christmas Eve, having done a 15-mile march, as usual, without a man falling out.

The Adjutant had gone to Brigade Headquarters as acting Staff Captain five days previously. Lieut. F. D. Parker took over the Adjutancy, and retained it without a break until the cadre was disbanded in July, 1919. Lieut. J. S. Pritchard, M.C., became Battalion Education Officer, and 2nd-Lieut. Holmes was placed in charge of the arrangements for demobilization. Lieut. A. G. Gilbert was now Quartermaster.

Col. Warde-Aldam returned in the middle of January to pilot the Battalion through its last months, and to remain with it until the last N.C.O. and man were demobilized. On July 13th, 1919, the date on which the cadre was disbanded, the 2/20th Battalion ceased to exist, save as a glorious memory.

CHAPTER XIX

GERMANY

WE have reached the final stages of our journey with the Battalion, and little now remains to be written. It is an accepted principle among authors and dramatists that a novel or a play should end on a note of happiness. The play which tells the story of the 2/20th Battalion shall be no exception. When the curtain falls for the last time it shall be on the happiest scene of the story, and much of the tragedy of the earlier scenes shall be forgotten in a last burst of happiness and enjoyment. The period of nine weeks spent at Sinzenich was undoubtedly the plum of the war for those concerned. It was the " rare and refreshing fruit " of four years' strain and toil, and the fruit was the sweeter for all the labour and sacrifice which had been expended on the planting and cultivation of the tree of victory.

For the Army as a whole the termination of hostilities on November 11th entirely changed everything, but for the battalions which were ordered to make hurried preparations to march on into Germany the change was not so immediate. The Army of Occupation saw little evidence of any change at all until units found themselves at the end of the year comfortably settled in excellent billets round Cologne. The march had been so arduous, and had been carried out under such difficulties of ration and boot supply, and often of suitable billet accommodation, that the conditions more closely resembled those of active service than of peace-time soldiering. To be more or less permanently established in a comfortable little German village, with no arduous military duties to perform, and with no responsibilities except those of keeping physically fit and waiting patiently for demobilization, was as pleasant as it was novel.

From the moment when the billeting party, under Major Watson, arrived, to be followed at midday on Christmas Eve by the rest of the Battalion, no trouble was spared to make the stay in Sinzenich as enjoyable as possible. Col. Craddock was very strong on this point, and he was well backed up by Col. Warde-Aldam, who towards the end of January returned from leave and took over temporary command of the Brigade from Col. England, Lord Hampden being on leave.

Sinzenich was none too large to accommodate so strong a unit as the 2/20th had become as a result of the several drafts which had been received since the Armistice, but at a pinch there was room for everybody; and, moreover, the village possessed a dancing-hall and a football ground, rare acquisitions which were worth a great deal of sacrifice in the way of personal billet accommodation. The 5th Devonshire Regiment at Schwerfen, and the 8th West Yorkshire Regiment at Kommern, were much less fortunate, though Brigade Headquarters in the chateau at Eicks had the best football ground in the neighbourhood. Sinzenich lies on the flat plain of the Rhine Valley. There is nothing to be said about the surrounding country except that it is monotonous, and that almost every inch was cultivated. The village itself, which consists of a wide main street with outlying houses and buildings, is compact, well kept, and clean, and has some picturesque corners. The attitude of the villagers was at first suspicious; it soon became friendly. Doubtless, like all their countrymen in the British occupied zone, they were at a loss to reconcile the British soldier in the flesh with all that they had been told about him. They were astounded to see the terms on which the officer stood with his men, to see officers walking through the village street in football clothes; and they could not believe their eyes when they saw the terrible British " Tommy " playing happily with the children or helping the housewife in the billet. There were no riots, no looting incidents, no violence of any sort—just a cheery army of smart, well-disciplined troops, who did their duty cheerfully, lived on the very best terms with each other, and regarded no honest man as their enemy. Perhaps the women at least thought sometimes of what would have happened to the people of England if the war had placed a German army of occupation in London, instead of a British army of occupation in Cologne. Some of *us* were proud to think of things in that light, anyway.

On the arrival of the Battalion in the Sinzenich area there were many things needed in the way of crockery, cutlery, tables, chairs, and saucepans, to make life comfortable. These were all obtained by requisition—a most convenient arrangement, which, besides furniture, was capable of providing briquettes for fuel, chickens and fresh eggs. All requisitioning was done officially on the Burgomaster, who personally received Col. Craddock's demands and was responsible for supplying them. Practically everything requisitioned was produced, though in some cases articles had to be obtained from other parts of the *kreis*. All food supplied on requisition was duly paid for.

Though military training rather took a back seat, it was by no means neglected. Battalion parades were frequent, and steady drill, musketry, and physical training all had their share of attention; and there was always a company or a battalion route march down on the week's programme. A great deal of time was spent on the Army education scheme, which enabled men to prepare themselves for their approaching return to civil life. Not the least pleasant feature of the scheme was a series of popular lectures. One of these, given by Major Lane-Fox, of the Scots Guards, in the village hall, will not soon be forgotten by those who heard it. The lecturer spoke for two hours and a half on his experiences as a prisoner-of-war in Germany, and he kept his audience spellbound throughout the time. On another occasion a lecture was given by Viscount Broome, R.N., who described the work of the British Navy during the war.

Afternoons were occupied in outdoor recreation, and many of the men went into Cologne " on pass." There were many good games of football both between companies and against other battalions, the 9th Durham Light Infantry being the most formidable opponents among the latter. On the whole, the Battalion side upheld its high reputation, though on occasions it suffered defeat. In cross-country running, however, the 2/20th was unbeaten. On a certain Sunday morning after church parade the 5th Devonshire Regiment was engaged over a course which included a good deal of ploughland. The 2/20th supplied ten out of the first twelve home. On a later occasion the Battalion easily beat the 8th West Yorkshire Regiment over the same course.

The days closed in all too rapidly, and employment had to be found for the long winter evenings. Col. Craddock set to work to solve the problem as soon as the Battalion arrived in Sinzenich. Social functions of all sorts were arranged, and the village hall was transformed into a comfortable recreation room. For the first time in the history of the Battalion, a regular concert party was formed, and the members were struck off all duties so as to have ample time for practice and rehearsals. 2nd-Lieut. F. A. Martin was in charge, and in addition the party comprised Lce.-Cpl. Darbourne, Sergt. Lymbery, Lce.-Cpl. Lunn (" Queenie "), who made an admirable " girl," Sergt. Johnson, Sergt. Crate, and Private Spencer. Scenery was by Pte. Court, and lighting effects by Pte. All-

SINZENICH UNDER SNOW, DECEMBER 1918.

wright. The party gave many excellent shows, which were thoroughly popular with the Battalion; and, moreover, it was much in demand by other units, and frequently gave performances at Euskirchen and other outlying villages. Besides concerts at Sinzenich, there were many other indoor entertainments, all of which went with a swing. The officers set to work keenly in the organization of whist drives, billiard and chess tournaments, and fancy dress dances; and on one occasion great interest and amusement was caused by an Old English Fayre, at which the officers—dressed as costers—were in charge of stalls of the Bank-Holiday-on-Hampstead-Heath type, much to the amusement (and amazement) of the German civilians who peered into the hall from the street. The N.C.Os. and men had nothing to do but to " pay their money and take their choice." The choice included, among other things, the " booth of the dwarf," successfully exploited by Capt. Woolfe; a " houp-la " stall, by Capt. Churchouse and 2nd-Lieut. D. C. McClure; a fishpond, by 2nd-Lieut. W. J. Rogers; " Aunt Sally," by 2nd-Lieut. J. Batty; and a darts stall, by Capt. Shepherd, besides many other attractions of a Bank Holiday nature. The whole affair was voted a huge success, and the whole Battalion thoroughly enjoyed the fun.

The two fancy dress dances provided an immense amount of amusement, many of the costumes being excellent, and not a few grotesque. The whist drives, in the organization of which Lieut. Gilbert and the Rev. H. C. Caswall figured prominently, were always well supported and much appreciated by the men as evening occupations.

The sergeants found an excellent mess, but there was no building in the village really suitable for an officers' mess. The sergeants settled down exceedingly comfortably in the upper room of a house in the main street. An ample supply of crockery and furniture was requisitioned, and the first dinner was held on the last night of the year, under the chairmanship of C.S.M. Martin. Lights were extinguished as 1918 became 1919, and all present, including Col. Craddock and the officers who had come in as guests, joined hands and sang " Auld Lang Syne." It was an ideal setting for the last of the special sergeants' dinners which have been referred to so frequently in this record.

The officers' mess was in the village estaminet—in many ways a suitable place, but the premises were not really large enough. Many a cheery evening was spent there, nevertheless.

Though demobilization was known to be more or less imminent, only very meagre details of the War Office scheme were published before the middle of January. Meanwhile leave to England continued on a liberal scale. It was made very different to leave in war-time by the comforting reflection that on return the Battalion would be found peacefully at home on the banks of the Rhine, instead of waiting to go into a battle or perhaps already in one. A similar remark applies to Cologne leave, which was not too liberally sanctioned, but which was, all the same, quite fairly easy to obtain. All ranks in the Army of Occupation travelled free on trains and trams, and this made a day in Cologne or Bonn a very inexpensive treat. The chief attractions of Cologne were its magnificent Cathedral and the Hohenzollern Bridge over the Rhine. But a very interesting time could be spent in studying the crowds in the Hohestrasse, looking at the cleverly camouflaged emptiness of the shop-windows, and watching the gaily-dressed and dignified Prussian policemen, whose punctilious saluting of British officers was quite remarkable. The salute, by the way, was invariably " the naval salute," as we should call it in this country. The cafés, too, were interesting studies, especially the " Rosenhof," and the opera was always worth a visit, if only to see the audience.

Food could not be bought by the troops in Cologne except at Army and other British canteens. There was an excellent officers' club with German waiters and a German orchestra at the "Ewige Lampe," and for the men there was the British Empire Leave Club and the invaluable hostels of the Y.M.C.A., the Church Army, and those other innumerable bodies who did such invaluable work in the war by providing refreshment and recreation huts.

For some reason leave to Bonn was not so popular as leave to Cologne, though Bonn is much the prettier town of the two and possesses a famous University. It is connected with Cologne by an electric train system, a swift and comfortable means of travelling which is very much used in Germany. Bonn and Cologne can be reached from Sinzenich by train from the neighbouring village of Zulpich or from Euskirchen. The only difficulty of either journey was in getting to Zulpich or Euskirchen, and in getting back from there at night. Apart from this difficulty, all was simple—and free !

All good things come to an end, and the happy days of Sinzenich finished on March 3rd, when the Battalion, under Col. Warde-Aldam, proceeded by train to Duren, and took over the staffing of the demobilization camp in the German barracks there. At the same time, a small detachment, under Capt. Woolfe, proceeded to Malmedy for a short period of special duty.

A few men—urgent cases—had already proceeded home for demobilization, and a great deal of work had been put in by the orderly-room staff under Sergt. Gathercole and Cpl. Pierce in the preparation of the many demobilization papers required for each officer and man in the Battalion. The orderly-room had had an exceedingly busy time during the last days at Sinzenich, and Capt. Parker, as Adjutant, had his hands full. Subsequently a special demobilization office had been formed under 2nd-Lieut. Holmes, and the orderly-room was able to concentrate on preparations for the imminent break-up of the Battalion.

The Concert Party gave a final concert in the Stadt Theatre, Duren, which was attended by a large audience gathered from all units of the corps. Within a few days after this only the cadre—4 officers and 90 men—remained.

The first party to leave was one of 11 officers and 250 N.C.Os. and men, under Capt. Elliot, consisting of volunteers for the Army of Occupation and those not available for demobilization. This party proceeded by train on March 12th to join the 10th Royal West Kent Regiment (Lieut.-Col. F. Wallis, M.C.) at Hennef, east of the Rhine. The draft was welcomed on the station platform by the Commanding Officer and a large number of officers and N.C.Os. of the 10th Battalion, and by the Battalion band, which struck up the regimental march as the train steamed in. These officers and men of the 2/20th subsequently played a prominent part in the life of their new Battalion while holding the bridgehead posts on the frontier between occupied and unoccupied Germany. " B " Company of the 10th West Kents, of which Capt. Elliot was placed in command, had C.S.M. Martin as Company Sergeant-Major, and C.Q.M.S. Chappell as Company Quartermaster-Sergeant. For a long time " B " Company had the village of Ingersauel to itself, and the company greatly distinguished itself both at football and cricket. Pte. J. Palmer, Sergt. Giannini, and Cpl. Minney, all of the 2/20th Battalion, largely contributed to its successes.

The party which proceeded to the 10th Royal West Kent Regiment was the only formed body which remained together after the Battalion had been dispersed. The remainder of officers and men proceeded to England from Duren in demobilization drafts, and were demobilized at the dispersal centres nearest to their homes.

The cadre, consisting of 4 officers (Col. Warde-Aldam, Capt. Parker, Lieut. F. W. E. Smith, and Lieut. Gilbert) and 90 other ranks, remained for two months at Jacobswullesheim with a remnant of Battalion stores and equipment, and completed the peripatetic career of the 2/20th Battalion by returning home via Antwerp. An account of the civic reception of the cadre by the borough of Lewisham on its return home appears elsewhere in this volume.

The story of the 2/20th Battalion ends here. The memory of what the Battalion accomplished should last for ever.

ROLL OF HONOUR

" Blow out, you bugles, over the rich Dead!
There's none of these . . . . . .
But, dying, has made us rarer gifts than gold—
These laid the world away; poured out the red
Sweet wine of youth; gave up the years to be
Of work and joy, and that unhoped serene
That men call age; and those who would have been,
Their sons, they gave, their immortality."
RUPERT BROOKE.

* *Killed in action.*   ‡ *Died of disease.*
† *Died of wounds.*   § *Accidentally killed.*

FRANCE (JUNE 25TH, 1916—DECEMBER 7TH, 1916).

*Pte. S. Eunson	12/7/16	*Cpl. F. T. Scott	13/8/16
†Pte. R. G. Owers	13/7/16	*Pte. O. Bishop	13/8/16
†Pte. J. Waterhouse	15/7/16	†Pte. W. Askew	15/8/16
*L./Cpl. F. L. Keating	16/7/16	*Sgt. L. C. Simpson	15/8/16
†Pte. A. E. Wilson	18/7/16	†Pte. J. Dawes	15/8/16
†Pte. A. E. Watts	20/7/16	*Pte. C. Triggs	23/8/16
*Pte. H. W. Barrell	22/7/16	*Pte. C. S. Sign	25/8/16
*Pte. S. Noakes	26/7/16	*Cpl. G. Peverall	26/8/16
*L./Cpl. B. Waterfield	2/7/16	†Pte. W. H. Buhl	8/9/16
*Pte. A. Smith	27/7/16	*Pte. J. K. Otter	10/9/16
*Pte. W. A. Chaplin	28/7/16	*Pte. P. Cutler	11/9/16
†Pte. F. Edmondson	28/7/16	*Pte. G. Johnstone	11/9/16
*Lt. T. Gardner	29/7/16	*Pte. A. L. Mears	11/9/16
*2/Lt. C. T. Hellicar	29/7/16	*Pte. A. N. Stevens	11/9/16
*Pte. J. W. Edwards	29/7/16	*Pte. W. J. Fordyce	11/9/16
*Pte. W. N. Davies	29/7/16	†Pte. F. W. Brewstar	13/9/16
*Cpl. N. S. Crouch	30/7/16	*Pte. A. E. Tollington	14/9/16
*Pte. E. Morgans	30/7/16	†Pte. L. E. Denton	18/9/16
*Pte. J. G. Burr	30/7/16	*L./Cpl. J. Snowden	19/9/16
*Pte. H. C. Ford	30/7/16	*Pte. B. A. Johnson	23/9/16
*Pte. R. Hosegood	30/7/16	†2/Lt. E. A. Clarke	1/10/16
*Pte. W. V. Oliver	11/8/16	†Pte. C. D. Newton	4/10/16
†Pte. J. Hoare	12/8/16	*Pte. E. B. Widders	5/10/16
*Pte. T. W. Yarnold	13/8/16	*Pte. J. Rice	14/10/16
*Pte. J. A. Wade	13/8/16	*Pte. B. Thomas	14/10/16

MACEDONIA (DECEMBER 8TH, 1916—JUNE 15TH, 1917).

*Pte. C. W. Pescud	...	25/3/17	*Pte. W. J. Jordan ...	25/4/17
‡Pte. T. R. Collar	...	30/3/17	*Pte. H. Walters ...	25/4/17
*Pte. F. D. Watts	...	23/4/17	*Pte. C. Shone ...	25/4/17
*Pte. G. S. Norris	...	23/4/17	*Pte. T. Sadler ...	25/4/17
*Pte. H. Taffs	...	23/4/17	*Pte. W. H. Appleton	25/4/17
†Pte. H. Wright	...	25/4/17	*Pte. S. Ellinor ...	25/4/17
†Sgt. W. O. Smyth	...	25/4/17	*Pte. J. Rosenberg ...	25/4/17
*Pte. F. Hooks	...	25/4/17	*Pte. A. W. Beadles ...	25/4/17
*L./Cpl. L. G. Nash	...	25/4/17	*Pte. H. Wade ...	25/4/17
*Pte. F. G. Snashull	...	25/4/17	*Pte. C. J. Carter ...	25/4/17
*Pte. H. J. Ellis	...	25/4/17	‡Pte. T. G. Helyer ...	—
*Pte. D. Conley	...	25/4/17	(Died of disease while prisoner of war in Bulgaria.)	
*Pte. F. L. Coney	...	25/4/17		
*L./Cpl. H. F. Goodwin		25/4/17		

PALESTINE (JUNE 18TH, 1917—JUNE 8TH, 1918).

‡Capt. W. G. Elder	...	—	*Pte. J. Collinson, M.M.	29/11/17
‡Pte. E. Buggy	...	2/11/17	*Pte. J. E. Porritt ...	29/11/17
*Pte. H. J. Deuchars		6/11/17	*Pte. E. G. Law ...	29/11/17
*Pte. C. T. Andrews	...	6/11/17	*Pte. A. E. Edwards	29/11/17
*Pte. N. Baddeley	...	6/11/17	†Pte. A. W. Parsons ...	2/12/17
*Capt. T. S. Travers, M.C.		7/11/17	‡Pte. N. E. Garden ...	7/12/17
*L./Sgt. S. B. Bayfield		7/11/17	*Pte. J. Evans ...	8/12/17
†Pte. A. Wheeler	...	7/11/17	*L./Cpl. W. Pullan ...	9/12/17
*Pte. J. A. W. Knott		7/11/17	*Pte. E. C. Groves ...	9/12/17
*Pte. H. W. S. Groom		7/11/17	†L./Cpl. H. C. Bland ...	18/12/17
*Pte. C. H. Walters	...	7/11/17	†Pte. E. Walker ...	19/12/17
*Pte. A. J. Billing	...	7/11/17	*Pte. S. R. Woolger ...	19/12/17
*Pte. W. Cole ...	...	7/11/17	*Pte. F. Bates... ...	29/12/17
*Pte. J. Hayes	...	7/11/17	*Pte. W. R. P. Blundell	29/12/17
*Cpl. J. H. Walker	...	7/11/17	*Lt. J. A. C. Hasslacher	29/12/17
*Pte. E. White	...	7/11/17	*2/Lt. M. Lane, M.C., M.M.	29/12/17
*Pte. J. White	...	7/11/17	*L./Sgt. A. Crossley ...	29/12/17
†Pte. G. A. Dampier	...	7/11/17	*Pte. R. H. Hart ...	29/12/17
*Pte. H. R. Higgins	...	7/11/17	*Pte. J. H. Tolhurst ...	29/12/17
*Pte. F. A. Stevens	...	7/11/17	†Pte. F. J. Cude ...	5/1/18
†Pte. C. D. Campbell		8/11/17	‡Pte. W. Mullett ...	15/1/18
†L./Sgt. J. Linklater	...	10/11/17	†Pte. J. T. White ...	16/1/18
†Sgt. G. Macdonald	...	19/11/17	‡Pte. W. P. Thomas ...	19/1/18
†Pte. W. Massey	...	23/11/17	*Pte. D. Calley ...	19/2/18
*Pte. T. A. Barber	...	27/11/17	*2/Lt. L. E. M. Weatherley	19/2/18
†Pte. P. J. Collins	...	28/11/17	*Lt. K. G. Malcolm ...	19/2/18
*L./Cpl. C. Doughty	...	29/11/17	*Pte. A. H. Crook ...	19/2/18
*Pte. A. E. Kiln	...	29/11/17		
*Pte. A. Barrett	...	29/11/17		

285

*Pte. H. Galinsky	...	19/2/18
*Pte. S. J. Howell	...	19/2/18
*Pte. F. Keveren	...	19/2/18
*L./Cpl. N. McDougall		19/2/18
*Pte. G. W. Milsom	...	19/2/18
*Pte. H. Seviour	...	19/2/18
*Pte. A. S. Simpson	...	19/2/18
†Cpl. L. Waring	...	19/2/18
*Pte. W. Paxton, M.M.		20/2/18
†Pte. R. W. Hodgson		21/2/18
†Pte. G. H. Lill	...	21/2/18
†Pte. M. Kassowitch	...	22/2/18
†Pte. L. A. F. Skan	...	22/2/18
†L./Sgt. W. Hoffman		26/2/18
*L./Cpl. J. W. Lamb		8/3/18
*Capt. R. C. Hearn, M.C.		30/4/18
*2/Lt. E. R. Spice	...	30/4/18
*L./Cpl. A. H. G. Crawley		30/4/18
*Pte. A. E. Osborne	...	30/4/18
*Pte. S. Symonds	...	30/4/18
*Pte. H. T. Walden	...	30/4/18
*Sgt. S. G. Giles	...	30/4/18
*Pte. G. Sweet	...	30/4/18
*Pte. S. F. Richardson		30/4/18
*Pte. L. G. Meyer	...	30/4/18
*Pte. M. N. Crawley	...	30/4/18
*Pte. A. Hunt	...	30/4/18
*Pte. A. J. Evans	...	30/4/18
*Pte. W. Wright	...	30/4/18
*Pte. P. H. Trinder	...	30/4/18
*Pte. F. S. Sutton	...	30/4/18
*Pte. A. Symons	...	30/4/18
*Pte. A. Jarvis	...	30/4/18
*Pte. A. W. G. Wall	...	30/4/18
*Sgt. J. G. Rennie	...	30/4/18
*Sgt. R. A. J. Saunders		30/4/18
*Pte. H. G. Allchin	...	30/4/18
*L./Cpl. C. G. Fox	...	30/4/18
*Pte. F. E. Webster	...	30/4/18
*Sgt. E. Strachan	...	30/4/18
*L./Cpl. R. C. Levett	...	30/4/18
*Pte. E. W. Coulson	...	30/4/18
*Pte. H. R. Rudd	...	30/4/18
*Pte. H. W. Harris	...	30/4/18
*Pte. H. J. Burton	...	30/4/18
*Pte. A. Bishop	...	30/4/18
*Pte. E. W. M. Bozie		30/4/18
*Pte. W. C. Cocklin	...	30/4/18
*Pte. J. T. Griffen	...	30/4/18
*Pte. L. Haynes	...	30/4/18
*L./Cpl. C. Marcer	...	30/4/18
*L./Cpl. J. F. Rainsbury		30/4/18
*Pte. C. A. Webster	...	30/4/18
*Pte. S. McLeod	...	30/4/18
*Pte. T. F. Wood	...	30/4/18
*Pte. J. W. H. Woodward		30/4/18
*Pte. J. Bennett	...	30/4/18
*Pte. J. H. Smith	...	30/4/18
*Cpl. A. Read	...	30/4/18
*Pte. N. Davy		1/5/18
†Pte. J. White	...	1/5/18
*Pte. B. Randall		4/5/18
†Pte. J. E. G. Cornet	...	8/5/18
†Pte. T. A. Johnstone		8/5/18
†Pte. W. Ferguson	...	13/6/18
§Pte. N. V. Hatt (Drowned)	...	18/6/18

FRANCE (JUNE 30TH, 1918—DECEMBER 31ST, 1918).

‡Pte. G. W. Miller	...	15/8/18
†Pte. C. Holtum	...	30/8/18
*Capt. R. G. Jones		30/8/18
*Sgt. J. Moger		30/8/18
*L./Cpl. A. Howe	...	30/8/18
*Sgt. J. H. Bowers		30/8/18
*L./Cpl. L. Wilkin		30/8/18
*Pte. A. M. Jeffs		30/8/18
*Pte. W. G. Pacy	...	30/8/18
*Pte. C. Grant		30/8/18
*Pte. J. T. Baker	...	30/8/18
*Pte. W. Crook	...	30/8/18
*L./Cpl. G. Owens	...	30/8/18
*Pte. B. Taylor		30/8/18
*Pte. A. J. Eddolls	...	30/8/18
*Pte. G. W. Pettitt	...	30/8/18
*Pte. J. J. Williams	...	30/8/18
*Pte. R. S. Sutherland		30/8/18
*Pte. H. G. Dawn		30/8/18
*Pte. A. H. Beesley	...	30/8/18
*Pte. W. H. Ward	...	30/8/18
*Pte. J. Snodden	...	30/8/18

*Pte. A. Hare	30/8/18	*Pte. S. W. Greenlees	15/9/18
*Pte. W. L. Wallin	30/8/18	†2/Lt. G. J. P. Holton	16/9/18
*Pte. J. J. Meloy	30/8/18	†Pte. J. P. Mott	17/9/18
*L./Sgt. O. Curran	30/8/18	†Pte. M. J. Kennedy	23/9/18
*Pte. A. J. S. Cobb	30/8/18	†Pte. J. Owens	23/9/18
*Pte. W. A. H. Graves	30/8/18	*Sgt. G. F. Hannam	26/9/18
*L./Cpl. H. Whelan	30/8/18	*Pte. C. Speller	26/9/18
*L./Cpl. E. H. Wallis	30/8/18	*Lt. V. Slaughter	27/9/18
*Pte. R. D. Hiddleston	30/8/18	*2/Lt. F. Jackson	27/9/18
*Pte. J. S. Cooper	30/8/18	†Pte. T. C. Birrell	27/9/18
†Pte. E. Coleman	31/8/18	*Cpl. S. G. Bird	27/9/18
†Pte. W. A. Cook	31/8/18	*L./Cpl. J. Mann	27/9/18
†Pte. D. Metcalfe	31/8/18	*Pte. H. H. Horsfall	27/9/18
†Cpl. G. W. Catley	2/9/18	*Pte. B. Harris	27/9/18
†Pte. R. Yeoman	2/9/18	*Pte. R. R. Reynolds	27/9/18
†Cpl. H. L. Smith	2/9/18	*Pte. E. Butler	27/9/18
†Pte. G. B. Yallup	4/9/18	*L./Cpl. G. Jackson	27/9/18
†Pte. J. W. Flewitt	7/9/18	*Pte. E. G. L. Hopcraft	27/9/18
†Pte. P. Musson	8/9/18	*Pte. E. J. W. Wren	27/9/18
†Pte. T. Hodder	12/9/18	*Pte. S. Tickle	27/9/18
†2/Lt. V. C. W. Sutton	14/9/18	*Sgt. J. W. Leeds	27/9/18
*2/Lt. H. J. Ellen, M.C.	14/9/18	*Pte. J. Greening	27/9/18
*2/Lt. J. Hirst, M.M.	14/9/18	*Pte. E. Cooper	27/9/18
*Pte. J. W. Hulse	14/9/18	*Pte. F. Butcher	27/9/18
*Pte. E. H. Chatten	14/9/18	*L./Cpl. W. Goodey	27/9/18
*Cpl. F. W. Knights	14/9/18	*Pte. W. C. Gibson	27/9/18
*L./Cpl. H. S. Stockman	14/9/18	*Sgt. W. P. Hemens	27/9/18
*Pte. T. German	14/9/18	*L./Cpl. A. J. Pridgeon	27/9/18
*Pte. C. A. Cruse	14/9/18	†Pte. B. P. C. Castle	27/9/18
*Pte. G. E. Plater	14/9/18	*Pte. J. E. Baker	27/9/18
*L./Cpl. L. Sicard	14/9/18	†Pte. A. E. Tree	28/9/18
*Pte. E. Twitty	14/9/18	†Pte. T. Byrne	28/9/18
*Sgt. A. Nash	14/9/18	†Pte. J. H. O. Fenn	28/9/18
*Pte. W. Griffiths	14/9/18	†Pte. F. S. Christie	29/8/18
*Pte. J. Hind	14/9/18	*Pte. J. H. Davies	30/9/18
*Pte. G. H. Hobbs	14/9/18	†Pte. A. J. Partner	30/9/18
*Pte. R. T. Bennett	14/9/18	*Pte. J. W. King	30/9/18
*Pte. S. E. Isaacs	14/9/18	*Pte. J. Pettman	30/9/18
*Pte. G. Haines	14/9/18	*Pte. W. Bateman	30/9/18
*Pte. A. G. Barton	14/9/18	*Pte. A. H. Town	30/9/18
*Cpl. C. L. Robinson, M.M.	14/9/18	*Pte. D. E. Shemming	30/9/18
*Pte. J. Sams	14/9/18	†Pte. V. C. Eschbacher	5/10/18
*Pte. H. A. J. Filliston	14/9/18	†Cpl. C. J. New	8/10/18
*Pte. G. C. Holden	14/9/18	†L./Cpl. R. Bell	10/10/18
*Pte. P. C. Martlew	14/9/18	†Pte. G. E. Boakes	20/10/18
†Pte. F. S. Ellen	14/9/18	*Pte. T. Gaunt	20/10/18
†Pte. O. G. Hendon	15/9/18	*L./Cpl. E. B. Elliott	20/10/18

*Pte. H. C. Trundley	20/10/18	‡Pte. J. Taylor	3/11/18
*Pte. F. H. Hodgson	20/10/18	‡Pte. G. Dawes	4/11/18
*Pte. J. S. Hodgson	20/10/18	*L./Cpl. W. Flatman	4/11/18
*Pte. E. Brown	20/10/18	†Pte. C. H. Pocock	5/11/18
*Pte. W. E. A. Beeney	20/10/18	*Pte. A. Howard	5/11/18
*Pte. L. E. Moore	20/10/18	†Pte. C. Hoare	6/11/18
*L./Cpl. J. Bradley	20/10/18	*Pte. C. F. Isaac	6/11/18
*L./Sgt. W. H. Oliver	20/10/18	*Pte. F. E. Scott	6/11/18
*Pte. H. A. George	20/10/18	*Pte. S. J. Avory	6/11/18
*Pte. J. H. Rogers	20/10/18	†Pte. A. H. Harrington	6/11/18
*Pte. A. E. Driver	20/10/18	†Pte. H. Woodcock	8/11/18
†Pte. F. J. G. Plumb	20/10/18	†L./Cpl. D. V. Thompson	9/11/18
†Pte. J. G. Maloney	20/10/18	‡Pte. F. Patterson	18/11/18
*Pte. H. C. Setchell	21/10/18	‡Pte. N. Mobsby	19/11/18
†L./Cpl. W. S. Glockler	21/10/18	‡Pte. S. Chitty	25/11/18
‡Pte. H. Elliott	21/10/18	§Pte. P. W. Hollamby	21/12/18
*Pte. F. Crew	22/10/18	‡L./Cpl. D. Murray	6/3/19
‡Pte. W. G. Stairmand	3/11/18		

APPENDICES.

[*Appendix I*

HONOURS AND AWARDS

TO BE BREVET MAJOR.
Capt. (temp. Lieut.-Col.) W. St. A. Warde-Aldam (Coldstream Guards).

TO BE BREVET LIEUTENANT-COLONEL.
Capt. (Brevet-Major) W. St. A. Warde-Aldam.

DISTINGUISHED SERVICE ORDER.
Lieut.-Col. W. St. A. Warde-Aldam. Major W. M. Craddock

MILITARY CROSS.

Major W. M. Craddock.
Capt. D. Watson.
Capt. T. S. Travers.
Capt. A. Reynolds.
Capt. R. C. Hearn.
Capt. M. Lane.
Capt. D. C. Bacon.
Capt. H. W. Wilson.
Capt. B. T. Woolfe.

Capt. W. K. Churchouse, R.A.M.C. (T.)
Capt. A. H. Hunt.
Capt. W. R. Elliot.
Lieut. C. R. Salter.
Lieut. D. R. Blundell.
2/Lieut. J. Crafter.
2/Lieut. J. S. Pritchard.
2/Lieut. P. L. Smout.
2/Lieut. H. J. Ellen.
2/Lieut. W. J. Rogers.

CHEVALIER DE LEGION D'HONNEUR.
Lieut.-Col. W. St. A. Warde-Aldam.

ORDER OF THE NILE.
Capt. W. R. Elliot.

DISTINGUISHED CONDUCT MEDAL

R.S.M. W. T. Skeer.
C.S.M. A. E. Dawes.
C.S.M. J. T. Hills.
C.S.M. S. N. Seager.
Sgt. A. Backhus.

Sgt. A. J. L. Smith.
L./Sgt. R. Pallister.
L./Sgt. E. G. Oliver.
Pte. T. L. M. Haynes.

MILITARY MEDAL AND BAR.

Sgt. J. Graney. Pte. G. Earl.
Pte. A. Barron.

MILITARY MEDAL.

C.S.M. J. B. Salkeld.
Sgt. E. J. Painter.
Sgt. J. McCafferty.
Sgt. E. H. Chappell.
Sgt. J. Tyler.
Sgt. F. Powell.
Sgt. F. W. Cook.
Sgt. H. M. Challis.
Sgt. H. F. Cannon.
Sgt. C. Dickens.
Sgt. C. R. Beckley.
Sgt. J. J. Eames.
Sgt. H. Hadlow.
Cpl. A. J. De Bolla.
Cpl. J. H. Gardner.
Cpl. W. G. Feaver.
Cpl. C. Smith.
Cpl. A. C. Crate.
Cpl. T. Smith.
L./Cpl. A. Smith.
L./Cpl. A. R. Greenaway.
L./Cpl. L. A. Pearson.
L./Cpl. J. McRobie.
L./Cpl. W. White.
L./Cpl. G. J. Shaw.
L./Cpl. J. F. Yare.
L./Cpl. A. M. Smith.
L./Cpl. G. Giddings.
L./Cpl. C. L. Robinson.
L./Cpl. G. F. Crawley.
L./Cpl. W. J. Tapsfield.
L./Cpl. W. Mardell.
Pte. W. G. Hubble.
Pte. W. Castel.
Pte. J. Collinson.
Pte. T. R. Newton.
Pte. W. Paxton.
Pte. A. H. Kent.
Pte. G. Earl.
Pte. A. Westall.
Pte. D. Woolfe.
Pte. S. G. Hales.
Pte. W. H. Taylor.
Pte. G. Critchell.
Pte. H. G. Roberts.
Pte. A. Bates.
Pte. J. D. Clark.
Pte. S. Timms.
Pte. B. J. Owen.
Pte. H. J. Meade.
Pte. C. G. Allsopp.
Pte. P. Ross.
Pte. J. T. P. Barnett.
Pte. T. R. Marrison.

MERITORIOUS SERVICE MEDAL.

R.Q.M.S. E. H. Clymo.
Sgt. O. W. Mahoney.
Sgt. J. Bose.
Sgt. J. W. Willgress.
Cpl. A. J. De Bolla.

MENTIONED IN DISPATCHES.

Lieut.-Col. W. St. A. Warde-Aldam (three times).
Major W. M. Craddock (twice).
Capt. T. S. Travers.
Capt. W. K. Churchouse (twice).
Capt. W. J. Dark (twice).
R.S.M. W. T. Skeer.
C.S.M. J. T. Hills.
C.S.M. S. J. Martin.
Sgt. C. J. Scouller.
Sgt. H. Osbourn.
Sgt. M. W. Gathercole.
L./Sgt. W. H. Oliver.
L./Cpl. H. A. Bean.
Pte. A. H. Beesley.
Pte. R. W. Jones.
Pte. M. C. Bell.

[*Appendix II*

NOMINAL ROLL OF OFFICERS WHO LEFT ENGLAND WITH THE BATTALION, JUNE 24TH, 1916.

Rank and Name.	Left Unit.	Reasons for Leaving
Lieut.-Col. W. St. A. Warde-Aldam	—	—
Major F. C. Bentley	29/11/16	Sick.
Capt. W. M. Craddock	1/4/19	Demobilized.
Capt. D. Watson	12/3/19	Demobilized.
Capt. C. M. Bullock	12/10/16	—
Capt. R. F. C. O'Brien (Inns of Court O.T.C.)	14/8/16	To U.K., sick.
Capt. A. Pritchard (Royal Berkshire Regiment)	10/7/16	To U.K., sick.
Capt. G. Cooper-Willis	14/12/17	Att. 180th Inf. Bde.
Capt. A. Reynolds	30/8/18	To U.K., wounded.
Capt. T. S. Travers	7/11/17	Killed in action.
Capt. H. C. Partridge	11/12/17	To hospital, injured.
Lieut. W. R. Elliot	12/3/19	To 10th R. W. Kent Regt.
Lieut. R. G. Jones	30/8/18	Killed in action.
Lieut. H. L. Goldby	9/6/18	Hospital, sick.
Lieut. D. C. Bacon	20/1/19	Demobilized.
Lieut. J. C. Hasslacher	29/12/17	Killed in action.
Lieut. B. T. Woolfe	12/3/19	Demobilized.
Lieut. H. C. Lovell	5/4/19	Demobilized.
Lieut. T. Gardner	28/7/16	Killed in action.
Lieut. W. G. Elder	27/9/17	U.K., sick.
Lieut. L. E. M. Weatherley	19/2/18	Killed in action.
Lieut. L. W. Kempe	25/4/17	Wounded.
Lieut. A. W. Pilbeam	19/2/18	Wounded.
Lieut. W. G. Thompson	27/3/17	Hospital, sick.
Lieut. A. M. Lane, M.M.	29/12/17	Killed in action.
Lieut. H. F. Baker	7/11/17	Wounded.
Lieut. E. F. Gunning	26/9/16	U.K., sick.
Lieut. E. J. C. Vint	10/7/16	Att. 180th T.M.B.
2/Lieut. G. T. Hellicar	29/7/16	Killed in action.
2/Lieut. G. S. Morris	15/8/16	Wounded.
2/Lieut. E. W. Haseldene	28/7/16	U.K., sick.
2/Lieut. W. Davies	28/1/17	Hospital, sick.
Capt. W. K. Churchouse, R.A.M.C. (T.)	16/3/19	M.O., Duren Barracks.
Lieut. and Q.M. W. J. Dark	29/7/18	Leave, Med. Bd. U.K.

[*Appendix III*]

NOMINAL ROLL OF WARRANT OFFICERS AND SERGEANTS WHO LEFT ENGLAND WITH THE BATTALION, JUNE 24TH, 1916 (INCLUDING THOSE WHO, WITH SOME LOWER RANK, EMBARKED ON THAT DATE AND SUBSEQUENTLY BECAME SERGEANTS).

RANK AND NAME.	LEFT UNIT.	REASONS FOR LEAVING.	FIRST APPOINTED SERGEANT.
R.S.M. W. T. Skeer, D.C.M.	12/3/19	Demobilized	R.S.M., 25/5/15
R.Q.M.S. E. H. Clymo, M.S.M.	18/1/19	Leave and demobilized	R.Q.M.S., 4/1/15
R.Q.M.S. J. Bose	12/3/19	Demobilized	Sgt., 21/10/16
C.S.M. A. E. Dawes, D.C.M.	3/9/18	Wounded	C.S.M., 30/1/15
C.S.M. F. J. Drayton	17/6/18	Left in Egypt	C.S.M., 30/1/15
C.S.M. E. Mullett	2/10/18	U.K., wounded	C.S.M., 15/5/15
C.S.M. J. Salkeld, M.M.	17/10/18	U.K., for commission	C.S.M., 19/6/15
C.S.M. J. T. Hills, D.C.M.	18/1/19	Demobilized	C.S.M., 24/6/16
C.S.M. R. J. Milton	13/9/18	U.K., sick	Sgt., 2/10/14
C.S.M. S. N. Seager, D.C.M.	12/3/19	Demobilized	Sgt., 13/6/16
C.S.M. S. J. Martin	12/3/19	10th Royal West Kent Regt.	Sgt., 14/4/16
C.S.M. A. J. L. Smith, D.C.M.	12/3/19	10th Royal West Kent Regt.	L./Sgt., 24/8/16
C.S.M. E. H. Chappell, M.M.	12/3/19	10th Royal West Kent Regt.	Sgt., 2/9/16
C.Q.M.S. W. J. Gill	9/10/18	U.K., sick	C.Q.M.S., 15/5/15
C.Q.M.S. H. F. Trevillion	27/6/17	U.K., for commission	C.Q.M.S., 17/12/15
C.Q.M.S. A. G. Robshaw	14/10/17	Commission	C.Q.M.S., 17/12/15
C.Q.M.S. W. Paterson	26/1/19	Demobilized	Sgt., 15/11/15
C.Q.M.S. H. W. Watts	12/3/19	Demobilized	Sgt., 14/2/15
C.Q.M.S. F. L. Pringle		Demobilized with Cadre	Sgt., 8/2/15
C.Q.M.S. H. Osbourn	7/3/19	Hospital, sick	Sgt., 26/10/14
Col./Sgt. A. Warren			Sgt., 30/1/15
Sgt. L. C. Fry	29/7/16	Wounded	Sgt., 17/12/15
Sgt. L. C. Simpson	15/8/16	Killed in action	Sgt., 22/7/16
Sgt. J. G. Flint	19/8/16		Sgt., 17/12/15

RANK AND NAME.	LEFT UNIT.	REASONS FOR LEAVING.	FIRST APPOINTED SERGEANT.
Sgt. R. W. Cresswell	28/8/16	U.K. for commission	Sgt., 17/12/15
Sgt. F. Speer	26/8/16	Wounded	Sgt., 17/12/15
Sgt. H. A. Walker	2/9/16	Wounded	Sgt., 17/12/15
Sgt. E. A. Funnell	4/10/16	U.K., sick	Sgt., 17/12/15
Sgt. G. W. Osborne	5/10/16	Wounded	Sgt., 17/12/15
Sgt. S. F. Cox	17/10/16	U.K., sick	L./Sgt., 17/12/15
Sgt. J. McCafferty, M.M.	12/10/16	Wounded	Sgt., 22/7/16
Sgt. W. R. Herbert	18/10/16	Wounded	L./Sgt., 2/9/16
Sgt. G. R. Maskell	30/11/16	Left in B.E.F.	Sgt., 17/12/15
Sgt. W. D. Francis	8/3/17	U.K., for commission	Sgt., 17/12/15
Sgt. E. J. Painter, M.M.	15/3/17	Transferred to R.O.D., B.S.F.	L./Sgt., 21/10/16
Sgt. W. O. Smyth	25/4/17	Died of wounds	L./Sgt., 17/12/15
Sgt. F. J. Barber	7/6/17	Left in Salonica	Sgt., 17/12/15
Sgt. F. N. Harding	16/6/17	U.K., for commission	Sgt., 24/8/16
Sgt. F. W. Watkins	30/5/17	U.K., wounded	L./Sgt., 17/12/15
Sgt. H. R. Garwood	27/6/17	U.K., for commission	Sgt., 17/12/15
Sgt. R. Yeates	27/6/17	U.K., for commission	L./Sgt., 10/5/17
Sgt. G. W. Phipps	15/7/17	Wounded	Sgt., 13/6/16
Sgt. G. McDonald	19/11/17	Died of wounds	Sgt., 25/9/16
Sgt. J. Linklater	10/11/17	Died of wounds	L./Sgt., 28/6/17
Sgt. W. J. Wiles	14/1/18	U.K., wounded	L./Sgt., 27/12/16
Sgt. S. B. Bayfield	7/11/17	Killed in action	L./Sgt., 5/3/17
Sgt. E. B. Gibbins	26/12/17	U.K., wounded	L./Sgt., 1/2/17
Sgt. G. E. Fielder	8/12/17	Commission	Sgt., 13/6/16
Sgt. A. Spittle	24/11/18	U.K., wounded	Sgt., 23/5/16
Sgt. G. F. Wale	29/11/18	U.K., wounded	L./Sgt., 27/9/18
Sgt. W. R. Doe	4/11/18	Posted to 3-20th	Sgt., 6/11/16
Sgt. W. G. Feaver, M.M.	12/3/19	Demobilized	L./Sgt., 20/1/19
Sgt. T. E. Davies	8/3/18	Commission, 2/20th	Sgt., 23/5/16
Sgt. A. Jones	25/4/18	U.K., wounded	L./Sgt., 26/12/17

RANK AND NAME.	LEFT UNIT.	REASONS FOR LEAVING.	FIRST APPOINTED SERGEANT.
Sgt. S. J. Giles	30/4/18	Killed in action	L./Sgt., 17/12/15
Sgt. J. G. Rennie	30/4/18	Killed in action	Sgt., 23/5/16
Sgt. E. Strachan	30/4/18	Killed in action	L./Sgt., 10/5/17
Sgt. F. T. Bottom	10/6/18	U.K., sick	Sgt., 28/6/15
Sgt. E. G. Oliver, D.C.M.	17/6/18	Left in Egypt (hospital)	L./Sgt., 21/10/16
Sgt. J. H. Mould	17/6/18	Left in Egypt (hospital)	Sgt., 14/10/14
Sgt. W. Narroway	17/6/18	Left in Egypt (hospital)	Sgt., 24/7/15
Sgt. H. J. Mitchell	17/6/18	Left in Egypt with R.A.F.	Sgt., 22/7/16
Sgt. W. J. Braddick	17/6/18	Farrier/Sgt., 60th Division	Sgt., 22/2/16
Sgt. T. A. Flood	25/7/18	U.K., sick	L./Sgt., 21/10/16
Sgt. G. V. Metcalfe	17/6/18	Left in Egypt (hospital)	Sgt., 23/5/16
Sgt. J. H. Cooper	28/8/18	U.K., sick	L./Sgt., 10/5/17
Sgt. J. Moger	30/8/18	Killed in action	L./Sgt., 25/9/16
Sgt. F. J. Hartshorn	28/8/18	U.K., sick	L./Sgt., 1/2/17
Sgt. O. Curran	30/8/18	Killed in action	L./Sgt., 14/6/18
Sgt. G. D. Myers	4/9/18	U.K., wounded	L./Sgt., 14/11/17
Sgt. P. Herrington	5/9/18	U.K., wounded	L./Sgt., 6/4/17
Sgt. A. E. Ludlow	5/9/18	U.K., wounded	L./Sgt., 2/9/16
Sgt. E. Barrett	1/9/18	Leave, Medical Board	L./Sgt., 14/11/17
Sgt. G. F. Hannam	26/9/18	Killed in action	L./Sgt., 28/6/17
Sgt. C. H. White	25/9/18	U.K., wounded	L./Sgt., 17/12/15
Sgt. E. F. Fuller	27/9/18	U.K., wounded	L./Sgt., 10/10/16
Sgt. W. W. Linnell	30/9/18	U.K., wounded	L./Sgt., 14/11/15
Sgt. J. Tyler, M.M.	2/10/18	U.K., wounded	L./Sgt., 10/5/17
Sgt. F. W. Cook, M.M.	29/9/18	Missing, death accepted	Sgt., 18/3/16
Sgt. W. P. Hermens	27/9/18	U.K., wounded	L./Sgt., 21/10/16
Sgt. J. Fowler	6/10/18	U.K., sick	Sgt., 23/5/16
Sgt. A. Reed	19/10/18	Killed in action	Sgt., 2/6/16
Sgt. W. H. R. Oliver	20/10/18	U.K., sick	L./Sgt., 15/1/18
Sgt. F. Powell, M.M.	6/12/18	U.K., sick	Sgt., 16/9/14

RANK AND NAME.	LEFT UNIT.	REASONS FOR LEAVING.	FIRST APPOINTED SERGEANT.
Sgt. G. E. Read	10/12/18	U.K., sick	L./Sgt., 16/10/18
Sgt. A. Wood	3/1/19	Demobilized	L./Sgt., 4/12/18
Sgt. M. W. Gathercole	6/1/19	U.K., sick	L./Sgt., 11/11/17
Sgt. G. I. Shaw, M.M.	12/1/19	Demobilized	L./Sgt., 4/12/18
Sgt. A. H. Figes	18/1/19	Demobilized	L./Sgt., 30/4/18
Sgt. W. G. Bartlett	16/1/19	Demobilized	Sgt., 16/9/14
Sgt. A. Backhus, D.C.M.	26/1/19	Demobilized	L./Sgt., 24/8/16
Sgt. A. E. Watkins	26/1/19	Demobilized	Sgt., 20/1/16
Sgt. S. J. Lucas	30/9/18	Wounded	L./Sgt., 21/10/16
Sgt. O. W. Mahoney, M.S.M.	13/11/18	Hospital	L./Sgt., 17/12/18
Sgt. H. M. Challis, M.M.	4/4/19	Demobilized; re-enlisted for four years Royal West Kent Regt.	
Sgt. C. R. Beckley, M.M.	28/3/19	Demobilized	L./Sgt., 17/1/18
Sgt. A. Smith, M.M.	12/3/19	Demobilized	L./Sgt., 30/10/18
Sgt. A. W. Hollands	12/3/19	Demobilized	L./Sgt., 12/6/18
Sgt. W. G. Thorncroft	12/3/19	Demobilized	L./Sgt., 6/4/17
Sgt. A. D. Barnard	12/3/19	Demobilized	L./Sgt., 27/9/18
Sgt. B. H. Lymbery	12/3/19	Demobilized	L./Sgt., 10/5/17
Sgt. J. J. Eames, M.M.	12/3/19	Demobilized	L./Sgt., 7/12/17
Sgt. E. G. Silvester	12/3/19	Demobilized	L./Sgt., 28/6/17
Sgt. J. Goreham	12/3/19	Demobilized	L./Sgt., 19/1/19
Sgt. J. C. Coles	12/3/19	Demobilized	L./Sgt., 30/10/18
Sgt. H. J. Hadlow, M.M.	12/3/19	Demobilized	L./Sgt., 4/12/18
Sgt. W. Fuller	12/3/19	Demobilized	L./Sgt., 20/1/19
Sgt. J. W. L. Johnson	12/3/19	Demobilized	L./Sgt., 4/12/18
Sgt. A. C. Crate, M.M.	12/3/19	Demobilized	L./Sgt., 2/9/16
Sgt. T. C. Richardson	12/3/19	Demobilized	L./Sgt., 4/12/18
Sgt. T. Vickery	12/3/19	Demobilized	L./Sgt., 27/9/18
Sgt. G. Buckmaster	12/3/19	Demobilized	L./Sgt., 25/9/16
Sgt. A. M. Smith	12/3/19	Demobilized	L./Sgt., 1/12/17
			Sgt., 20/1/19

296

RANK AND NAME.	LEFT UNIT.	REASONS FOR LEAVING.	FIRST APPOINTED SERGEANT.
Sgt. F. W. Todd	12/3/19	Demobilized	L./Sgt., 12/1/19
Sgt. A. B. S. Crummey	12/3/19	Demobilized	Sgt., 16/9/14
Sgt. E. L. Hobbs	12/3/19	Demobilized	L./Sgt., 18/10/18
Sgt. L. C. Dickens, M.M.	12/3/19	Demobilized	L./Sgt., 28/6/17
Sgt. F. G. Watts	12/3/19	Demobilized	Sgt., 15/11/15
Sgt. A. Giannini	12/3/19	10th Royal West Kent Regt.	L./Sgt., 13/5/18
Sgt. A. E. White	12/3/19	10th Royal West Kent Regt.	L./Sgt., 6/4/17
Sgt. S. L. Smith		180th T.M.B. (Q.M.S.)	Sgt., 18/2/16
Sgt. J. Forbes	12/3/19	Demobilized	L./Sgt., 13/1/19
Sgt. R. E. Frost	12/3/19	Demobilized	L./Sgt., 8/1/19
Sgt. L. Debonnaire		Demobilized with Cadre	L./Sgt., 17/1/18
Sgt. J. W. Willgress, M.S.M.		Demobilized with Cadre	L./Sgt., 4/12/18
Sgt. J. S. Pierce	16/4/19	Demobilized	L./Sgt., 20/1/19
Sgt. H. C. Cooper	9/4/19	Demobilized	L./Sgt., 10/5/17
Sgt. R. T. Jones	9/4/19	Demobilized	L./Sgt., 10/10/16
Sgt. G. W. Wood	12/3/19	Demobilized	A./Sgt., 20/1/19
Sgt. S. G. Bird	27/9/18	Killed in action	L./Sgt., 17/12/15
Sgt. W. J. Lee	20/10/18	Hospital, sick	L./Sgt., 17/12/15
Sgt. S. Collins	20/8/18	Hospital, sick	L./Sgt., 25/9/16
Sgt. C. P. Oakshott	30/4/18	Wounded	L./Sgt., 14/11/17
Sgt. A. Lewis	22/11/18	Hospital, sick	L./Sgt., 10/5/18
Sgt. W. J. Harris	10/11/18	Hospital, sick	L./Sgt., 27/9/18
Sgt. H. L. Smith	2/9/18	Wounded	L./Sgt., 13/6/18
Sgt. A. W. Swinburne	20/1/19	Demobilized	L./Sgt., 22/10/17
Sgt. W. S. Irish			L./Sgt., 21/10/16

[*Appendix IV*

Nominal Roll of Officers who Joined the Battalion Overseas.

RANK AND NAME.	JOINED UNIT.	LEFT UNIT.	REASONS FOR LEAVING.
Lieut. R. C. Hearn	8/8/16	30/4/18	Killed in action.
Lieut. G. J. Edwards	23/8/16	31/10/16	Left in B.E.F.
Lieut. A. H. Hunt	17/10/16	12/2/19	Demobilized.
Lieut. F. D. Parker	11/11/16		Demobilized with Cadre.
Lieut. M. F. C. Willson	29/12/16	20/2/18	Wounded.
Lieut. H. W. Wilson	17/2/18	4/11/18	Wounded.
Lieut. A. C. Hardie (19th London Regt.)	16/10/18	12/3/19	10th Royal West Kent Regt.
Lieut. B. B. Shepherd (City of London Yeo.)	18/10/18	28/3/19	Demobilized.
Lieut. J. B. West	16/7/16	9/12/17	Hospital, sick.
Lieut. J. Crafter	25/8/16	31/10/16	Left in B.E.F.
Lieut. F. E. Manico	7/9/16	31/10/16	Left in E.E.F.
Lieut. G. Tweedie	8/9/16	15/6/17	180th Machine Gun Corps.
Lieut. R. G. Grant	10/9/16	31/10/16	Left in B.E.F.
Lieut. A. Stone	13/9/16	26/3/18	Sick in E.E.F.
Lieut. D. R. Blundell	15/9/16	4/11/18	Wounded.
Lieut. D. F. P. Spurgeon	30/9/16	30/4/18	Wounded.
Lieut. W. F. Stroud	4/10/16	6/8/17	18th T.M.B.
Lieut. C. R. C. Salter	4/10/16	9/8/18	Leave, Medical Board, U.K.
Lieut. V. Slaughter	8/10/16	27/9/18	Killed in action.
Lieut. S. P. Pattison	9/10/16	23/3/18	Royal Flying Corps.
Lieut. J. S. Pritchard	6/2/18	12/3/19	10th Royal West Kent Regt.
Lieut. F. A. R. Smith	3/8/18	10/10/18	Hospital, injured.
Lieut. A. P. Cole	16/10/18	25/1/19	Demobilized.
Lieut. D. C. McClure	23/11/18	12/3/19	Demobilized.
Lieut. F. W. E. Smith	23/11/18		Demobilized with Cadre.
Lieut. and Qr.Mr. A. G. Gilbert	1/12/18		Demobilized with Cadre.
Lieut. A. Haywood	18/12/18	12/3/19	10th Royal West Kent Regt.

RANK AND NAME.	JOINED UNIT.	LEFT UNIT.	REASONS FOR LEAVING.
Lieut. W. T. Jezzard	6/1/19	12/3/19	10th Royal West Kent Regt.
2/Lieut. Cresswell	8/8/16	15/8/16	U.K., sick.
2/Lieut. E. K. James	23/8/16	30/8/17	Royal Flying Corps.
2/Lieut. E. A. Clarke	13/9/16	1/10/16	Died of wounds.
2/Lieut. B. Edgar	22/9/16	31/10/16	Left in B.E.F.
2/Lieut. F. C. Long	4/10/16	15/11/17	Wounded.
2/Lieut. T. E. Durban	13/8/17	2/12/17	Hospital, sick.
2/Lieut. K. J. Malcolm	10/2/18	19/2/18	Killed in action.
2/Lieut. H. K. Holmes	16/2/18	16/3/19	Demobilized.
2/Lieut. F. Barnes	25/2/18	31/8/18	Wounded.
2/Lieut. W. L. Bright	25/2/18	31/8/18	Wounded.
2/Lieut. E. R. Spice	25/2/18	30/4/18	Killed in action.
2/Lieut. J. Hirst, M.M.	25/2/18	14/9/18	Killed in action.
2/Lieut. P. S. R. Marshall	25/2/18	12/3/19	10th Royal West Kent Regt.
2/Lieut. S. G. Cumner	25/2/18	17/6/18	Left in E.E.F.
2/Lieut. R. A. Baker	1/3/18	17/6/18	Surplus to Establishment.
2/Lieut. T. E. Davies	8/3/18	15/3/19	Demobilized.
2/Lieut. W. L. Sutton (West Surrey Regt.)	12/4/18	31/4/18	Wounded.
2/Lieut. E. B. Jones (Royal W. Kent Regt.)	12/4/18	30/12/18	Demobilized.
2/Lieut. J. Priest (Royal W. Kent Regt.)	12/4/18	12/3/19	10th Royal West Kent Regt.
2/Lieut. R. H. Rose (Royal W. Kent Regt.)	15/4/18	7/5/18	Hospital, sick.
2/Lieut. P. W. Robinson (Royal W. Kent R.)	15/4/18	3/5/18	Wounded.
2/Lieut. W. J. Rogers (Royal W. Kent Regt.)	5/5/18	12/3/19	10th Royal West Kent Regt.
2/Lieut. V. C. W. Sutton (Royal W. Kent R.)	8/5/18	14/9/18	Died of wounds.
2/Lieut. E. F. Tiffin (Royal W. Surrey R.)	21/5/18	17/6/18	Left in E.E.F.
2/Lieut. H. W. G. Dillingham	21/5/18	12/3/19	Demobilized.
2/Lieut. B. P. O'Dowd (7th London Regt.)	4/6/18	12/3/19	10th Royal West Kent Regt.
2/Lieut. F. E. Read	3/8/18	2/9/18	Wounded.
2/Lieut. S. W. Prestidge	3/8/18	11/2/19	Leave and demobilization.
2/Lieut. H. J. Ellen	3/8/18	1/10/18	Killed in action.

RANK AND NAME.	JOINED UNIT.	LEFT UNIT.	REASONS FOR LEAVING.
2/Lieut. A. F. Dyball	3/8/18	31/8/18	Wounded.
2/Lieut. J. Batty, M.M.	3/8/18	12/3/19	10th Royal West. Kent Regt.
2/Lieut. G. J. P. Holton	10/8/18	16/9/18	Died of wounds.
2/Lieut. P. L. Smout	11/8/18	31/8/18	Wounded.
2/Lieut. F. Jackson	22/8/18	27/9/18	Killed in action.
2/Lieut. W. H. Trethewey (12th London R.)	2/9/18	29/12/18	Demobilized.
2/Lieut. F. H. Dowdell (25th London Regt.)	11/9/18	12/3/19	10th Royal West Kent Regt.
2/Lieut. W. J. Cottis	17/9/18	30/9/18	Wounded.
2/Lieut. S. Herbert	17/9/18	27/9/18	Wounded.
2/Lieut. J. C. McKee (16th London Regt.)	17/9/18	12/3/19	10th Royal West Kent Regt.
2/Lieut. W. J. S. Hooper	18/9/18	6/10/18	Trans. to Canadian M.G.C.
2/Lieut. H. L. Wermig (16th London Regt.)	18/9/18	12/3/19	10th Royal West Kent Regt.
2/Lieut. A. T. Darby (City of London Yeo.)	16/10/18	31/3/19	10th Royal West Kent Regt.
2/Lieut. H. T. Musto (12th London Regt.)	16/10/18	13/3/19	Demobilized.
2/Lieut. E. E. L. Tinsley (19th London R.)	16/10/18	12/3/19	Demobilized.
2/Lieut. A. H. Urry (11th London Regt.)	16/10/18	12/3/19	Demobilized.
2/Lieut. W. R. Taylor	22/11/18	18/1/19	Demobilized.
2/Lieut. W. A. Chappell	23/11/18	27/1/19	Demobilized.
2/Lieut. M. W. Smith	2/12/18	18/1/19	Demobilized.
2/Lieut. F. A. Martin	18/12/18	15/3/19	Demobilized.

[*Appendix V*

NOMINAL ROLL OF WARRANT OFFICERS AND SERGEANTS WHO JOINED THE BATTALION OVERSEAS.

RANK AND NAME.	JOINED UNIT.	LEFT UNIT.	REASONS FOR LEAVING.	FIRST APPOINTED SERGEANT.
Sgt. A. G. Chitty	31/7/16	13/1/19	Demobilized	L./Sgt., 14/11/17
Sgt. J. B. Lancashire	31/7/16	20/10/18	U.K., wounded	L./Sgt., 7/12/17
Sgt. A. Kenney	31/7/16	18/1/19	Demobilized	L./Sgt., 4/12/18
Sgt. C. J. Scouller	31/7/16	12/3/19	10th Royal West Kent Regt.	L./Sgt., 14/1/19
Sgt. B. Parmley	31/7/16	16/1/19	Demobilized	L./Sgt., 13/5/18
Sgt. J. W. J. Johnson	31/7/16	12/3/19	10th Royal West Kent Regt.	L./Sgt., 16/1/19
Sgt. G. C. Stocker	5/8/16	12/3/19	Demobilized	L./Sgt., 20/1/19
Sgt. E. Owens	8/8/16	30/11/16	Left in B.E.F.	Sgt., 8/8/16
Sgt. R. I. McGuire	8/8/16	30/8/18	Wounded	L./Sgt., 30/4/18
Sgt. K. W. Crimp	8/8/16	6/11/18	Wounded	L./Sgt., 27/9/18
Sgt. H. G. Legg	29/8/16	21/1/18	U.K., wounded	L./Sgt., 15/7/17
Sgt. C. F. Bishop	10/11/16	12/3/19	10th Royal West Kent Regt.	L./Sgt., 27/9/18
Sgt. J. Graney	10/11/16	12/3/19	10th Royal West Kent Regt.	L./Sgt., 14/11/17
Sgt. W. J. Burne	10/11/16	17/11/18	Hospital	L./Sgt., 14/11/18
Sgt. W. H. Mashman	25/1/17	5/11/18	Wounded	L./Sgt., 27/9/18
Sgt. A. Crossley	2/2/17	29/12/17	Killed in action	L./Sgt., 7/12/17
Sgt. H. K. Holmes	16/2/17	16/2/18	Commission, 2-20th	Sgt., 16/2/17
Sgt. Pallister R.	16/2/18	14/4/18	U.K., wounded	L./Sgt., 26/4/17
Sgt. W. J. Tapsfield	16/2/17	12/3/19	10th Royal West Kent Regt.	L./Sgt., 18/1/19
Sgt. L. Walters	16/2/17	15/9/18	U.K., wounded	L./Sgt., 17/1/18
Sgt. A. Howland	16/2/17	12/1/19	Demobilized	A./Sgt., 4/12/18
Sgt. E. A. Reavell	13/4/17	17/6/18	Left in Egypt	L./Sgt., 15/6/17
Sgt. A. Read	20/7/17	30/4/18	Killed in action	L./Sgt., 20/7/16
Sgt. E. Mottram	20/7/17	12/3/19	Demobilized	L./Sgt., 30/10/18
Sgt. P. Ion	18/8/17	12/3/19	Demobilized	L./Sgt., 22/1/19

RANK AND NAME.	JOINED UNIT.	LEFT UNIT.	REASONS FOR LEAVING.	FIRST APPOINTED SERGEANT.
Sgt. H. F. Cannon	20/10/17	5/11/18	Wounded	L./Sgt., 30/6/18
Sgt. F. W. Harris	20/10/17	17/9/18	Wounded	L./Sgt., 30/6/18
Sgt. W. C. Dimon	8/8/18	26/1/19	Demobilized	L./Sgt., 4/12/18
Sgt. C. C. Nicholls	8/8/18	19/1/19	Demobilized	L./Sgt., 8/8/18
Sgt. G. Kain	8/8/18	3/9/18	U.K., wounded	Sgt., 8/8/18
Sgt. A. Nash	8/8/18	14/9/18	Killed in action	Sgt., 8/8/18
Sgt. H. Milford	8/8/18	16/11/18	Transferred to 11th Hussars	Sgt., 16/10/18
Sgt. R. O. Nicholas	8/8/18	4/1/19	Demobilized	L./Sgt., 4/12/18
Sgt. J. H. Gardner	8/8/18	24/1/19	Demobilized	L./Sgt., 4/12/18
Sgt. J. H. Bowers	11/8/18	30/8/18	Killed in action	Sgt., 11/8/18
Sgt. J. W. Leeds	12/8/18	27/9/18	Killed in action	Sgt., 12/9/18
Sgt. G. L. Kay	12/8/18	13/1/19	Demobilized	Sgt., 12/9/18
Sgt. H. S. S. Keyse	7/11/18	20/1/19	Demobilized	Sgt., 7/11/18
Sgt. C. R. King	7/11/18	8/1/19	Demobilized	L./Sgt., 27/11/18

[Appendix VI

THE RETURN OF THE CADRE

THE following account of the return of the Battalion cadre and its civic reception at Lewisham on Friday, June 13th, is quoted, by kind permission, from the *Kentish Mercury* of June 20th, 1919 :—

" Four officers and 30 men, forming the cadre of the 2/20th Battalion County of London Regiment (T.F.), reached Catford Bridge Station by the 1.38 p.m. train on Friday, and were welcomed by the Mayor of Lewisham, the Mayoress, and the Misses Hume Nicholl, Captain Hamilton Benn, R.N.V.R., C.B., D.S.O., M.P. (honorary colonel of the 20th), Lieut.-Colonel Pownall, M.P., Major Eric Ball, L.C.C., Captain W. F. Marchant, Captain W. J. Dark, Mr. R. Jackson, L.C.C., Alderman Ball, J.P., Councillor Harry Chiesman, the Town Clerk (Mr. J. W. Shuter), and the Rev. F. C. Bainbridge-Bell. Lieut.-Colonel Warde-Aldam, D.S.O., of the Coldstream Guards, who commanded the 2/20th from March, 1916, travelled down with the cadre, whose officers were Captain F. D. Parker, Lieut. and Quartermaster A. G. Gilbert, and Lieut. F. W. E. Smith, who went out with the 1st Battalion. Lieut.-Colonel B. L. Hooper (commanding the Reserve Battalion), Lieut. H. W. Hallett (in charge at Holly Hedge House), and R.S.M. Chesney, D.C.M. (of the 1/20th), were also present, as were representatives of the following Voluntary Aid Detachments : Nos. 164 (Commandant Lee), 216, 218, 228 (Mrs. Chapman), 238 and 240 (Quartermaster Mrs. Norris).

The band of the Deptford branch of the Discharged and Demobilized Sailors' and Soldiers' Federation, under Bandmaster A. E. Jackson (a former bandsergeant of the 1/20th) played ' See the Conquering Hero

Comes' as the cadre marched into the station yard, and afterwards headed a procession, which marched by way of Canadian Avenue and Bromley Road to the Town Hall, where lunch was served.

The Mayor of Lewisham, who presided, said Lewisham was extremely proud to welcome back the cadre, nearly all of whom belonged to the borough. The 2/20th had seen a great deal since it went out in 1916. Colonel Warde-Aldam had been telling him of the parts of the world to which they had been. The people of Lewisham had been trying to follow them and the other units which were representative of the borough. They had, he found, seen service in France, Salonica, Palestine, again in France, and as part of the victorious army which marched into Germany (applause). That was a record of which to be proud. Lewisham was intensely proud that they had won honours in those different parts of the world, and so had brought honour to Lewisham. He was perfectly certain from what he had heard that their officers were proud of them, and if that was so it followed that they were proud of their officers (applause). Those who had seen, as he had done, the hardships and sufferings that men on active service had to undergo realized that they were living peaceful lives to-day as the result of what they had done. He wished them all health and happiness in the civilian life to which they were returning (applause).

Captain Hamilton Benn, who followed, said he was very glad to have the opportunity of endorsing what the Mayor had said, of offering his hearty congratulations on their safe return home, and of extending a very warm welcome from the people of Lewisham and Greenwich. As the Mayor had said, they were proud of the 20th London—proud of the record the Regiment had made. It was one of which any regiment in the British Army might well be proud. He believed they had a quite exceptional case : the Colonel was credited with having captured a battery by himself, and brought it home ;

anyway, it was a very good story. But it had been a very tough time. This war had shown which were the fighting peoples of Europe, and he did not think there was any doubt as to who was on top to-day. ' I think it's Tommy,' said Captain Benn amid hearty applause. There was every reason why people should be proud of what the men had done. What we had to be careful about now was that, having won the war, we won the peace : that we did not lose, by quarrelling among ourselves at home, what we had won by the force of arms abroad. (Hear, hear.) ' You have been,' he went on, ' through troublesome, through trying and exhausting times, but it was worth it—worth it to each one of you ! Life can never be the same again to any one of you men. You have seen a great deal of the world. They say that travelling broadens the mind : it also elongates the tongue (laughter). Every one of you must feel that you have had your part in the greatest enterprise, in the greatest events, that the world has ever seen, and in days to come you will always have your memories and thoughts of the great days of the great war, and it will be an asset in the lives of each one of you. I wish you a very hearty welcome home, and I wish you the best of luck in your homes.' (Applause.)

" Lieut.-Colonel Warde-Aldam, replying for the Battalion, said when he joined it in 1916 the 2/20th had sent, during 1915, over 1,000 men to the 1/20th. When they first went abroad they received a large draft of men drawn from the R.A.M.C. Since then they had received large drafts from the R.A.S.C. and from other battalions of the London Regiment, but what had actually happened had been that the nucleus of officers and non-commissioned officers and the permanent staff of the Battalion during the whole three years they had been abroad had been composed of men from the borough of Lewisham and its surroundings. Those men—of whom, perhaps, the best known was Captain Elliot, Adjutant for two years—had imbued the spirit of the neighbourhood and of the regiment—the three battalions of the 20th London—into all the enormous number of men who had joined the battalion from all over England, and as much into himself as into anyone. Again, right away through the whole three years they had kept up their connection with the Royal West Kents—had always kept up the tradition of being part of the Royal West Kents. In Egypt they came across another battalion of that regiment, and met them on cordial terms, and when the 2/20th was broken up he sent 14 officers and 250 men to the 10th West Kents, where they were received as if they had come from another battalion of the West Kents, and made to feel very welcome. (Applause.) He claimed the privilege of coming home to Lewisham, though he had never been there before ! Speaking as an outsider—as a regular soldier—who knew what the men had done, he wished to tell one or two things about them. They had been a most extraordinarily lucky battalion—had been saved all the monotony that battalions which had spent their whole three or four years in France had gone through. They had not fought absolutely annihilating battles, as the 1/20th had done, but he did not wish to infer that they had not fought battles : they had had some very stiff ones, and had gone through some hardships. They had, as had been said, seen a great deal of the world. The first six months in France was practically all spadework, and then their luck began. They went to Palestine, and had more than their share of the fighting there.

After telling the story of his mess-cook, Pte. Church, who was the first man in Jerusalem, Colonel Warde-Aldam went on to observe that when they left Palestine they were told, ' You have helped to win the war here, and are going back to win it in France '—another instance of a remark made in jest proving true. From August, 1918, they went over the top five times, and captured eight guns and over 1,000 prisoners. (Applause.) They marched into Germany at the head of the 62nd Division, and were lucky again, because only two London battalions—the London Scottish and the 2/20th—were part of the Army of Occupation. They had been lucky in keeping a nucleus of regimental officers, and probably 80 per cent. of the men who had returned that day went out with the battalion and came from Lewisham or its neighbourhood. Nearly all of them volunteered to stop out in Germany in order to come home with the cadre as being local men. (Hear, hear.) Another point of which they were very proud was that they had lost only six prisoners. While they had carried abroad the reputation of Lewisham as a fighting people, he thought they had done more—a thing which was much harder : they had carried abroad its reputation as breeding a people who were gentlemen. (Applause.) That, to his mind, was very important, especially for a battalion that had been in so many places : that ' we people from London ' should show what the English word 'gentleman' meant. He appealed to all the people of Lewisham to do their best to keep up the reputation which the two battalions of the 20th London had made during the war. There would be a future 20th London, and he was most anxious, although that was the last time he should wear the uniform, that the deeds of the two battalions should be handed down. In this, he was sure, the Mayor could do a great deal to help. Lastly, on behalf of all ranks, he wished to thank them for their magnificent reception.

Hearty cheers for the Mayor and Mayoress followed. The cadre marched by way of Rushey Green, High Street, and Belmont Hill to headquarters at Holly Hedge House, where tea was served. There were decorations on houses and business premises on the route, and everywhere there was cheering, renewed when the cadre marched to the New Cross Empire to receive a warm welcome from the audience."

[*Appendix VII*

THE PRESENTATION OF THE KING'S COLOUR BY
H.R.H. PRINCE ALBERT, ON APRIL 10TH, 1920

SOME months after the 2/20th was disbanded, Col. Warde-Aldam obtained information from the War Office that a King's Colour had been allotted to the Battalion in token of its war services. It was not possible for a presentation ceremony to be arranged at that time, and a convenient opportunity was awaited. When Saturday, April 10th, 1920, was fixed as the date of the unveiling of the Regimental Memorial at Holly Hedge House, it was decided to ask H.R.H. Prince Albert to present the 2nd Battalion Colour on the same day. The ceremonies duly took place on April 10th, and the first Regimental Reunion Dinner followed in the evening at Greenwich Borough Hall.

The undermentioned ex-officers, N.C.Os. and men of the 2nd Battalion, under command of Capt. W. R. Elliot, M.C., formed a guard of honour to Prince Albert and acted as Colour Party :—

Capt. F. D. Parker	Lieut. J. Batty, M.M.
Sergt. A. E. Watkins	Sergt. F. W. Watkins.
Sergt. E. F. Fuller	Sergt. G. F. Wale
Sergt. G. Buckmaster	Sergt. J. W. Johnson
Sergt. F. Powell, M.M.	Sergt. H. J. Hadlow, M.M.
Sergt. J. Graney, M.M.	Lce.-Cpl. L. R. Marriott
Lce.-Cpl. E. A. Dubois	Lce.-Cpl. C. H. Wheeler
Lce.-Cpl. L. A. Pearson, M.M.	Lce.-Cpl. W. Mardell, M.M.
	Lce.-Cpl. H. A. Bean.
Lce.-Cpl. G. D. Draycott	Pte. F. Staplehurst
Pte. E. E. Tracey	Pte. J. Airey

Pte. H. Stewart

The following account of the afternoon ceremonies and of the speeches at the Reunion Dinner is quoted from the *Kentish Mercury* of April 16th, by kind permission of the Editor :—

" H.R.H. Prince Albert visited Holly Hedge House, Blackheath, on Saturday afternoon to present the King's Colour to the 2/20th Battalion, and to unveil the regimental memorial to all ranks of the 1/20th and the 2/20th who gave their lives on the various fronts. Attended by Commander Louis Greig, His Royal Highness (who wore the uniform of a Major of the Royal Air Force) arrived by motor-car, was received by Lieut.-Col. Eric Ball, L.C.C. (commanding the 20th), and was loyally greeted by the many thousands of spectators who had assembled to witness the proceedings. The Prince inspected the Colour party—under Capt. W. R. Elliot, M.C.—and presentations were then made, these including Major-General Sir Neville Smyth, V.C. (commanding the 2nd London Division), Col. A. Hubback, C.M.G. (commanding the 5th London Infantry Brigade), Col. H. W. Studd (commanding the Coldstream Guards, first Brigadier of the 180th Brigade, of which the 2/20th was a constituent Battalion), Capt. Hamilton Benn, C.B., D.S.O., M.P. (Hon. Colonel of the 20th), Lieut.-Col. Assheton Pownall, M.P., Lieut.-Col. W. St. A.Warde-Aldam, D.S.O. (late commanding the 2/20th), Lieut.-Col. H. A. Christmas, V.D., Major B. L. Hooper (late commanding the Reserve Battalion), Lieut.-Col. W. Parker, D.S.O. (late commanding the 1/20th), Major Dolphin, D.S.O. (late commanding the 1/20th), the Mayor of Greenwich (Alderman Sir Charles Stone, J.P.), the Mayor of Lewisham (Councillor Harry Chiesman, M.B.E., J.P.), Capt. Rochfort, D.S.O., M.C. (Adjutant of the 20th), and Lieut. H. W. Hallett.

" The band of the Coldstream Guards, under Lieut. W. Evans, rendered selections before the arrival of His Royal Highness, and it was on the drums that the Colour rested during its consecration by the Bishop of

Woolwich. Capt. Elliot handed the Colour to Prince Albert, who then presented it, 2nd-Lieut. J. Batty, who served in the 1/20th as a sergeant and was granted a commission in the 2/20th, receiving it on behalf of the Regiment. R.S.M. W. T. Skeer, D.C.M., was in charge of the Colour escort.

"Proceeding to the extremity of the enclosure, His Royal Highness addressed those taking part in the ceremony and a large number of ex-members of the 20th who were formed up, in the following terms :—

"'Col. Eric Ball, officers, warrant officers, non-commissioned officers and men of the 20th Battalion London Regiment,—It affords me great pleasure to have the privilege of presenting this King's Colour on behalf of His Majesty the King, as a testimony both to you and to future generations of the loyal services so nobly rendered by the members of your 2nd Battalion on the field of battle in the Great War. It is a symbol which will ever call to mind the arduous duties so heroically performed by your 2nd Battalion. Your Regiment has a splendid record. Prior to the formation of the Territorial Force, as the 2nd and 3rd Volunteer Battalions of the Royal West Kent Regiment, it served in the South African War. The services which the 1st Battalion performed in many a hard-fought field on the Western front—including Loos, Vimy, High Wood, Bourlon Wood—are well known. To-day I would more especially allude to the record of the 2nd Battalion. It was formed in September, 1914, as part of the 60th London Division ; embarked for France in June, 1916, and served in the Vimy Ridge trenches. Transferred to Salonica in December of the same year, it carried out an important raid in April, 1917. From there the Battalion went to Egypt, and took part in the Palestine offensive in June of the same year, capturing the water-supplies of Sheria, and fighting at Nebi Samwil. One company assisted in the assault which delivered Jerusalem. The Battalion was present again in the battles at Er Ram, Shab Salah, Arak Ibrahim, and in two raids east of Jordan. In July, 1918, the Battalion returned to France in time to take part in the final counter-offensive, fighting at Vraucourt, Havrincourt, Solesmes and Flesquieres, and eventually ended up as part of the Army of Occupation in Germany—a truly splendid record of service, and one of which you may all be proud. Your Regiment has gained many honours, on which I offer my congratulations. The Regiment has suffered heavy casualties, and with you I mourn the loss of the 900 gallant men whose memory we are here to-day to honour, and to whose relatives I offer my deepest sympathy. I confide this emblem, consecrated by the Bishop of Woolwich, to the care of the 20th County of London Battalion. I am very glad to have met you all. I congratulate you on having come through the great struggle, and I wish you every success in the future.'

" A move was next made to the enclosure surrounding the memorial—a massive Celtic wheel cross of rough-hewn silver-grey Cornish granite, rising to a height of 20 feet, its base 10 feet by 8 feet. On a panel of white marble set in granite is carved the White Horse of Kent —the regimental emblem—while on the step is the inscription :—

> IN MEMORY OF THE OFFICERS, WARRANT OFFICERS, NON-COMMISSIONED OFFICERS AND MEN OF THE 1/20TH AND 2/20TH BATTALIONS THE LONDON REGIMENT WHO FELL FOR THEIR COUNTRY DURING THE GREAT WAR, IN BELGIUM, FRANCE, SALONICA, EGYPT, PALESTINE AND GERMANY, 1915-1919. THIS MEMORIAL HAS BEEN ERECTED BY THEIR COMRADES.

"The Bishop of Woolwich pronounced the simple formula : ' In the faith of the Lord Jesus Christ, and in memory of the officers and men of the 20th Battalion of the London Regiment who fell in the late war, I hereby dedicate this cross ; in the name of the Father, and of the Son, and of the Holy Ghost.' The ' Last Post ' and the ' Réveillé ' were sounded, and then the Prince pulled the cord which released the Union Jack which had been draped about the cross, and the unveiling was completed.

"Among the many beautiful wreaths deposited at the base of the memorial, pride of place was given to one in which the regimental badge and motto were picked out in white on a crimson background, and to which was attached a card inscribed : ' To the ever-glorious memory of our comrades who gave their lives for their country in the Great War. From all ranks, past and present, of the 20th London Regiment. Invicta !' "

At the Reunion Dinner in the evening Col. Hamilton Benn, C.B., D.S.O., M.P., presided over a gathering which included 340 old members of the three Battalions of the Regiment and their guests. After the Royal toast had been honoured, and Col. Hubback had proposed ' The 1st Battalion,' Col. H. W. Studd gave ' The 2nd Battalion.' He said he could speak quite personally and intimately, because he knew the Battalion at the comparative beginning of its career. The 1/20th had gone away to France, taking away from the two Battalions what they thought was best. They must have had a jolly hard task, because he did not think they could have found anything much better than they left behind. A second reason why he could speak was that he—and he alone—was responsible for the Commanding Officer they had with them in France, in Palestine, and again in France at the end of the war. (Cheers.) It was really something to be proud of to have chosen Col. Warde-Aldam, and to have got him for the Battalion with a great deal of difficulty. (Hear, hear.)

He (the speaker) went out with them, and they were for six months holding trenches on the Vimy Ridge. At one time it was settled that they were to attack, and he thought they would have been successful. Unfortunately, the troops that were to have come to assist were taken away, and they had to leave the taking of it to the Canadians. The latter won it gloriously, and while he did not think the 180th Brigade could have done it better, he thought they could have done it as well. (Cheers.) Then they were ordered to Salonica, and he knew it was felt most deeply by every man of the Brigade. Then the greatest blow that had fallen on him in his life fell: Sir Douglas Haig inspected the Brigade, and said he was going to give him a Staff appointment. He replied that he did not want a Staff appointment, and that he wished to remain with his old comrades, but within a week he had to say farewell to them. At that time the Battalion had established its reputation, but had still to work out all the details of that picture of glory which had made up the record of the 2/20th. He followed very closely their performances in Salonica and Palestine. Perhaps one of the finest things they did was the charge of the ridge which resulted in the taking of Jerusalem. And who were actually the first into Jerusalem? A cook and an orderly! When cooks and orderlies took cities, there was nothing one could draw the line at! (Laughter and applause.) In his heart would always be the memory of his old friends of the 2/20th: a man could not forget the people on whom he had had to make great calls—calls that were never made in vain, that were always responded to up to the hilt. There was nothing he ever asked the 2/20th to do that they did not do. Among them was an extraordinary feeling of union and self-sacrifice, each man helping the other—the only relation in which it was worth living this life at all. He was proud to say that spirit animated the whole of the 180th Brigade—(Hear, hear)—and it would be a great pity if that feeling were allowed to die out simply because they were not now actively engaged in killing other people. They still had their struggles : could they not undertake them in the spirit of helping those who were around them—their comrades ? He was sure if they did so everything would be easier. (Applause.)

" Lieut.-Col. W. St. A. Warde-Aldam, who was accorded a reception second to none in heartiness, observed that the 20th had always been very lucky in its Brigadiers and Major-Generals, and this was going to be kept up in the future in Col. Hubback. (Applause.) Col. Studd taught the 180th Brigade to march, to dig, and to fight. The night after they got into Jerusalem there was a historic dinner-party, at which it was agreed that what won Jerusalem was the training given them by Col. Studd. (Hear, hear.) Alluding to the history of the 2/20th, shortly to be published, the speaker said no one could have better qualifications to write it than Capt. Elliot, who was taking an absolutely unlimited amount of trouble over it. He had been in hopes that a joint history might have been brought out, but that proved impossible. They still hoped, however, that the 1/20th would bring out a companion history. The question of a memorial at Jerusalem had been in abeyance, because they had to fit in with the cathedral authorities there. It was a question between a stained glass window and a picture, and he thought the memorial would probably have to take the form of a picture. In the record of the 1/20th and the 2/20th they had a great tradition, which it was most desirable they should carry on, and a great many of them could do so by joining the new Territorial Battalion. He wished Col. Ball and the future 20th Battalion the very best of luck. (Cheers.)

" Some of the speakers referred to the fact that a gun which had been captured by the 2/20th Battalion at Solesmes, and had been given to the Greenwich Borough Council for public exhibition, was in the Council's dustyard. The announcement was greeted with cries of

' Shame !' ' Let's go and get it back !' ' It's our gun !' and ' Direct Action !' After dinner a large number of the guests—probably 200 in all, including a small sprinkling of ex-officers—assembled outside the Borough Hall about 10.30 p.m., and, formed in fours, marched to the Borough Council depot in Shooters' Hill Road, where the German gun had been deposited. The gates of the depot were closed, but they offered only a slight obstacle to men determined to wipe out what they undeniably felt to be an insult, and were speedily forced. Ropes were attached to the gun, which was dragged back in triumph to Holly Hedge House, which was reached about midnight."